Making a Scene in the Pulpit

Making a Scene in the Pulpit

Vivid Preaching for Visual Listeners

Alyce M. McKenzie

WESTMINSTER
JOHN KNOX PRESS
LOUISVILLE · KENTUCKY

First edition
Published by Westminster John Knox Press
Louisville, Kentucky

18 19 20 21 22 23 24 25 26 27—10 9 8 7 6 5 4 3 2 1

Book design by Sharon Adams
Cover design by designpointinc.com

Library of Congress Cataloging-in-Publication Data

Names: McKenzie, Alyce M., 1955- author.
Title: Making a scene in the pulpit : vivid preaching for visual listeners / Alyce M. McKenzie.
Description: First edition. | Louisville, Kentucky : Westminster John Knox Press, 2018. | Includes bibliographical references and index. |
Identifiers: LCCN 2018025273 (print) | LCCN 2018034305 (ebook) | ISBN 9781611648966 | ISBN 9780664261566 (pbk.)
Subjects: LCSH: Preaching. | Imagination--Religious aspects--Christianity.
Classification: LCC BV4211.3 (ebook) | LCC BV4211.3 .M (print) | DDC 251--dc23
LC record available at https://lccn.loc.gov/2018025273

Most Westminster John Knox Press books are available at special quantity discounts when purchased in bulk by corporations, organizations, and special-interest groups. For more information, please e-mail SpecialSales@wjkbooks.com.

*To all those who have committed their lives
to preaching the gospel to a hurting world*

Contents

Introduction

"Don't make a scene." This command is usually hissed through clenched teeth. Maybe spoken by a mom to a toddler at Target: "No, we're not buying that. Put it back. Don't make a scene." Maybe spoken by a man or woman to a date in an elegant restaurant: "Keep your voice down. We'll talk about this later. Don't make a scene!" Maybe spoken by a lawyer to her client on the way into the courtroom: "Let me do the talking when we get in there. Don't make a scene."

"Don't make a scene" means "Don't draw bystanders into our drama." My advice to preachers these days is exactly the opposite: "Make a scene. Do everything you can to draw bystanders into our drama. For God's sake, make a scene in the pulpit!"

The narrative preaching of the past thirty-five years or so has assumed that human beings are hardwired to be story makers, engaged in a life-long project of making a coherent plot out of the disjointed scenes and situations of our daily lives. There is a growing conviction that many people may not have the skill or even the will to be engaged in this ongoing, plot-building project. Our ubiquitous handheld devices have shrunk our screens from panoramic to palm size. Our attention spans have likewise shortened and become more diffuse. We used to yearn for the ability to be in more than one place at a time. Now we have it. We have the ability to be sitting in a coffee shop with friends while checking scores, texting other friends, verifying a fact on Wikipedia, and catching up on scenes from our favorite shows. This has led to a condition some social commentators call *Continuous Partial Attention (CPA)*. Rather than being in more than one place at one time, we can now be fully present nowhere at one time.

The dynamics of shrinking screens and shortened, divided attention spans have shaped people's perception of God at work in the world. It is becoming harder and harder to sell the panoramic biblical narrative of salvation from creation, fall, and redemption to new creation. Understandably, given the violence and chaos of our day, it's hard not to be more attuned to the randomness and injustice of life than to instances of justice, mercy, and order in our world. As screens and attention spans have shrunk, so has the faith of many people in panoramic salvation metanarratives.

While not everyone is skilled at crafting a narrative arc out of their life experiences, just about everyone seems to love sharing moments of their lives with others. We still love scenes, small segments of a larger story. We upload scenes from our lives for others to experience. We watch and rewatch scenes from others' lives on YouTube, Facebook, and Instagram.

The scene as a unit of human perception appears across many different disciplines. The advertising executive uses scenes from daily life to persuade viewers to invite her product into their daily lives. The sportscaster covers scenes, not only on the field, but also from the personal lives of players. The lawyer is skilled in crafting compelling closing arguments that paint a scene of innocence or guilt. The psychotherapist helps patients reframe or reclaim scenes from their past. Teachers in many fields use case studies, scenes held up as cautionary tales or as positive examples. Scenes are everywhere. Biology has mitosis and photosynthesis. Chemistry has reactions. Math has equations, and music has measures and movements.

In the pages that follow, I zoom in on that segment of story called a scene. I define a *scene* as novelists, playwrights, and screenwriters do: the action that takes place in one physical setting in more or less continuous time. Scenes are similar to the anecdotes that have traditionally been used to illustrate the points of a sermon. But they are a more vivid version. Rather than tell us about something, they invite us into somewhere (setting) to identify with someone (characters). They use sensory detail and dramatic energy to invite us in as participants, rather than leave us standing on the porch or sitting in the stands as spectators. They are designed to create experiences rather than report them.

There are sound anthropological, biblical, and communicational grounds for giving attention to that segment of story known as the scenes. Preaching in scenes is congruent with how people experience life today. It honors the authority of Scripture, not primarily as divine data, but as an unfolding divine drama with acts and scenes within those acts. Just as story has been shown to be a genre that has cross-cultural, cross-generational appeal, the same can be said for scenes. They gain and hold attention, providing compelling conveyances for exegetical and theological teaching. Scenes in sermons can function, as they often do in literature and film, as ethical simulation chambers for dealing with real-life challenges, drawing us in to identify with characters, undergo changes with them, and take that changed perspective back into our world.

Chapter 1, "Scene Is the New Story," explores the dynamics of our culture's fascination with scenes, from Instagram to movie trailers to viral YouTube videos. Whether it's a sorrowful scene—a young Iraqi woman Neda, dying in the street in Iraq in 2009; a natural disaster—a tornado in Joplin, Missouri; an everyday, adorable pet trick—a dog helping a puppy down the stairs; or an everyday human interaction—like "Uncle Henry gets surprised at Christmas," we love scenes. In the narrative arc of popular television dramas, it is the suspenseful, forward moving dynamic of individual scenes that keeps viewers on the hook for the whole season of episodes . . . and then for the next season.

Chapter 1 traces the rise of the narrative preaching of the "New Homiletic" and makes the argument that *narrative*, the foundation of preaching theory and practice in many circles since the final quarter of the twentieth century, needs to give more attention to the smaller unit of a story known as a *scene*. *Narrative* and *story* are terms that are often blurred in contemporary usage. For example, a lawyer might say to his client, "We need to create a convincing narrative." In that popular usage, *narrative* and *story* are viewed as identical. But for our preaching purposes, we distinguish them from one another. I find Fred Craddock's distinction helpful. "Narrative refers to the shape or movement of the sermon. It is not a piece of the sermon. It describes the whole, not a component."[1] A narrative sermon, then, isn't narrowly understood as a sermon on a biblical story, or a sermon that contains a story. As Eugene Lowry puts it, "A narrative sermon is any sermon in which the arrangement of ideas takes the form of a plot involving a strategic delay of the preacher's meaning."[2] Essentially, he is identifying narrative with plot.[3]

The narrative shape, or plot, of sermons is most often, though not always, a movement from tension to resolution, from ambiguity to clarity, from bad news to good news, from guilt to grace, from death to life.[4] A story, by contrast, is a specific sequence of events (or scenes) with a beginning, a middle, and an ending. For example, the story of the three little pigs has a narrative plot that moves from equilibrium to upsetting the equilibrium to the reestablishment of equilibrium. Within the story are several scenes: The story begins with the three little pigs being sent out into the world by their mother to "seek out their fortune." The first little pig builds a house of straw, but a wolf blows it down and devours him. The second little pig builds a house of sticks, which the wolf also blows down, and he devours the second little pig.

Each dialogue between wolf and pig features these memorable lines:

"Little pig, little pig, let me come in."

"Not by the hair on my chinny chin chin."

"Then I'll huff, and I'll puff, and I'll blow your house in."

The third little pig builds a house of bricks. The wolf is unable to blow his house down, so he tries unsuccessfully to trick the pig out of his house. Finally, the wolf comes down the chimney and lands in a cauldron of boiling water the pig has set there. The pig cooks and eats him. In milder versions, the first and second little pigs escape out the back door of their houses and run to their brother's house for safety; the wolf, after falling into the water, runs away and never returns. Whichever version of the story you prefer, there are several scenes within it. I know that for a fact, having dramatized them for three children and a grandchild, complete with huffing and puffing!

I offered the Beecher Lectures on the theme of "Making a Scene in the Pulpit" in 2015; following my final lecture, a man raised his hand and asked, "What is the difference between a scene and a story, illustration, or anecdote in a sermon?" It was one of those moments when the question is so basic that your mind, even after months of reflecting on a topic, goes blank! Here is what I wish I had said: "What I mean by a scene is a story event within a story.[5] For example, the story of the prodigal son has at least six scenes or story events: (1) the boy asking for his inheritance, (2) his squandering it in various forms of excess, (3) his decision to return home as he sits with the pigs; (4) his trip home rehearsing what he will say to his father, (5) his father's greeting; (6) his father's encounter with the older son. To use a contemporary example, the story of your relationship with a close friend is composed of several scenes: how you met, a time you got each other in trouble, a time one of you came to the other's defense, and so forth. To qualify as a scene, a brief story, anecdote, or illustration in a sermon must have a healthy dose of "show" and not just "tell." Like an extroverted host, a scene invites us to come into the house rather than stand out on the porch looking in. By means of memorable sensory detail, emotional appeal, and a significant theme, often involving conflict, it invites us to identify with the characters and the action and to be affected by our participation. A scene makes spectators into participants.

Think of it in terms of a play. The play has an overall plot or narrative movement. It is a story with a beginning, a middle, and an ending, which is why many plays have three acts. Within each act are several scenes. To qualify as a scene, the theater goer, novel reader, or sermon listener must be able to pull it out of its larger context. Even if listeners/viewers don't know the whole story, there should be enough detail and energy in a scene to make them want to explore the broader story. This is precisely the dynamic of "making a scene in the pulpit!" It is a method tailor-made for those unfamiliar with, or even indifferent to, the plot (narrative) of God's saving dealings with humankind and the stories that make it up. We draw them into one scene and pique their interest in its broader story.

Chapter 2, "The Preacher as Scene Maker," deals with the identity of the scenic preacher and the habit of attentiveness key to the preaching task. It traces the ability to craft scenes back to the sages of Scripture who brokered their close observation of life around them into scenic wisdom teachings (proverbs and parables) for their communities. In order to preach in scenes, preachers need first to be able to discern scenes within and around them. This chapter commends the model of the preacher as sage for today's preachers. It highlights the fundamental habit of the preacher that, in my book *Novel Preaching: Tips from Top Writers on Crafting Creative Sermons*, I named the "knack for noticing." This habit of noticing elements of character, scene, and conflict applies to the preacher's inner life, the life of his/her congregation and community, and the biblical text. I've named these three arenas "inscape," "landscape," and "textscape."[6]

Chapter 2 also treats the reader to scenes from sermons preached by pulpit masters of the past. Much traditional preaching has been three-point preaching, using scenes in a somewhat limited way as illustrative anecdotes for logical points. People couldn't always remember all the points, but their favorite story lived on in their imaginations. Some of the best preachers throughout the ages of Christian preaching have been those who have known how to make a scene in the pulpit.

Chapter 3 is entitled "Making a Scene in the Scriptures." The ultimate Scene Maker is God, and this chapter offers a biblical grounding for the use of scenes in our preaching.

Chapter 4, "Making a Scene in the Sermon," begins with a theological basis for scenic preaching in the theo-drama of Kevin Vanhoozer's

The Drama of Doctrine. It goes on to describe the reasons why scenic sermons are tailor-made for serial-tasking audiences who find sustained reflection on a single topic to be a challenge. It shows why scenic sermons today need to be clear, compelling, and, at the same time, to acknowledge the complexity and ambiguity in people's lives. It offers three models for the use of scenes in sermons. One is the *deductive sermon* that gains hearer attention by opening with a scene, a form that is especially suited to teaching those who are theologically and biblically untutored. The other two sermon models, the *multi-scene sermon* and the *single-scene sermon*, are primarily inductive, not giving away the full theme at the outset, but designed to unfold with high-definition clarity. The multi-scene sermon begins with an attention grabbing scene from either the Bible or today. It works well in preaching to distractible serial taskers, capturing and holding their attention and unfolding from scene to scene with a clear connective theme. Yet another model is the single-scene sermon that takes as its home screen a scene from Scripture, the preacher's personal life, an historical scene or a contemporary scene. Designed for those experiencing CPA (continuous partial attention), it seeks to pull them into one scene and then repeatedly draws them back into it. That scene becomes the stage setting for a one-act play in which all the action takes place in the same setting on stage, with no curtains or blackouts. The preacher invites listeners to join the scene onstage and points to connections between their experiences and Scripture.

Chapter 4 depicts the characteristics of successful scenes: clarity of purpose, imagery, and significant detail, to name just a few. It offers examples of these characteristics from the sermons in chapter 5. Chapter 4 highlights two key benefits to preaching in scenes: (1) "Scening" our teaching portions vivifies exegetical and theological teaching by placing it in the context of a scene. (2) Preaching in scenes can help the preacher avoid common pitfalls in delivery.

Chapter 5, "Scenic Sermons," offers several sample sermons that illustrate the use of scenes in sermons as described in chapter 4.

Rather than chastise contemporary people for their shortened attention spans, *Making a Scene in the Pulpit* encourages preachers to harness the human fascination with scenes for the development and delivery of our sermons. Its core strategy is to invite listeners into scenes—from Scripture, history, literature, or contemporary life—and, once they are there, to point them toward the larger story of God's forgiving, transforming relationship with humankind. The dynamic of making a scene becomes the golden thread that glimmers through the whole process of preaching, from observation of scenes from the preacher's daily life, to interpretation of texts from Scripture, to sermon shaping and sequencing, to sermon delivery. Finally, it provides a wonderfully precise portrayal of the purpose of the sermon: to send listeners out into the scenes they'll play in their lives during the next week, equipped to act out their parts in ways that are kinder, more just, and more courageous, than last week.

Chapter One

Scene Is the New Story

The house lights dim. The audience stops rustling candy wrappers. The curtains open. There is the Grinch in a Santa hat, standing by a mantle hung with stockings, loading a family's Christmas gifts into a sack. A little girl in footie pajamas enters the room. We are about to be drawn into a scene.

The defendant is being escorted by the police from courthouse to jail. An angry crowd is gathering, trying to block their way. Somebody throws a rock. That's all it takes. We are about to be drawn into a scene.

"No one wants her in this town. She doesn't belong here," the women were saying as she stepped in line behind them at the post office. As soon as they spotted her, their faces flushed and they offered a syrupy greeting. We are about to be drawn into a scene.

He sends both of his wives, his two maids, and his eleven children across the Jabbok River and is now alone, by the river, in the dark, dreading the encounter with his brother that will occur the next day. Out of nowhere, a man hurtles toward him and grabs him in a death hold. The struggle that will last all night begins. This is Genesis 32:22–32, and we are about to be drawn into a scene.

Scenes. They are everywhere: in our daytime thoughts and nighttime dreams, in plays, books, contemporary and historical experiences, and in the Bible. In a stage play or film, a scene is a unit of story or a story event within a larger story; it is "an action through conflict in more or less continuous time and space" that has a significant impact on a character's life.[1] I've shortened the definition to this: "the action that takes place in one physical setting in more or less continuous time." A scene has a setting, a plot, characters, and a degree of conflict. In the hands of a skilled novelist, playwright, or preacher, it has one theme—not three, not five, but one.

Here is the scene that depicts how I first came to be fascinated with scenes. The class was held on the top floor of Stuart Hall at Princeton Theological Seminary. You know Stuart Hall even if you've never been in Stuart Hall: dark red stone exterior, high ceilings, dark paneling, the smell of layers of lemon oil consistently applied since 1876. It was the fall of 1990. I trudged up the stairs, twelve-pound "portable" computer in hand. I was late for class, a graduate seminar in the practical theology PhD program on the subject of Old Testament Hermeneutics, co-taught by professors Thomas G. Long and Patrick D. Miller. It was a bad day to be late. It was the day we were to sign up for our thirty-page papers on interpreting a genre of Old Testament literature for contemporary life. It was to be due in three weeks. By the time the clipboard came to me, someone had already nabbed the patriarchal narratives. Someone had purloined the psalms. Someone had appropriated the apocalyptic passages. Someone had even lapped up the legal codes. This left one lone, unclaimed genre: proverbial wisdom. Of course! This was a group of budding practical theologians; what use did they have for proverbial wisdom? A fellow student, whom, up until that point, I had regarded as a friend, leaned over and said, "Good luck getting a sermon out of a one-liner, McKenzie!"

After class I headed directly to the seminary library. What I discovered there made my situation seem much brighter. I discovered that proverbs had the shortest bibliography of all the genres! I checked out an armful of books and headed for home. That evening, after I put my children to bed, I opened the Bible to the book of Proverbs. I couldn't help but remember a witticism by William H. Willimon, who had remarked more than once in oral presentations that "reading the book of Proverbs is like taking a long road trip with your mom." With a long suffering sigh, I began to read.

> Can fire be carried in the bosom
>   without burning one's clothes?
>   6:27

> There is a way that seems right to a person,
>   but its end is the way to death.
>   14:12

It is not good to eat much honey,
  or to seek honor on top of honor.
                        25:27

Like a city breached, without walls,
  is one who lacks self-control.
                        26:28

The crucible is for silver, and the furnace is for gold,
  so a person is tested by being praised.
                        27:21

The fear of others lays a snare,
  but one who trusts in the LORD is secure.
                        29:25

At breakfast the next morning, I read a couple of proverbs to my then seven-year-old daughter, Rebecca. My second grader was clearly under-whelmed: "That's just what everybody already knows, only in words you can picture."

The sages responsible for coining and collating the book of Proverbs in the years following the Israelites' exile from Babylon certainly did not follow the advice, "Don't make a scene!" They trained their laser wisdom vision on multiple scenes in daily life around and within them and crafted their observations into vivid proverbs to guide the young and foolish and to remind the older and wiser. Centuries later, Jesus took a page out of the sages' playbook and preached, not only in short sayings, but also in parables, a genre that is a longer narrative cousin to the proverb. The sages' (including Jesus) homiletical example became the inspiration for my career-long passion for scenes.

The Rise of Story

Early Christian preachers imitated the homiletic of Jesus and the sages, preaching in scenic proverbs and parables, challenging listeners to discern how to apply them to situations in their daily lives. But when the preaching of the gospel entered the mission field of the Greco-Roman world, the scenes—which drew you in, changed you, and sent you out to play your part on the world stage—suffered a demotion. Their new role was to serve as anecdotes that illustrated the sermon's conceptual points.

The expectations of non-Jewish audiences were shaped by several centuries of rhetorical training, the art of persuasive public address, perfected by Greek and Roman teachers. They drummed into their young students' heads that speeches should teach, delight, and persuade.[2] Unfortunately, they divided reason from imagination, relegating the former to teaching and persuading and the latter to delighting. It was the function of the content, the logical argument, to teach and persuade. It was the function of style, word choices, and flourishes of delivery, to delight. Metaphor and imagery were seen as ornamental, as sugar sprinkled on ideas to make the medicine go down. This "great divide" between reason and imagination has influenced centuries of preachers to separate images, stories, scenes, and metaphors from ideas, concepts, and lines of thought.[3]

For the first several centuries, the purpose of Christian preaching, modeled after the rhetorical models of the Greeks and Romans, was persuasion. As the centuries rolled on, it morphed to explanation, as propositional preaching came to the fore. Such preaching took a couple of different forms. One that arose in the late medieval period was known as the "university sermon," in which the preacher takes a central theme and divides it into three parts with explanations of each. Yet another was the Puritan Plain style sermon, which has its roots in earlier rabbinic strategies of exegesis/application. The preacher begins by offering background on the ancient text, then draws from it several doctrinal points, finally applying them to the contemporary congregation. The "three points and a poem" became the sermonic form of choice, with some notable exceptions, until the fourth quarter of the twentieth century. It is a time-honored form, still viable today.[4] The sermon, "Finding Faith amid Your Fears," in chapter 5 is a two-point deductive sermon that opens with a scene.

In the early 1970s, a movement arose that came to be called "the New Homiletic"; it focused on narrative and plot rather than propositions in preaching. It became the dominant approach to preaching from the mid-1970s to the early twenty-first century. It based its reliance on narrative on theological and biblical grounds; God's interactions with humankind as reflected in Scripture have an interactive narrative shape. Texts are not reducible to propositions but are language events that seek to impact the existential experience of readers.[5] So much for a theological, biblical rationale for narrative. Now all that was needed was an anthropological one. And in 1971, Stephen Crites, religion and philosophy professor at Wesleyan University in Connecticut, provided it in an influential article titled "The Narrative Quality of Experience." In it, he claimed that "The formal quality of experience through time is inherently narrative."[6] He argued that human beings experience and process life in a narrative shape, attempting to craft a coherent, continuous plot out of the disjointed scenarios of daily life. His article contributed to the ongoing work of theologians, philosophers, ethicists, and biblical interpreters who believed that narrative was more than a faddish interest in storytelling. Rather, it was central to theological interpretation, ethical reflection, and biblical hermeneutics.

As Crites was writing his article in the early 1970s, I was sitting in church in New Cumberland, Pennsylvania, the small town on the Susquehanna River where I grew up. I was listening to three-point sermons, which, though they had their moments, often left me wondering, "When life is so interesting, why is preaching so boring?" Fred Craddock, a young New Testament scholar and preacher, was wondering the same thing. In 1971, he self-published a critique of modernist, propositional preaching with a title tailor made for the recalcitrant, authority-averse 1970s: *As One without Authority*.[7] His book described traditional preaching as the preacher going on the whitewater rafting trip of biblical exegesis for the sermon and bringing the congregation back a keychain. He advised preachers to take the congregation along on the trip. He advocated preaching that encouraged listeners to be active participants rather than passive recipients, nodding in intellectual assent, what he called "javelin catchers" for the preacher's ideas. Craddock instigated a move away from propositional, didactic, authoritarian sermons toward sermons with plots. The narrative preaching that dominated homiletics from 1971 to 2000 was shaped by the dynamics of plot, moving from the bad news of how the human condition is to the good news of how it could be, by God's grace.[8] Throughout the 1980s and 1990s, other preachers and teachers of preaching joined in Craddock's critique, offering their own versions of the whitewater rafting trip. Eugene Lowry's "Lowry Loop" followed the narrative flow of Aristotle's *Poetics*: from equilibrium, to disequilibrium, to resolution and transformation.[9] Henry Mitchell's classic *Black Preaching* recommended that the preacher "start low, strike fire, end high,[10] His work, and that of Frank Thomas in *They Like to Never Quit Praisin' God*, sought to offer the genius of African American preaching to preachers of all ethnicities. Says Thomas, "The nature and purpose of African American preaching is to help people *experience the assurance of grace* (the good news) that is the gospel of Jesus the Christ."[11]

David Buttrick's "moves" mapped out a line of thought, carefully segmented and sequenced to arrive at a liberating destination.[12] Paul Scott Wilson's *Four Pages of the Sermon* moved from trouble in the text to trouble in the world to good news in the text to good news in the world. Patricia Wilson-Kastner, in her book, *Imagery for Preaching*, offered Ignatian meditation as the form of the sermon plot. Guided by it, the preacher and people enter into the biblical story with an intention, ask for God's grace, experience the story, and gives thanks for the resulting insight. All these sermon forms are variations on the plot of complication-resolution or problem-resolution. They are microcosms of the overarching Salvation Plot of creation, fall, redemption, and recreation.

Not everybody got on board the narrative train as it moved out of the homiletical station. Richard Lischer, in an essay in 1984, "The Limits of Story," questioned the privileging of narrative as the most appropriate rhetorical mode for the discovery of the self and the experience of God.[13] He pointed out that there are expanses of both Scripture and human experience that are not narrative in shape, and that stories need interpretation. In an era when many people are biblically illiterate, he asked, why jettison the teaching function of preaching in favor of a story that supposedly speaks for itself? He was suspicious of the complication-resolution plots of the New Homiletic, quoting literary critic Hugh Kenner, who called plot "a broom which sweeps everything in the same direction."[14] Finally, he noted that "stories can provide a desperately needed sense of order or they may arrogantly impose order on the disorder and anarchy of life as it is."[15] A more recent criticism of narrative preaching comes from theologian Francesca Aran Murphy in her book *God Is Not a Story: Realism Revisited.* She warns that narrative theology runs a danger of shrinking God to the confines of an anthropological appetite.[16]

The Erosion of Story

We have a lot to thank the New Homiletic for: its respect for the listener, its understanding of the sermon as dialogue, not monologue, and its view of the people as partners in the message, not passive recipients. But it was founded on two assumptions that, in recent years, have been called into question from a number of quarters. One is that listeners are biblically literate. Listeners know the stories, themes and overarching Salvation Story (metanarrative) of the Bible well enough to make connections with their ongoing life stories without much help from the preacher. The second assumption is that listeners have the narrative competence to be crafting ongoing life stories they can access and connect to biblical themes and stories.

Biblical Illiteracy/Indifference

It's not 1971 anymore. People don't know the biblical stories that make up the metanarrative of salvation. Some would argue they didn't then. Be that as it may, an even more formidable obstacle today is that not everyone is all that interested in learning the biblical stories. The Pew Research Center's recent statistics on "America's Changing Religious Landscape" show that the number of people who identify themselves as Christians has dropped sharply over the past seven years, while those who list themselves as having no religious affiliation (the "nones") are increasing, and not just in the under-thirty-five age group. Everybody has their reasons. Some people consider themselves to be "spiritual but not religious," not wishing to affiliate with any institutional religious organization. Others self-identify as atheists or agnostics. Still others regard religion as irrelevant. They don't feel it is a necessary requirement for surrounding themselves with a supportive community or living an ethical life that includes a commitment to social justice.[17]

Unimpressed by Christian Public Witness/Damaged by Church

Still others aren't buying our metanarrative because they don't find us Christians to be particularly compelling advertisements for our own story. Rather, they find us to be judgmental and joyless.[18] In 1971, the same year Stephen Crites wrote his article "The Narrative Quality of Experience," and Fred Craddock wrote *As One without Authority*, John Lennon wrote "Imagine," a track on the album of the same name. The song's lyrics encourage the listener to imagine a world at peace and a world with no religion. The impediments to a world at peace, according to the song, are living for fear of punishment or hope of reward rather than focusing on the present. Other impediments include religion, violent nationalism, and materialism. These factors are presented as divisive, working against unity and peace.

In 1971, when *Imagine* was released, the U.S. was just entering the second decade of involvement in Vietnam. Eighteen-year-olds had just gotten the vote. Carroll O'Connor was portraying a sexist racist on the CBS sitcom *All in the Family*. It was just three years after the assassination of Dr. Martin Luther King Jr. That year, the U.S. Supreme Court upheld the use of busing to achieve racial desegregation in schools. Several major cities—including Chattanooga, Tennessee, and Camden, New Jersey— experienced incidents between police and ethnic minority citizens that sparked riots. While a majority of Americans identified themselves as Christian and as churchgoers, *Imagine* appealed to a growing dissatis- faction with rigid governmental, religious, and social authority. *Imagine* became the most commercially successful and critically acclaimed album of Lennon's solo career. In 2012, *Imagine* was voted number eighty of the top five hundred albums of all time.[19]

In the almost fifty years that have passed since 1971, lots of people have joined Lennon in imagining no religion. Many people view religion as the culprit in the woes of our world. When religious extremists, on an almost weekly basis, slaughter innocent people in public places, it is not hard to understand this perspective. Others name religion's role in discrimina- tion against lesbians, gay, bisexual, transgendered, queer, and intersex persons. David Kinnaman's 2007 book, *Unchristian: What a New Gen- eration Thinks about Christianity . . . and Why It Matters*, lists the reasons for the disaffection with institutional religion felt by those younger than thirty-five. One reason is that they view the church as judgmental with regard to persons who do not self-identify as heterosexual. Yet another group of people want nothing to do with Christianity because they have experienced abuse at the hands of church leaders charged with nurturing and protecting them.[20]

We should not be surprised at these weighty challenges to our Chris- tian narrative. They call us to accountability, especially when our story factors out our complicity in ongoing discrimination and inequity in our society. Making a scene is not just a rhetorical strategy the preacher dem- onstrates to the people from the pulpit. It is a way of congregational life in the world in which both preacher and people participate. For ten years I attended a church in Yardley, Pennsylvania, that had the same small sign over every exit. You couldn't walk out of any door without reading it: "When the worship is over the service begins."

The Appeal of Alternative Stories

In his book *Preaching at the Crossroads: How the World and Our Preach- ing Are Changing*, homiletician David Lose points out that we preach to postmoderns, secularists, and pluralists, each of whom, for differing reasons, is not buying our metanarrative of creation, fall, redemption, and recreation. Postmoderns aren't buying our claim that God can be known. Secularists aren't buying our claim that daily life is an arena in which God can be known. Pluralists aren't buying our claim that Christians have a distinctive story of human identity and divine activity in the world.[21]

Others aren't buying our metanarrative because they've already bought into a competing one. Among several options offered by Steve Wilkens and Mark Sanford in their recent book *Hidden Worldviews: Eight Cultural Stories that Shape Our Lives* are: individualism ("I am the center of the universe"), consumerism ("I am what I own"), nationalism ("My nation, under God"), and scientific naturalism ("Only matter matters).[22]

Our Story Is Too Neat and Tidy

A lot of people, especially under thirty-five years old, aren't buying the complication-resolution metanarrative of salvation anymore. Rather, many people's view of life mirrors the title of a macabre series of children's books by American author Dan Handler writing under the name Lemony Snicket: *A Series of Unfortunate Events.* One of his more famous quotes is this: "Fate is like a strange, unpopular restaurant filled with odd little waiters who bring you things you never asked for and don't always like."[23]

A couple of years ago, I was teaching an elective class on narrative preaching with a group of twenty-somethings. I was trying to get them to break down a theme for a sermon into smaller units and brainstorm how they would flesh it out. "So, class," I began, "Let's look at Matthew 8:23–27, Jesus calming the storm. The focus that we will be using for our sample sermon was inspired by my research into Jesus' pet name for the disciples in Matthew: 'Little faith ones.' Unlike Mark's Gospel, the disciples in Matthew do have a little faith, and it can grow, so it's not a pejorative nickname. So here is our sermon focus: 'Our faith grows, when, in the high gales of life, we turn to Jesus and find that he is present and able to help us.'"

As I turned to write it on the whiteboard, the barrage of questions began.

"What do you mean by *faith*?"

"What do you mean by the *high gales*? They aren't the same for everyone!"

"How can we assure people of calm seas when life is so dangerous and uncertain?"

"Why should I trust someone who falls asleep when I need him the most?"

At that point, I was calling on our Lord for assistance myself! But, given our current cultural context, I shouldn't have been surprised at my young students' unwillingness to fall in line with my plot without question.

Atrophy of Story-Making Skills

Some cultural theorists are saying that the issue is not that contemporary people don't want to buy into our salvation narrative. It is that they can't, because they have lost the narrative competence to make connections between the "Story" and the disjointed episodes of their daily lives. These days not everyone agrees with Stephen Crites and the New Homiletic that human beings are hard-wired to process life by crafting a coherent life story. One of these is Galen Strawson, a British analytic philosopher and literary critic. In a recent essay, "Against Narrativity," Strawson posits that, while some people, whom he calls "diachronics," process life through narrative, others, whom he calls "episodics," live from moment to moment and in no way see themselves as crafting a coherent, ongoing narrative."[24]

In a recent essay, "Out of the Loop," Thomas G. Long contests Strawson's dismissal of narrativity. Long understands the episodic phenomenon, not as a description of a type of person, but as a description of our cultural context that has eroded our innate story-shaping skills. To put it bluntly, many people's narrative chops have atrophied. They aren't in the habit of creating holistic narratives out of the disparate events of their daily lives. Rather, they (or maybe "we") are immersed in the episodic experiences of life with neither the skills nor the will to look beyond them. In our attention deficit, high-tech, visual culture, many have lost the skill to be engaged in an ongoing process of making a story of their lives. Long suggests, rather, that many people are living in "random bursts, our attention fleeting from *American Idol* to the troop movements in the Middle East to the desire to purchase a more powerful cell phone, a kind of cultural attention deficit disorder."[25]

Amid the talk about episodics and loss of narrative competence these days, story is still hanging in there. Findings in recent years, from neuroscience, biology, and psychology, support the view that we are indeed hardwired to make cause-and-effect connections between the scenes of our lives. This view is reflected in scholarly works like that of the late Nobel Prize winner, Dr. Gerald Edelman's 2006 book *Second Nature: Brain Science and Human Knowledge.*[26] It also appears in popular works, like English professor Jonathan Gottschall's 2012 book, *The Storytelling Animal: How Stories Make Us Human*; and writer and writing coach Lisa

Cron's *Wired for Story: The Writer's Guide for Using Brain Science to Hook Readers from the Very First Sentence.*[27]

Jonathan Gottschall, a young English professor at Washington and Jefferson College, was driving down the highway on a brilliant fall day, spinning the FM dial on the radio. A country music song came on. He was not a country music fan, but there was, he says, something heartfelt in the singer's voice. Instead of turning the channel, he listened to a song about a young man asking for his girlfriend's hand in marriage. The girl's father makes him wait in the living room, where he stares at pictures of a little girl playing Cinderella, riding a bike, running through a sprinkler, and dancing with her dad. The young man in the song suddenly realizes that he is taking something precious from the father. He is stealing Cinderella. Before the song was over, Gottschall was crying so hard he had to pull off the road. Chuck Wicks' song "Stealing Cinderella" captured the bittersweet experience of being a father to a daughter and knowing you won't always be the most important man in her life.

> I sat there for a long time feeling sad but also marveling at how quickly Wicks' small, musical story had melted me—a grown man, and not a weeper—into sheer helplessness. How odd it is, I thought, that a story can sneak up on us on a beautiful autumn day, make us laugh or cry . . . , alter the way we imagine ourselves and our worlds. How bizarre it is that . . . the story maker penetrates our skulls and seizes control of our brains.[28]

So the idea came to him for a book called *The Storytelling Animal: How Stories Make Us Human*, published in 2012, in which he uses insights from biology, psychology, and neuroscience to understand why we love stories. More than loving them, we need them to make us human. They are "the flight simulators of human social life."[29] Our love for story is an anthropological appetite with an important social function. I am convinced that we are still story makers—plot providers—but that our skills have atrophied. Drawing people into one episode or scene and then helping them connect it to God's encompassing story exercises their weakened story-making skills.

The Scenic Quality of Experience

While many people are suspicious of our tidy, metanarrative plot and may even have lost their narrative chops, they still love being drawn into scenes. That's why movies use trailers. That's why YouTube has three billion video views a day. That's more than twenty-five times the audience of the Super Bowl. Every minute, three hundred hours of new video are uploaded to YouTube. That's way more than all the TV networks' combined airings in a year."[30] People get drawn into scenes. That's why, even though you can fast forward through the commercials, you still watch some of them—maybe more than once. The prevailing wisdom is that an online video should run a maxium of three minutes. Then there are microvideos, called *vines*, six-second videos with infinite looping capability. There is Instagram, with its newly increased limit of sixty seconds, up from fifteen seconds. There are "60 second docs," described as "a diverse series of documentaries that provide a new look into the most unique characters, expressions and practices that make up the world. Life. One minute at a time."[31] Many people enjoy inviting others into brief scenes from their own lives and being drawn into scenes from others' lives.

On the web, just as in life and the Bible, scenes run the gamut from touching to terror-filled, from humorous to horrific. A dog helps a puppy down the stairs. A man with a scimitar stands next to a man kneeling, his head shrouded in a black hood. A duck steals a bag of chips from a 7-11 store. Neda Agha-Soltan bleeds out in Kargar Street in the 2009 Iranian election protests in Tehran, in what may be the most widely witnessed death in human history. More recently, scenes that have gone viral have been musical—like the choreography to Ed Sheeran's "Shape of You"—or humorous—Ping Pong Trick Shots, Ed Sheeran Carpool Karaoke, and Bad Lip Reading of the 2017 Inauguration. I confess it took all the self-discipline I have at my disposal to extract myself from these engrossing YouTube scenes and return to writing about them!

I'm thinking about writing a new version of Stephen Crites' 1971 article, "The Narrative Quality of Experience." I would call it "The Scenic Quality of Experience." Maybe before we ever graduate to story, human existence and experience is fundamentally scenic in form. Maybe we are hardwired to be drawn into scenes (the action that takes place in one physical setting in more or less continuous time) before we ever make connections to a larger story.

The Ubiquity of Scenes

A former generation of homiletical thinking argued that narrative runs through all human disciplines. I make that case for scenes. Scenes abound in the Bible. I was introduced to scenes through my study of biblical wisdom literature's genres of proverbs and parables.[32] But the wisdom literature has no cornered market on scenes; they appear in every genre of Scripture. Think, for example, of the vivid scenes in the patriarchal narratives. Think of the metaphorical scenes and actions of the prophets: Ezekiel's valley of dry bones (Ezek. 37), Amos' plumb line (Amos 7:8), Isaiah's naked walkabout (Isa. 20:2), and Jeremiah's trip to the potter's house (Jer. 18). There are accounts of Paul's conversion on the road to Damascus (1 Cor. 15:3–8; Gal. 1:11–16; Acts 9:3–9), and his portrayal of a scene of Eucharistic corruption (1 Cor. 11:17–22). There are the vivid apocalyptic scenes like the one from Daniel 7: a vision of the Ancient One on his throne and the "one like a human being / coming with the clouds of heaven" (Dan. 7:13). There is Revelation's scene of "a new heaven and a new earth . . . coming down out of heaven from God," complete with a divine voiceover (Rev. 21:1–4). The Gospels offer scenes of healings, exorcisms, conflictual encounters, miraculous calming of storms, and multiplication of loaves and fish. They depict the scene of Mary running from her encounter with the Risen Lord to tell the good news to disbelieving disciples. There are also violent, visceral scenes: the mass slaughter of those who get in the way of God's chosen people (1 Sam. 15); a king killed on the toilet (Judg. 3); a woman gang raped and cut in pieces (Judg. 19); a couple who drop dead because they withhold part of their church offering (Acts 5:1–11); a man stripped down, beaten, and nailed up on a cross. All these scenes throughout the canon deserve the attention of what chapter 2 will introduce as the sage's (the preacher as wisdom seeker and teacher) "knack for noticing" in preaching.

Scenes function in a variety of disciplines beyond the usual suspects of novels, plays, movies, and short stories. Music has measures. Math has equations. Education, psychology, and forensic anthropology have case studies. Law has closing arguments. The hard sciences are characterized by scenes invisible to the naked eye, which reside at the center of our physical world. Biology has mitosis and photosynthesis. Chemistry and physics have actions and reactions, which can rearrange the reactants' atoms to produce new substances.

Scenes also abound in the arts and social sciences. To find them requires only a short walk around the campus of Southern Methodist University in Dallas, Texas, where I teach in the Perkins School of Theology.

Last spring, students in my Creative Sermon Design course gathered in the lab at the Temerlin Advertising Institute at SMU's Meadows School of the Arts. Institute Professor Carrie La Ferle told my students: "The goal of a television commercial is to get viewers to invite your product into their life story." She went on, "In the early days of television, advertising was about a pitch person telling you facts about the product. Today's ads are mini-narratives, scenes that depict characters who need the product with whom (we hope) viewers identify. They have to be better than ever since people can fast forward through them."

Over at SMU's Guildhall, in the graduate, video-game education program, students' screens glow with the video games they are designing, complete with scenes and levels and passwords to move from level to level.

Last year I invited Gretchen Smith, theater historian, performance studies scholar, and playwright from the Meadows School of the Arts, to lead us in a workshop on crafting scenes in sermons. Half the class was working on sermons on the Prodigal Son. Half were working on Jacob wrestling with the man on the banks of the Jabbok River. Professor Smith began with this advice, "In any scene, you must first ask the question, 'What is at stake for the character(s)?' If there is nothing at stake for them, why should we, the audience, care? It will not be a memorable scene. Nor will it propel us to the next scene."

Anthropology Professor Ronald Wetherington stands at the front of his classroom in Heroy Hall. Next to him is a human skeleton hanging on a hook. This is a course called "Forensic Anthropology: Stories Told by Bones." The class recreates death scenes from autopsy reports. "All right, people," says Professor Wetherington. "Two bullet wounds to the back of the head from a distance of 1–2 feet. Homicide or suicide?"

Millicent Johnnie, Director, Choreographer and Filmmaker, in a dance class at SMU several years ago, explained that, while movies and plays have scenes, freestyle dance has cyphers. A cypher is the circular dance space that forms naturally once a freestyle session begins. Johnnie's research traces the cypher to the bantaba in Africa giving expression to the thoughts, values, beliefs, and knowledge of African people and their descendants brought to the New World through the Atlantic slave trade. In a recent email exchange with Johnnie, she had this to say about the cypher in relation to the scene (email exchange July 13, 2018): "The movement expressed in the cypher is a microcosm of the bigger story of struggle, resistance and the liberation of African and Caribbean people. Like in street dance, rather than tell people about the social conditions of economically poor black and brown people, we draw them a bite size scene using movement reflective of our social conditions and our cultural values. The nature of a circle is inclusive—that is, there is no hierarchy in a circle and because of this cyphers feel more egalitarian in spirit. If one understands the values of the circle and the values of the people that make up the circle, one will understand how the circle/cypher functions as a kinetic experience of liberation." She added, "The importance of the circle/cypher for storytelling in Africanist cultures and communities is summed up in an excellent quote from South Africa, 'Until the lion learns to write, all stories will glorify the hunter.' Consider the cypher as the platform for the lion to tell its story."

I got permission to sit in on a painting class recently at SMU. I had never taken a formal art class, and I was absorbed in the sights and sounds of the scene: cathedral ceiling studio, smell of paint, students all around with their easels and canvasses. During the break, the graduate assistant for the class talked with me about scenes in painting. She told me that, in painting a scene, the artist seeks to direct your eye to something within it. "If it is an apple, for example, lines will direct your eye to the apple. Light will hit the apple. The apple will appear with definition and clarity amid the rest of the contents of the canvas." She continued, "The question an artist asks is, 'Where is the light in the scene?'"

For the past few years, I've invited Kevin Paul Hofeditz, Professor of Theatre at Meadows School of the Arts, to come to my class and give my preaching students some performance coaching. He tells them, "Actors have to know the bigger story, but act it one scene at a time. You don't want to play the end at the beginning. When Juliet first meets Romeo, there can't be a veil of sadness over her eyes at her knowledge of the outcome. She is fifteen, and she's in love!"

Good Reasons to Preach in Scenes

The New Homiletic generation of preachers made the case that there were good anthropological, biblical, and theological reasons to employ narrative in preaching.

In the chapters that follow this one, I make the same case for scenes. In this time when our screens and attention spans have shrunk, preachers are called, not to give up on conveying the larger story, but to invite people into palm-sized segments of it, from there to connect them to the bigger view.

If we want to be heard by people who have minimal biblical knowledge and are living from episode to episode with rusty connective skills, some would recommend preaching lengthy teaching sermons (sometimes referred to as "six points and a PowerPoint") to fill in the gaps in their biblical knowledge. Still others would suggest we tell a string of loosely related stories to touch hearers' hearts. The necessary homiletical response, I believe, is one that combines teaching and touching emotion and will.[33] It is to draw people into a scene that connects them with a story we could never have invented ourselves, a story that can connect the disjointed episodes of our distracted lives, that offers something to live and die for beyond ourselves. Over twenty years ago, David Buttrick, in *Homiletic: Moves and Structures*, asserted that the biblical narrative of salvation provides an encompassing master story into which we can place our individual stories. It gives our often incoherent, episodic lives a new prelude and a new closing chapter.[34] Preaching can invite people, even people with little knowledge of or interest in our story, to enter into it, scene by scene.

Speaking of scenes, we turn now to the closing scene of *this* chapter, which I have titled "Close Encounter on the DART Train." I have permission to share this scene from my friend and colleague Dr. Rebekah Miles, Professor of Ethics and Practical Theology at Perkins School of Theology, Southern Methodist University, Dallas, Texas.

During the spring semester, Dr. Miles was teaching a graduate seminar called "Twentieth Century Ethical Thought." She lives in Fort Worth and was riding the DART train (Dallas Area Rapid Transit) to Dallas to teach one afternoon. She had the book that would provide the basis for discussion in her class on her lap, her notes spread out on the seat beside her. She was staring out the window, mentally tweaking her lesson plan—Do I want to start with my lecture, then respond to questions, and then break into small groups to discuss them or . . . Glancing to her right, she noticed a woman staring at her. From observing details of the woman's appearance and other sensory clues, Dr. Miles inferred that she was down on her luck, perhaps homeless. The woman nodded toward the book on her lap: "That book looks interesting. What's it about?" Dr. Miles looked down at her copy of Reinhold Niebuhr's *The Nature and Destiny of Man* and for a moment, she says, her mind went completely blank—and then she said, "Well, it's about our creatureliness and how we are bound by it, within it, to some degree, but how, at the same time we have the capacity for self-transcendence, how we are limited by social structures that have both corrupt elements and, at the same time, liberative possibilities." To which the woman responded . . . "Oh" and turned her gaze away to look out her window at whatever happened to be passing by. Dr. Miles arrived at class with a new version of her lesson plan for her graduate ethics students: "Today we begin with this question: How would you convey the metanarrative of *The Nature and Destiny of Man* to a homeless woman on the DART train so that you offer a word that might make a difference in her life?"

Chapter Two

The Preacher as Scene Maker

Who Should We Be Today?

I teach preaching and worship at Perkins School of Theology at Southern Methodist University, in Dallas, Texas. Many of my students are young, some, just out of college, are as young as twenty-one. During the Introduction to Preaching class, I coach them on claiming their identity, voice, and authority as preachers and on offering the good news through their own unique lens on life. The youngest preacher I have ever coached was my grandson Graham, who was almost three years old when this scene occurred. Like most children, he tries on in his mind different people he'd like to be when he grows up. One visit it was a basketball player. The next time it was a baseball player. Another day it was a firefighter. Then he wanted to be a painter. On a recent visit to Gigi's (my grandmother name), he started the day off by asking, "Gigi, who should I be today?" I shrugged and asked him, "Who do you want me to be?"

His answer was to solicit my help dragging a little table from the living room into the corner of my home office, where I'm now sitting typing this book. He then began gathering objects to put on the table. They included a small brass bell, a little standing cross, a figure of John Wesley on his horse, a Bible, and a home Communion set that had belonged to my husband's grandfather, a Methodist preacher on the Maryland Line in the 1940s. It had somehow caught Graham's eye in the china cabinet in the dining room. Finally, he placed his grandpa's bobblehead figure of Dallas Mavericks' power forward Dirk Nowitzki on what I now realized was an altar. I convinced him that, while Dirk sacrifices himself on a regular basis, it is on the basketball court, not an altar. He reluctantly put Dirk on a nearby bookshelf to observe the proceedings.

Graham then went into my closet and got a black sweater that came down to his ankles. Coming back into my office he said to me, "Gigi, today I am going to be a priest. Sit quietly while I preach." At that point, the thought crossed my mind that maybe he is a reincarnated medieval cleric, perhaps even someone mentioned later on in this chapter. But more likely he is just a bright little boy whose parents take him to an Episcopal Church in Houston every week. I sat down obediently and folded my hands in my lap, prepared to give my full attention to this precious little priest. He raised his arms and then got a lost expression on his face. "Gigi, what should I preach?"

"What do you want to say to me?" I asked.

He thought for a moment and then said, "Jesus is walking by the seashore telling people that he loves them."

Not bad for a first sermon!

Graham's question echoes in my mind: "Who should I be today?" The last third of the twentieth century held several answers to that question for us preachers. The 1960s said, "Be an activist!" The 1970s said, "Be a therapist!" The 1980s said, "Be a church-growth consultant." The 1990s said, "Be a CEO and a player-coach." The twenty-first century says, "Be a Bible teacher."

The Preacher as Sage

I contend that it is time for the homiletical spotlight to hover over the sage, the seeker and teacher of wisdom.[1] The preacher as sage is not someone who only preaches on biblical wisdom texts. The sage is a seeker of wisdom, attentive to God's presence and guidance in the inner life (inscape); the text (textscape); and the congregational, community text of daily life (landscape).

Feminist biblical scholar Elisabeth Schüssler Fiorenza offers this helpful description of *wisdom*:

> Wisdom is a state of the human mind and spirit characterized by deep understanding and profound insight. . . . Wisdom is the power of discernment . . . the ability . . . to make the connections, to savor life and to learn from experience. Its root meaning comes to the fore in the Latin word *sapientia*, which is derived from the verb *sapere*=to taste and to savor something. Wisdom is intelligence shaped by

experience and sharpened by critical analysis. It is the ability to make sound choices and decisive decisions.[2]

In his book *The Journey and Promise of African American Preaching*, preaching professor and author Kenyatta Gilbert calls for contemporary African American preaching, while honoring the roles of prophet and priest, to recover the sagely voice. The sage keeps alive the scenes, stories, and values of the community that are enshrined in its folklore, idiom, and history. When the preacher functions as a sage, he or she recognizes that the true resident theologian is the community itself. What Gilbert affirms for African American preaching is instructive for all preaching.[3]

Why is now the time for the preacher as wisdom teacher? Because we live in a culture in which there is plenty of information but a paucity of wisdom. In our distractible state, we are losing the ability for sustained reflection on our spiritual identity and purpose in daily life. The preacher needs to be one who, amid all the demands of daily life, cultivates a spiritual focus that can be a source of refreshment for others. People seek guidance on how to make the connections between the disparate episodes of their daily lives. These days, many people resist granting any one person or institution the authority to define truth for them. More deeply, they may question whether there is such a thing as universally applicable truth. They need preachers who, like the sages of Scripture, recognize the limitation of individual human knowledge, including their own. They need preachers who, like the sages of Scripture, respect the need for a communal context for wisdom reflection; which is to say they respect their congregation's wisdom and are open to learning from it.

At the same time that contemporary listeners are reluctant to grant preachers' truth-prescribing authority, they are eager to experience the preacher's authenticity. The sage as wisdom teacher is both a trail guide and a fellow pilgrim on the way. The sage models how to discern and live by wisdom in the multiple scenarios of daily life, a vocation to which everyone, not just the preacher, is called. The egalitarian model of the preacher as sage is tailor made for our authority-suspicious, authenticity-craving context.

The Knack for Noticing

In my book *Novel Preaching: Tips from Top Writers on Crafting Creative Sermons*, I recount how, some years ago, I was having lunch with C. W. Smith, then the chair of the English department at SMU. I asked him, "What can preachers learn from fiction writers?" He thought for a moment and then said, "As a teacher of creative writing, much of my time is spent in trying to get students to notice what they see. And then, the next step is to get them to trust that there may be some significance in their observations."[4] After my conversation with Professor Smith, I began to think of this habit as a "knack for noticing." It is the core capability of the preacher as sage, scene noticer and scene maker, one who surveys his or her inner life (inscape), context (landscape) and the canonical sweep of Scripture (textscape), noticing what she or he sees.

One of the students in my Introduction to Preaching class a few years back was a former park ranger. He took visitors on a variety of nature walks through the park: one was a wildflower walk; one was a fossil walk; another was an animal track walk. Depending on the kind of walk it was, he would look for and point out different things. The authors of various genres of Scripture walked through life, looking for and pointing out different things, depending on their purpose. The sages looked for patterns of behavior that led to positive and negative outcomes as a source of ethical guidance for the community, offering insight into how God, the Giver of Wisdom, wants us to live in the everyday scenes of our lives (i.e., wisdom).[5] The authors of the patriarchal narratives were attentive to human disobedience continually rerouted by the forgiveness of God. The authors of the legal codes were on the alert for ritual and legal obligations in response to God's covenant. The prophets were attentive to God's demand for justice and promise of restoration. The psalmists were attentive to the whole range of human emotion in the context of divine sovereignty and reliability. In apocalyptic texts, the authors were attentive to the prospect of divine intervention in their current helpless, hopeless situations. In the epistles of the New Testament, the authors were attentive to the vulnerabilities of congregations and the overcoming power of what God has done in Jesus Christ. The Gospel authors, with their interweaving of healing stories, teachings, miracles, and exorcisms, were attentive to how Jesus' identity and teachings could fortify their communities in the face of their particular challenges. The knack for noticing is a dynamic by which any genre of Scripture comes into being and by which we enter into dialogue with it for preaching. But no genre offers a clearer, more practical exercise regime for our knack for noticing than the wisdom literature of Scripture.

The knack for noticing that was perfected by the sages, including Jesus, can be traced back to the biblical paradigm of the wise person: King Solomon. In 1 Kings 3, young King Solomon has inherited his father's kingdom and some big shoes to fill. He feels that odd mix of emotions we often feel when starting a new venture: profound appreciation for the opportunity and sheer panic at the prospect. When I picture this Gibeon scene, I see, next to King Solomon, Henry Ward Beecher on the afternoon of January 31, 1872, when he gave the first of the Beecher Lectures, established in memory of his even more famous father, Lyman Beecher. At age fifty nine, Henry was a lot older than young King Solomon but just as unsure of himself—so nervous he cut himself shaving![6] When I picture this Gibeon scene, right next to Henry Ward Beecher and King Solomon is a colleague from my days in pastoral ministry in Pennsylvania whose bishop moved him from an associate pastor position to senior pastor at a much larger church. He told me, "Alyce, for the first year, I felt like a little boy going into work carrying Daddy's briefcase."

At Gibeon, the Lord appeared to Solomon in a dream by night and invited him to make a request: "Ask what I should give you" (1 Kgs. 3:5).

Solomon suspects that dicey days lie ahead, scenes of conflict that will cry out for wise counsel. And so he gives this answer to God's offer: "Give your servant . . . an understanding mind [*lev shomea*] . . . , able to discern between good and evil" (1 Kgs. 3:9). Professor Roland Murphy, my Old Testament professor at Duke Divinity School in the late 1970s, pointed out in his book *The Tree of Life* that "discerning mind" could just as well be rendered "listening heart."[7]

I like the mixed metaphor of the listening heart. It expresses the fact that mind and heart are not, in the Bible, placed into separate, sealed containers. Throughout the Bible, the heart is not just emotions but also the seat of decision making and character. It is, as Jesus later points out, the source of thought and emotion and the wellspring of actions, either good or evil.[8]

God grants Solomon's request and gives him the gift of wisdom to navigate the complex scenarios that a king will encounter, like the conflictual scene that awaits him at the foot of the mountain as two women approach him, both laying claim to the same baby.

The Knack for Noticing in Proverbs

The sages of Israel would be quite helpful as guest speakers in Professor Smith's freshman Creative Writing classes and in my Introduction to Preaching classes as well. They excelled at the knack for noticing. They noticed the ruins of the temple, the empty palace, the bands of aimless youth in the street, and the now-slumped shoulders of elders who had once stood tall in the community.[9] The crisis brought about by the Babylonian destruction of Jerusalem in 586 BCE served as a jolt of caffeine to the sages' vocational senses. They began to collect, collate, and in some cases, coin scenic wisdom sayings to help the gullible young moderate their impulses for the good of the community. They compressed their observations of patterns of cause and effect in their postexilic context into scenes through which to convey wisdom to the young: "Like somebody who takes a passing dog by the ears/is one who meddles in the quarrel of another" (Prov. 26:17). "Like the glaze covering an earthen vessel / are smooth lips with an evil heart" (Prov. 26:23). With priests and king deported, the sages envisioned one whose authority did not depend on temple or palace, but who flourished by the hearth in the home. She was Woman Wisdom, a personification of an aspect of the character of God. They envisioned her as being present at creation and delighting in humankind (Prov. 8). The sages placed their wisdom on her lips, depicting her as a proactive prophetess with limited patience for being ignored (Prov. 1:20–33; 8:1–21).[10] She is not afraid to make a scene, standing at the crossroads and inviting every kind of fool off the path of folly onto her path of wisdom: "Gullible fool—come on. Know-it-all fool—come on. Malicious fool—come on. Come right now, because it's almost too late for you. Don't be wise in your own eyes. Trust God's wisdom. Control your appetites for food, drink, amassing wealth, sloth, anger, and sex. Act for the long-term good of the community, not your own short-term gratification!"[11]

The Knack for Noticing in Job

The sages of Job turned their knack for noticing on their postexilic surroundings. From 587 BCE on, the southern kingdom of Judah was under the control of the Babylonians; their educated elite deported, their traditional institutions of monarchy and temple destroyed. The Persians under Cyrus overcame the Babylonians and, in 538 BCE, Cyrus issued a decree allowing Judeans to return to their homeland and rebuild the temple at Jerusalem. The books of Job and Ecclesiastes may well date from the period of Persian rule. In different ways, each addresses the question of how the nation can continue to survive from day to day in a context of apparent futility and undeserved suffering.[12] Job's authors can't help but notice the discouragement and sense of futility of their nation. Job is perhaps a representative figure for the whole nation. As the drama unfolds, inadequate explanations of innocent suffering are struck down, until finally, Job is confronted from the whirlwind by the God before whose transcendence he has the good sense to tremble (Job 38–42).

The Knack for Noticing in Ecclesiastes

The sages of *Qoheleth*, the name given to the person or group that collected the wisdom of Ecclesiastes, turned their knack for noticing on their surroundings. Their people were under the rule of capricious Persian kings, who doled out plots (portions) of ground on the basis of favoritism. The wisdom Qoheleth offered was realistic and focused on the present: Enjoy your portion. Your relationships, work, food, and drink are all the more precious because they are precarious. Give daily thanks to God, who, though distant, is the giver of these gifts. But don't avert your eyes from the shadow side of the street. "Wisdom is better than weapons of war, / but one bungler destroys much good" (Eccl. 9:18). "Wisdom excels folly as light excels darkness. . . . Yet I perceived that the same fate befalls all of them [the wise and the fools]" (Eccl. 2:13–14). His wisdom subverted the naïve assumption that if you live wisely, things will go well. He warned that such assumptions would be disappointed at every turn. They are *hebel* (vapor). His advice was that we remember we are human and God is God, and live in each present moment, respectful of our transcendent God.[13]

Jesus' Knack for Noticing

Jesus learned from the subversive sages Job and Qoheleth as he turned his knack for noticing on his context. He observed the religion of his ancestors reduced to external, legalistic observances, having lost its heart for the poor and excluded. As theologian Elizabeth Schüssler Fiorenza puts it:

> Since the reality of the *basileia* for Jesus spells not primarily holiness but wholeness, the salvation of God's *basileia* is present and experientially available whenever Jesus casts out demons (Luke 11:20), heals the sick and ritually unclean, tells stories about the lost who are found, the uninvited who are invited, of the last who will be first. . . . Not the holiness of the elect but the wholeness *of all* is the central vision of Jesus.[14]

It falls to Jesus, the subversive sage, to overturn traditional wisdom by projecting scenes of counter-order wisdom on the screens of our imaginations through his one hundred two aphorisms and proverbs. "It is not what goes into the mouth that defiles . . ." (Matt. 15:11; Mark 7:15); "Those who want to save their life will lose it, and those who lose their life for my sake will find it" (Matt. 16:25; Luke 9:24; 17:33; Mark 8:35). Add to that his forty parables, scenes that begin with: "The kingdom of God is like . . ." and invite us to realize how far from that vision our lives really are.[15]

Jesus' version of "Imagine" was not John Lennon's "Imagine no religion" but "Imagine a world in which the kingdom of God has come on earth!"

"No One Like You!" 1 Kings 3:12

The first day of class each semester in Introduction to Preaching, I read the story of Solomon on the heights of Gibeon to my students. I read it to them because, sooner or later, when I'm working at my desk in my campus office, I'll look up and see a frustrated face framed by the privacy window. It will be a student in the throes of struggling with a sermon. He or she will come in, sit down in one of my less than comfortable chairs, and say, "Dr. McKenzie, so many preachers have preached on this text in the past. I don't think I have anything new to say." To which I reply, "But it has never before been said by *you*."[16]

That's why I read the scene of Solomon and God on Mount Gibeon the first day of class every semester. I don't want new preachers ever to forget God's response to Solomon's request for a discerning mind/listening heart. "Because you have asked this, and have not asked for yourself long life or riches, or for the life of your enemies, but have asked for yourself understanding to discern what is right, I now do according to your word. Indeed I give you a wise and discerning mind"; and then comes the best part, the answer to the question of why God says God gives this gift to Solomon. The answer, as the story goes, is this: "Because no one like you has been before you and no one like you shall arise after you" (1 Kgs. 3:11–12). The metaphor of *voice* for one's unique perspective is valuable for preachers. It is true in a physiological sense that your voice is unique in its physical production. That's why we recognize the voices of people we know well, and even can often identify which actor is doing the voiceover in a commercial. In a metaphorical sense, your voice is your unique perspective on things. Nancy Lammers Gross, in *Women's Voices and the Practice of Preaching*, addresses the question of why many women struggle to speak up, why it is so difficult for many women to claim their space in the pulpit and speak with confidence in their call and the conviction of their hearts. She denotes the literal, physical speaking voice as "voice" with a lower case *v*. She uses "Voice," with an upper case *V*, to refer to the metaphorical Voice, a woman's fundamental right to speak and the unique perspective God has called her to express.[17]

She explores the multiple ways a women can lose her Voice: gender bias, cultural norms for women's appearance and behavior, and sexual abuse. The Voice, in my understanding of the preacher as sage, is the product of what we notice. Women need to be free to speak with precision and courage about what they have noticed and experienced, that which is both life-affirming and death-dealing. That freedom is essential to any preacher's exercise of the knack for noticing. No force within or outside the preacher deserves to be given the power to silence the Voice.

Contemporary homileticians and theologians, reflecting on their own preaching and that of great preachers through the centuries, have their own names for the knack for noticing. Lucy Lind Hogan calls it "theological mindfulness."[18] Paul Scott Wilson calls it the "imagination of the heart."[19] Barbara Brown Taylor calls it being a "detective of divinity."[20] African American preaching traditions call it exercising the "sanctified imagination."[21] Frank Thomas calls it the exercise of "moral imagination."[22] Theologian Mary Catherine Hilkert calls it "Naming Grace and naming ungrace."[23] Roman Catholic nun and spiritual writer Macrina Wiederkehr calls it the exercise of "Real Presence."[24]

It's time to take our place in the company of preacher-sages, scene noticers, and sermonic scene makers. We will be in grand company. Throughout homiletical history, there have been many wise preachers who knew how to make a scene in the pulpit! Legend has it that Leonard Sweet, author and theological educator, used to begin his preaching classes with the question, "Who was the greatest preacher of all time?" To which someone would inevitably respond: "Jesus?" "That's right," he would say. "So why don't we preach like Jesus?" As Barbara Brown Taylor says it, "The Incarnate Word preached an incarnate word."[25]

Jesus, taking a page out of the sages' playbook, taught in aphorisms and their longer narrative cousin, parables. While he seems to have often left it up to listeners to set his stories in the soil of their everyday lives, the Gospel writers had a penchant for putting a "the moral of the story is . . ." ending on many parables.[26] From the moment the gospel climbed the hill to the Areopagus and encountered the Greco-Roman world, the purpose of preaching began to morph from invitation to persuasion. Christian preaching became persuasion for several centuries, followed—with the advent of the Enlightenment—by a couple of centuries of preaching as explanation. The scene that drew you in, changed you, and sent you out to play your role better in your own life's scenes became the anecdote that stood beside the point with a flashlight to prove the point or to explain the exegesis: hence, the term *illustration*, from *illustrare* ("to bring light"). Even though scenes had been demoted to anecdotes to illumine points, they still sometimes stole the show!

The historical examples of scenic preaching that follow do not presume to be a thorough historical survey of scenes from sermons through the ages. Their far more modest purpose is to offer examples that will inspire further exploration and imitation. I invite the reader to explore for themselves the preachers they wish I had included. For reasons of space and time, the sampling stops with Martin Luther King Jr. almost a decade before the advent of the New Homiletic. I've included some more recent sermon collections under "For Further Reading." With the multiplicity of sermons available online, I encourage you to reflect on the use your favorite contemporary preachers make of scenes. And now for a stroll down the portrait gallery of scenic preaching from centuries past, as we observe how preachers trained their knack for noticing on the various arenas of God's work in the world: inscape (preacher's inner life), landscape (preacher's context), and textscape (the world of the text).

A Portrait Gallery of Scenic Preachers

John Chrysostom (349–407)

There was a preacher from the fourth and fifth centuries who knew how to make a scene. John Chrysostom (nicknamed John Goldenmouth) could describe an imperial procession with high-definition (HD) precision, taking listeners along as he walks through the marketplace: beggars, children playing tug of war, knife throwers, and prisoners loaded with chains, the poor sleeping in the ashes of the furnace outside the baths, gladiators drowning their sorrows in drink, a rich home filled with borrowed furniture, guests inside gorging themselves until their temples throbbed and their bowels ached. Homiletical historian David Dunn Wilson says of him, "He used his imagination and powers of observation to make it difficult for any listener, whatever their economic status or walk of life, to escape his message."[27]

And there were some who would have preferred to escape his message! He turned his HD knack for noticing on Constantinople like an infrared germ detector in a cheap hotel room. He condemned the temptations of wealth, theater, horse track, and circus, alienating the city's ruling class and rival clergy. He was exiled to a remote village on the Black Sea, where he died September 14, 407.[28]

Silent Preaching

Some of the greatest preachers of all were visual artists skilled in drawing, and workers in wood and glass. Medieval apologists used the term "silent preaching" (*muta predicatio*) to describe murals and wall paintings that depict biblical scenes as well as contemporary legends. As the medieval preacher stood, announcing the divisions of his theme, listeners, literate or illiterate, could look around them and experience a rich visual feast.[29]

Likewise, today's scenic preacher knows how to appeal to the senses by painting word pictures. Homiletician Henry Mitchell, drawing on the long and vivid tradition of African American preaching, advises preachers to reach the total person—mind, heart, and will—by bringing all five senses to the text.[30] I would add this: bring your inner life (inscape) and life around you (landscape) as well.

If the power fails in the building and the preacher's PowerPoint and movie clips flicker out, the preacher still stands in the power of the Word, projecting its scenes onto the screen of listeners' imaginations.

Franciscan and Dominican Preaching

Two groups of preachers arose in the Catholic Church in the twelfth and thirteenth centuries. One was the Dominicans, the Order of Preachers founded by Spanish priest Dominic of Caleruega (1170–1221). Their mission was to address an increasingly well-educated urban class of laity with doctrinal teachings. At about the same time, the Franciscan order began, founded by Francis of Assisi (1181–1226), an Italian Catholic friar and preacher. His ministry was in response to a hunger among laity in villages and rural areas for vivid, heartfelt preaching by priests who modeled the simplicity of Jesus' own life.[31]

In response to this spiritual hunger among the laity, the Franciscans produced illustrated guides for the laity, filled with devotional scenes. Francis defined himself and his followers as "troubadours of God" (*loculatores Dei*). They preached penance to craftsmen, artisans, and shopkeepers. The Franciscan *sermo humilis* (ordinary speech) relied on narrative and *exempla* (examples). Their goal was to appeal to the emotions and excite listeners to action more than to instruct them in doctrine. Says homiletician Michael Pasquarello,

> In keeping with the Gospel story, such preaching often took place outside the church, in town squares, homes, roadsides, wherever there were people. Such humble preaching created its own space, transforming public space into the space of the Word of salvation. This homiletical activity reveled in narrative, emotion and the commonplace. It focused on the very human Christ, on the Incarnation and the mystery of his passion.[32]

St. Francis himself was the master of scene making. Legend has it, he preached to the birds, tamed a wolf, and, on his deathbed, thanked his donkey for his years of faithful service.

Throughout homiletical history, preachers have used scenes to challenge or subvert the status quo. They have also used them to support it. An example of the latter is the Crusade preachers (1095–1270) of both the Dominican and Franciscan orders. They were enlisted by various popes to persuade men that "to take the cross" (embark on a crusade) was to perform a penance crucial to their salvation, which garnered indulgences for their families. In some cases, they used dramatic gestures and demonstrations of piety. In one memorable scene, Franciscan preacher Robert of Lecce, part of a crusade preaching tour of Wales in the late twelfth century, tore off his habit to expose the armor underneath.[33]

Thomas Aquinas (1225–1274)

Thomas Aquinas is best known as master theologian of the Middle Ages. He was also a Dominican preacher who preached sermons on the basic doctrines of the Church, not only for scholars and theological students, but also for the burghers, merchants, housewives, shopkeepers, and artisans of Naples. His sermons follow the form of medieval sermons, the *sermo modernus* in which, rather than explicating a passage verse by verse, the preacher began with a theme taken from a verse of Scripture, divided it into parts, and expounded on each one. A number of his sermons, which come to us from the notes of listeners, are filled with scenic similes. For example, in explaining how difficult it is for unaided human understanding to grasp the workings of providence, he uses the example of someone who knows nothing about medicine seeing a physician administering water to one patient and wine to another. Aquinas points out that the observer who concluded that the physician acted in this way because he was ignorant of the medical arts would be foolish. It is the same way with God. We do not know why it is God does this or that or allows things to happen the way they do, so we assume things happen by chance.[34]

Hugh Latimer (1487–1555)

Flipping the pages of history forward, we come to the English Reformation and the bold, scenic preaching of Hugh Latimer. Latimer was a Fellow of Clare College, Cambridge; Bishop of Worcester before the Reformation; and later Church of England chaplain to King Edward VI. Latimer's sermons masterfully use irony, ridicule, personal reminiscence, simile, metaphor, and alliteration. Latimer often used a creative metaphor as a package for his sermon's message. In his famous "Sermon on the Cards," he pulled a deck of cards out of his preaching gown and used it to make his points. The son of a yeoman farmer, Latimer kept a rustic touch in his preaching, drawing on his experiences of farming on his father's Leicestershire estate.

His best known sermon is "The Sermon on the Plough," preached in St. Paul's Cathedral on January 18, 1548. In this sermon, Latimer said the preacher should be like the ploughman, because he should "labour [at] all seasons of the year." He lamented the fact that the clergy had forsaken ploughing for "lording and loitering." And then he launched into this famous passage:

> And now I would ask a strange question: who is the most diligent bishop and prelate in all England? . . . I know him well . . . it is the devil. He is the most diligent preacher of all other; he is never out of his diocess [*sic*] . . . ye shall never find him unoccupied. . . . [H]e is ever at his plough. . . . Where the devil is resident, and hath his plough going, there away with books, and up with candles; away with bibles, and up with beads; away with the light of the gospel, and up with the light of candles, yea, at noon-days. . . . [U]p with man's traditions and his laws, down with God's traditions and his most holy word. . . .
>
> [I]f you will not learn of God, nor good men, to be diligent in your office, learn of the devil.[35]

His bold scenic preaching gives us a strong hint as to why he became a martyr of the English Reformation. In 1555, under the Catholic Queen Mary, he was burned at the stake.

Ignatius of Loyola (1491–1556)

Another scene-making preacher was Ignatius of Loyola, a Spanish knight from a Basque noble family, later a priest and theologian, who founded the Society of Jesus (Jesuits) as part of the Counter Reformation. As a soldier, he was hit by a cannon ball in the femur, laid up for months with little reading material beyond the Bible. He began entering with his imagination into the events recounted in Scripture, invited into the scenes by the sensory details of the texts. He developed the highly imaginative "Spiritual Exercises": meditations, using all five senses, on a series of sacred images of eternal realities, from incidents in the life, death, and resurrection of Jesus as well as the Last Judgment. The purpose of these exercises is to help Christians see how and where God is active in their everyday lives, to purify their motivations, ridding them of idolatry and living in trust and obedience to God with gratitude, humility, and joy.

Women Preachers through the Centuries

Examples of women teaching and preaching publically abound in biblical stories and legends, and women preachers played a role in the leadership of the early Church. The scene of Mary Magdalene running from the tomb to tell the good news to the male disciples was imprinted in the mind of the early Church. For the first few centuries, Mary Magdalene and Catherine of Alexandria, a fourth-century martyr, were held up as examples of admirable and effective women preachers. But as the Church moved from movement to institution, patriarchal values reasserted themselves, and women's teaching and preaching were largely relegated to the private sphere. Early church fathers argued that women were responsible for original sin, intellectually inferior to men, and created for a purely subordinate role. Their objections were codified in Church councils of the fourth century, and restrictions on women's preaching and teaching, regardless of their learning, became even tighter as time rolled on.

Women mystics and scholars—like German Benedictine Abbess Hildegard of Bingen (1098–1179), English Anchoress Julian of Norwich, and Italian Catherine of Siena (1347–1380)—were respected for their visions and writings, but male clergy tended to attribute these more to divine inspiration than to learning and intellectual keenness.[36]

Despite this denigration of their abilities and prohibition of their preaching, women have taught and preached in both their homes and communities throughout every century. Examples include the women preachers of the Cathars and Waldensians of Southern Europe in the twelfth and thirteenth centuries, the radical Protestant Lollard women of England in the fourteenth and fifteenth centuries, the Catholic Ursulines of the sixteenth century, Anne Marbury Hutchinson's outspoken preaching in Puritan New England (1591–1643),[37] and the eighteenth-century women teachers and preachers of the Moravian and Quaker movements. They include the preaching of Jarena Lee (1783–1864), the nineteenth-century itinerant preacher—the first woman licensed to preach in the African Methodist Episcopal Church—and Sojourner Truth (1797–1883) and her "Ain't I a Woman?" speech of 1851, at the Ohio Women's Rights Convention in Akron, Ohio.[38]

They include Mother Leafy Anderson's (1887–1927) gender-bending preaching and prophesying in the black spiritualist churches of New Orleans of the 1920s, and the fervent, spiritually inspired public pageantry of suffragist gatherings in the early 1900s.[39] They also include Pentecostal evangelist Aimee Semple McPherson's (1890–1944) dramatic sermons, staged as scenes, complete with costumes and sets.

Julian of Norwich (1342–1416)

Julian of Norwich was an English anchoress who devoted her life to spiritual contemplation in a small room attached to the outer wall of the Church of St. Julian. She is venerated in the Anglican and Lutheran churches.[40] She turned her knack for noticing on her rich inner experience of a Trinitarian God. Her *Revelations of Divine Love* (also known as *A Revelation of Divine Love in Sixteen Shewings*, or simply *Showings*), written in 1395, is the first theological book in English known to have been written by a woman. Julian entered a religious order at a young age. Seriously ill at age thirty, Julian received sixteen different visions (or *showings*) of the love of God over a twelve-hour period. She recorded her visions in what is known as the "Short Text" of the *Showings*. Some twenty years later, she produced the "Long Text," which includes theological and devotional reflections on each vision. Though her ministry did not include public proclamation, her *Showings* eventually disseminated to an audience far beyond her cell. *Showings* displays many different literary genres, some reminiscent of the medieval sermon, with divisions and subdivisions. It also includes parables and allegorical dramas that use imagery and details common to medieval drama of the time, drawing readers into an experience of God's love, often portrayed as maternal in nature. Julian's writings reveal her knowledge of Scripture and classical spiritual writings of her day, as well as her literary skill. She painted scenes of Christ as mother, comparing the motherhood of God with earthly motherhood, involving childbearing, nourishing, caring, comforting, and disciplining.[41]

> So Jesus Christ who sets good against evil is our real Mother. We owe our being to him—and this is the essence of motherhood!—and all the delightful, loving protection which ever follows. God is as really our Mother as he is our Father. (p. 295)
>
> So Jesus is our true Mother in nature by our first creation, and he is our true Mother in grace by his taking our created nature. (p. 296)
>
> The mother can give her child to suck of her milk, but our precious Mother Jesus can feed us with himself, and does, most courteously and most tenderly, with the blessed sacrament, which is the precious food of true life. . . .
>
> The mother can lay the child tenderly to her breast, but our tender Mother Jesus can lead us easily into his blessed breast through his sweet open side. (p. 298)[42]

Julian's scene making had a subversive dynamic in a patriarchal church and society. Says homiletician Eunjoo Kim, in her study of women preachers through the centuries,

> By placing feminine images of God in the center of Christian theology, Julian challenged the rigid concepts of God in the medieval church and its theology. Her description of God in such feminine images was truly a subversive voice from the margins, chipping away at the masculine-centered Christianity.[43]

Martin Luther (1483–1546)

The Reformers favored biblical exposition and catechetical instruction in their preaching, but there was at least one among them who knew how to make a scene.[44] In his 1522 sermon, "The Gospel for Christmas Eve," Martin Luther turned his knack for noticing on the text itself, vividly portraying the manger and the young mother:

> . . . nobody took pity on this young woman who was about to give birth for the first time; nobody took to heart the heaviness of her

body; and nobody cared that she was in strange surroundings and did not have any of the things which a woman in childbirth needs. Rather, she was there without anything ready, without light, without fire, in the middle of the night, alone in the darkness. Nobody offered her any of the services which one naturally renders to pregnant women. Everyone was drunk and roistering in the inn, a throng of guests from everywhere, and nobody bothered about this woman.

Then comes the next sentence from this gifted preacher:

Therefore see to it that you derive from the Gospel not only the enjoyment of the story as such, for that will not last long. . . . But see to it that you make his birth your own.[45]

Says homiletician John C. Holbert of this scene, "No preacher since has combined the two elements of the gospel, its mystery and its earthy reality, better than Martin Luther."[46]

John Donne (1572–1631)

John Donne was an Anglican poet, royal chaplain, popular preacher, and, for the decade prior to his death, the dean of St. Paul's Cathedral. He put his knack for noticing, a hallmark of poets, together with his gift for language in what are some of the best known lines in the English language. He combines his observations about his inner pain with external stimuli in these moving yet simple words.

No man is an island, entire of itself; every man is a piece of the continent, a part of the main. If a clod be washed away by the sea, Europe is the less, as well as if a promontory were, as well as any manner of thy friend's or of thine own were: any man's death diminishes me, because I am involved in mankind, and therefore never send to know for whom the bells tolls; it tolls for thee.[47]

These lines come from a prose work, *Devotions upon Emergent Occasions, and severall* [sic] *steps in my Sicknes* [sic], written in 1624. The book expresses his reflections in light of his very serious bout with spotted fever.[48] Donne had been lying in illness, isolated from others due to his infection, listening to the church bells tolling the deaths in the community and wondering who had died. Says homiletician Paul Scott Wilson:

"It is such simple, poignant images of the world about us that we might seek to isolate in our own sermons to imaginative effect."[49]

John Bunyan (1621–1688)

Puritan allegorist John Bunyan knew how to make a scene. His allegory of the Christian life from a state of lost sinfulness to salvation, *The Pilgrim's Progress*, became, after the Bible, the single most popular book of Reformed Piety. In addition to this popular work, Bunyan wrote more than sixty sermons. As a teenager, he joined the Parliamentary Army in the early stages of the English Civil War. After he returned to Bedford, he took up his father's trade as a tinker and brazier, making and repairing household pans and kettles as well as farming implements and harnesses. He traveled through the countryside in the course of his work, collecting items that needed repair and selling others. The anvil a traveling tinker would carry on his back, along with other tools, weighed sixty pounds. It is not surprising that Bunyan's metaphor for sin was a great weight or "burden" on the back.[50]

He joined a nonconformist group and became a preacher. When King Charles was restored to the throne in 1660, nonconformists were put on a short leash. Bunyan spent the next twelve years in prison. He wrote *The Pilgrim's Progress* during his imprisonment.[51]

Bunyan trained his knack for noticing on his everyday surroundings, the landscape of his life. The images Bunyan uses in *The Pilgrim's Progress* are reflections of images from his own world; the "strait gate" is a version of the wicket gate at Elstow Abbey Church. The "Slough of Despond" is a reflection of Squitch Fen, a wet and mossy area near his cottage in Harrowden. The "Delectable Mountains" are an image of the Chiltern Hills surrounding Bedfordshire.[52]

Historian Monica Furlong, in her book *Puritan's Progress: A Study of John Bunyan*, points out that:

> Images of the traveler occur constantly in Bunyan's work. Christian and Faithful in *The Pilgrim's Progress* take a forbidden route because "the way from the River was rough, and their feet tender by reason of their Travels." The women in the second part of *The Pilgrim's Progress* have the alarming experience of being attacked by a fierce dog when they try to knock at the wicket-gate. Mud on the road, boggy ground, sweat, physical exhaustion, the comfort of good lodgings, the sight of men hanging on a gibbet, encounter with a harlot,

encounter with footpads, are all mentioned in Bunyan's writings and suggest some of the practical hardships of the life of a travelling tradesman or "mechanick."[53]

Commenting on his work, homiletician Thomas Troeger says this: "In the absence of the stained glass and statuary, this author's imaginative fusion of Scripture and scenes from the English countryside created the slough of despond, the hill of difficulty, vanity fair, and the castle of doubt. It supplied to the imagination what was denied to the eye.[54]

Today's scenic preacher can take a page out of Bunyan's book, noticing concrete details in her own surroundings and bringing them into her sermonic scenes to make them realistic and familiar to listeners.

In 1899, Rev. John Brown, B.A., D.D., was asked to offer the Beecher Lectures. Rev. Brown's topic was "Puritan Preaching in England: A Study of Past and Present." He ended his lecture on John Bunyan with a poem of his own composition. For Brown, Bunyan is a spiritual guide who shows us the way:

> We want *our* Bunyan to show the way
> Through the Sloughs of Despond that are round us to-day,
> Our guide for straggling souls to wait,
> And lift the latch of the wicket-gate.
> We fain would listen, O Preacher and Peer,
> To a voice like that of this Tinker-Seer,
> Who guided the Pilgrim up, beyond
> The Valley of Death and the Slough of Despond,
> And Doubting Castle and Giant Despair,
> To those Delectable Mountains fair,
> And over the River, and in at the Gate
> Where for weary Pilgrims the Angels wait.[55]

George Whitefield (1714–1770)

George Whitefield was the leading Reformed Evangelical clergyman of the eighteenth century, the driving force behind evangelical revivals on both sides of the Atlantic. He combined deeply felt religious conviction, a charismatic personality, dramatic flair, storytelling skills, and a voice that was coveted by the greatest actors of his day. The coalescence of his gifts, fired by the Holy Spirit, made him an oratorical phenomenon; he once drew a crowd of up to eighty thousand in Hyde Park. This son of

Gloucester innkeepers could speak to uneducated laborers as well as the wealthy and the intellectual elite of his day. In his lifetime, he preached at least eighteen thousand times to perhaps ten million hearers. He knew how to dramatize portions of Scripture, how to use humor to lower defenses, and how to use everyday stories and impromptu illustrations. His sermons, transcribed from the notes of listeners, hardly do his oratory justice. Still, a few scenes shine through.

An American gentleman once went to hear Whitefield, having heard of his reputation as a spellbinding preacher. The day was rainy, the congregation thin, and the beginning of the sermon rather heavy. The American began to say to himself,

> "This man is no great wonder after all." He looked around and saw the congregation as little interested as himself. One old man, in front of the pulpit, had fallen asleep. But all at once Whitefield stopped short. His countenance changed. And then he suddenly broke forth in an altered tone: "If I had come to speak to you in my own name, you might well rest your elbows on your knees, and your heads on your hands, and sleep; and once in a while look up and say, What is this babbler talking of? But I have not come to you in my own name. No! I have come to you in the name of the Lord of Hosts." There he brought down his hand and foot with a force that made the building ring, "and I must and will be heard." The congregation started. The old man woke up at once. "Ay! Ay!" cried Whitfield, fixing his eyes upon him, "I have waked you up, have I? I meant to do it. I am not come here to preach to stocks and stones: I have come to you in the name of the Lord God of Hosts, and I must, and will, have an audience." The hearers were stripped of their apathy at once. Every word of the sermon after this was heard with deep attention.[56]

On another occasion, the statesman and man of letters Lord Chesterfield was among Whitefield's hearers. The great preacher, in describing the miserable condition of an unconverted sinner, illustrated the subject by painting a scene of a blind beggar: a dark night, a dangerous road. The poor beggar had been deserted by his dog near the edge of a cliff and had nothing to help him, groping his way along with only his cane. Whitefield warmed to his subject, conveying the man's dangerous plight with such graphic power that the whole audience was kept in breathless silence, as if it saw the movements of the poor old man. Finally, "when the beggar was about to take the fatal step that would have hurled him down the precipice to certain destruction, Lord Chesterfield actually made a rush forward to save him, exclaiming aloud, 'He is gone! He is gone!' The noble lord had been so entirely carried away by the preacher, that he forgot the whole was a picture."[57]

Whitefield was known to inject his sermons with impromptu examples and scenes. Once, when preaching on eternity, he suddenly stopped his message, looked around, and exclaimed, "Hark! Methinks I hear [the saints] chanting forth their everlasting Hallelujahs, and echoing triumphant songs of joy. And do you not long, my brethren, to join this heavenly choir?"[58]

> In 1770, the 55-year-old continued his preaching tour in the colonies as if he were still a young itinerant, insisting, "I would rather wear out than rust out." He ignored the danger signs, in particular asthmatic "colds" that brought "great difficulty" in breathing. His last sermon took place in Newburyport, Massachusetts, in the fields, atop a large barrel.
>
> "He was speaking of the inefficiency of works to merit salvation," one listener recounted for the press, "and suddenly cried out in a tone of thunder, 'Works! works! A man gets to heaven by works! I would as soon think of climbing to the moon on a rope of sand.'"
>
> The following morning he died.[59]

Preaching in the Hush Harbors

Slave preachers presided over the slaves' religious lives. Often illiterate, dramatically called and oratorically gifted, they held prayer meetings, preached, and ministered in difficult conditions, often in secret. Under close surveillance, they had to live in the tension between the demands of conscience and the orders of their masters. One slave preacher recounts how the master told him to tell his people that if they obey the master they go to Heaven. He continued, "but I knowed there's something better for them, but daren't tell them 'cept on the sly. That I done lots. I tell 'em iffen they keeps prayin' the Lord will set 'em free.[60]

Slaves devised several techniques to avoid detection of their meetings. One practice was to meet in secluded places: woods, gullies, ravines, and thickets (aptly called "hush harbors"). "Kalvin Woods remembered preaching to other slaves and singing and praying while huddled behind quilts and rags, which had been thoroughly wetted 'to keep the sound of their voices from penetrating the air' and then hung up 'in the form of a little room,' or tabernacle."[61]

Slave preachers' sermons were characterized by vivid imagery, dynamic delivery, and vivid dramatizations of biblical narratives. "What wonderful preachers these blacks are!" exclaimed one correspondent from Georgia in a letter to the editor of *The American Missionary* in 1868, three years after the Civil War ended.[62]

> I listened to a remarkable sermon or talk a few evenings since. The preacher spoke of the need of atonement for sin. "Bullocks c'dn't do it, heifers c'dn't do it, de blood of doves c'dn't do it—but up in heaven, for thousan and thousan of years, the Son was saying to the Father, 'Put up a soul, put up a soul. Prepare me a body, an I will go an meet Justice on Calvary's brow!'" He was so dramatic. In describing the crucifixion he said: "I see the sun when she turned herself black. I see the stars a fallin from the sky, and them old Herods coming out of their graves and goin about the city, an they knew 'twas the Lord of Glory."[63]

Women Preachers of the Methodist Movement

John Wesley's sermons, at least in their written form, are not in themselves particularly well known for scenic anecdotes and illustrations, being mostly composed of rational argument and explanation. His knack for noticing his inner life and context show up more often in episodes from his life recounted in his journals. There, today's preachers can find a rich anecdotal feast! When you read Wesley's sermons you have to wonder how he drew crowds of up to twenty thousand. There is, of course, a difference between written and oral communication. It would appear that Wesley made strong emotional appeals in his oral preaching, which his published sermons do little to suggest.[64]

Over the course of his lifetime, John Wesley (1703–1791) gradually came to the conclusion that women's preaching should be authorized for his movement. The egalitarian quality of the Wesleyan revival springs from several principles it shared with other renewal movements that emerged from the Protestant Reformation: the value of individual souls, the possibility of direct communion with God, the emphasis on the present activity of the Holy Spirit in the life of the believer, the importance placed on shared Christian experience, and the Reformation doctrine of the priesthood of all believers. Add to this Wesley's dynamic view of salvation as a gift of unmerited grace, and we should not be surprised that he came to believe that "no one, even a woman, ought to be prohibited from doing God's work."[65] Wesley viewed his movement as God's use of exceptional means (including lay preaching) to revive the Church of England. He was led to embrace the ministry of exceptional women who clearly produced great fruit, naming it "an extraordinary call."[66]

When John Wesley offered his cautious endorsement of women preachers in 1761, Methodist women began preaching to female and mixed audiences with great impact. Their preaching was characterized by plain speech and emotional fervor.[67] Unfortunately, after Wesley's death, institutionalizing, patriarchal forces reasserted themselves. The 1803 Annual Conference prohibited women from preaching, because so many people opposed it, and because there were judged to be enough male preachers. Women, if they were certain they had an "extraordinary call," could preach to other women, but only with the permission of the male clerical authorities in their circuits.[68]

The following excerpt is from the opening of a sermon (precise date unknown) by Mary Bosanquet Fletcher, a Methodist preacher active in Madeley, England in the 1780–1790s. She displays both her knack for noticing details of the text and her congregation's concerns as she invited listeners to bring their inner storms into the scene depicted in the text.

"Fearing that we might run on the rocks, they let down four anchors from the stern and prayed for day to come." (Acts 27:29)

The situation of the ship wherein Paul and his companions were, seems to me to illustrate the state and situation of many of us here.—We are told,—"There arose a tempestuous wind called, in that country, Euroclydon,"—a kind of hurricane, not carrying the ship any one way, but driving her backwards and forwards with great violence. So it is in general with those who enter the voyage of life. Satan, who is called the Prince of the power of the air, and who ruleth in the hearts of the children of disobedience, keeps the mind in a continual agitation. Sometimes they are sunk, and almost crushed, under a weight of care; and again raised high in the waves of some expected pleasure. . . . Sometimes the most idle and extravagant fancies so deeply involve it, that no message from heaven could find any more entertainment than the Saviour could find in the Inn at Bethlehem. By all this, the soul becomes restless, and knows not where it is, nor which way it is going. . . . Dear souls, is not this the case with some of you? . . . But I hope those of you who are this night within the reach of my voice, are in a degree awakened, and most of you earnestly longing to be brought out of the storm into the quiet harbor of Jesu's breast. To these I feel chiefly my message to be, though I was not willing to leave the sleepers wholly disregarded.[69]

Jarena Lee (1783–1864)

Around the same time that Mary Fletcher was preaching in England, a baby girl, Jarena Lee, was born in Cape May, New Jersey. Born February 11, 1783, of free but financially struggling parents, she was hired out as a servant girl at age seven. At age twenty-one, she was converted to Christianity and entered into a time of spiritual struggle and discernment. In 1811, she began to feel a call to preach and shared her sense of calling with Rev. Richard Allen, then founder and minister in charge of the Bethel African Methodist Episcopal Church in Philadelphia. He refused to recognize her in any official preaching capacity but authorized her to hold prayer meetings or exhort congregations after the licensed ministers had preached their sermons.[70] She approached now Bishop Richard Allen several years later and got a warmer response. She was accepted by the A.M.E. hierarchy, not as a licensed preacher, but as an official traveling exhorter. She traveled all over the Middle Atlantic and Northeastern States, preaching to both black and white audiences. In 1835, she traveled over seven hundred miles and preached almost the same number of sermons. She wrote her autobiography out of a conviction that her record of God's work in her life would lead others to Christ. She paid $38 to have one thousand copies of her *Life* printed, handing them out at camp meetings and on the streets. The A.M.E.'s book committee turned down her request to publish a revised version, and so she financed the printing of her *Religious Experience and Journal* in 1849, which covered the story of her life up to her fiftieth birthday.[71] It describes the setting and outcome of her various sermons more than their content. The most vivid scene of all is to be found in her description of her call to preach and her initial visit to Rev. Allen:

> Between four and five years after my sanctification, on a certain time, an impressive silence fell upon me, and I stood as if someone was about to speak to me, yet I had no such thought in my heart. —But to my utter surprise there seemed to sound a voice which I thought I distinctly heard, and most certainly understand, which said to me, "Go preach the Gospel!" I immediately replied aloud, "No one will believe me." Again I listened, and again the same voice seemed to

say—"Preach the Gospel; I will put words in your mouth, and you will turn your enemies to become your friends."

At first I supposed that Satan had spoken to me, for I had read that he could transform into an angel of light for the purpose of deception. Immediately I went into a secret place, and called upon the Lord to know if he had called me to preach, and whether I was deceived or not; when there appeared to my view the form and figure of a pulpit, with a Bible lying thereon, the back of which was presented to me as plainly as if it had been a literal fact. . . .

Two days after I went to see the preacher in charge of the African Society, who was the Rev. Richard Allen . . . to tell him that I felt it my duty to preach the gospel. But as I drew near the street in which his house was . . . my courage began to fail me; so terrible did the cross appear, it seemed that I should not be able to bear it. . . . Several times on my way there, I turned back again; but as often I felt my strength again renewed, and I soon found that the nearer I approached to the house of the minister, the less was my fear."[72]

Reverend Allen, in this initial visit, informed Jarena that their Discipline did not allow for women preachers. At that point, says Lee,

[T]hat holy energy which burned within me, as a fire, began to be smothered. . . . And why should it be thought impossible, heterodox, or improper for a woman to preach? Seeing the Saviour died for the woman as well as for the man.[73]

Catherine Mumford Booth (1829–1890)

Turning our attention back to England, in the last third of the nineteenth century, the Salvation Army "Hallelujah Lasses," revived the tradition of women preaching beyond ecclesial walls. They were inspired by Catherine Mumford Booth, who, with her husband William Booth, founded the Salvation Army. Catherine, for a time, ambivalent about women's public proclamation, gradually became a fervent advocate of women's right to preach, an activist and evangelist.[74] She was, in part, inspired by American holiness theologian and preacher Phoebe Palmer. In response to male clergy criticism of Mrs. Palmer's British revival, Catherine, in December of 1859, wrote her impassioned defense of a woman's right to preach.[75]

A few months later, she recounts in her journals, she experienced the following scene.

> On Pentecost 1860 at Bethesda Chapel in Gateshead, England, as the service was concluding, she signaled to her minister husband William Booth who was standing at the front that she "wanted to say a word." She later reports that "A strange compulsion seized me. I felt I must rise and speak. An inner voice taunted me. 'You will look like a fool and have nothing to say.' I recognized this as the Devil's voice and replied "That's just the point. I have never yet been willing to be a fool for Christ. And now I will be one."[76]

Her sermon was so impressive that her husband changed his mind about women preaching. She soon developed a reputation as an outstanding speaker and could often be seen leading revival services on the docks of East London, protesting outside sweat shops where women and children worked long hours for a pittance, and standing outside match warehouses where the match women died painful, disfiguring deaths from exposure to yellow phosphorus. She preached the gospel with her words and the scenes of her life. In her pamphlet "Female Ministry: A Woman's Right to Preach the Gospel" she asked the compelling question: "Why would God endow a being with powers he never intended for her to use?"[77]

Martin Luther King Jr. (1929–1968)

A hundred years or so later, a magnificent orator arose who could paint a panoramic picture of standing on the mountain, looking over the Promised Land. But he could also, in the same address, zoom us in to view a poignant, small-screen scene:

> It came out in the *New York Times* the next morning, that if I had sneezed, I would have died. Well, about four days later, they allowed me, after the operation, after my chest had been opened, and the blade had been taken out, to move around in the wheel chair in the hospital. They allowed me to read some of the mail that came in, and from all over the states, and the world, kind letters came in. . . . I had received one from the President and the Vice-President. I've forgotten what those telegrams said. . . . But there was another letter that came . . . and I'll never forget it. It said simply, "Dear Dr. King. I am a ninth-grade student at White Plains High School. . . . While

it should not matter, I would like to mention that I am a white girl. I read in the paper of your misfortune, and of your suffering. And I read that if you had sneezed, you would have died. And I'm simply writing you to say that I'm so happy that you didn't sneeze."

And I want to say tonight, I want to say that I am happy that I didn't sneeze. Because if I had sneezed, I wouldn't have been around here in 1960, when students all over the South started sitting-in at lunch counters. And I knew that as they were sitting in, they were really standing up for the best in the American dream. And taking the whole nation back to those great wells of democracy which were dug deep by the Founding Fathers in the Declaration of Independence and the Constitution. If I had sneezed, I wouldn't have been around in 1962, when Negroes in Albany, Georgia, decided to straighten their backs up. And whenever men and women straighten their backs up, they are going somewhere, because a man can't ride your back unless it is bent. If I had sneezed, I wouldn't have been here in 1963, when the black people of Birmingham, Alabama, aroused the conscience of this nation, and brought into being the Civil Rights Bill. If I had sneezed, I wouldn't have had a chance later that year, in August, to try to tell America about a dream that I had had. If I had sneezed, I wouldn't have been down in Selma, Alabama, to see the great movement there. If I had sneezed, I wouldn't have been in Memphis to see a community rally around those brothers and sisters who are suffering. I'm so happy that I didn't sneeze.[78]

Noticing and Failing to Notice

You will notice that these preachers, in crafting scenes in their sermons, drew from their own inner experience (inscape), their attentiveness to the text (textscape), and events and places in the world around them (landscape). If we take a page out of their book, we will fine tune our knack for noticing the elements of scene, character, conflict, and setting, in life within and around us.

What scenes have you used recently in your sermons? If you are like me, there are just as many that you have missed. The English mystic Evelyn Underhill writes, "For lack of attention, a thousand forms of loveliness elude us every day."[79]

Sometimes our failure to notice is due to a lack of discipline. We notice a scene or experience a flash of insight, a "that'll preach!" moment;

but, since we don't record it, it slips away. Thomas Troeger challenges preachers that "it takes discipline to see and to hear the visions and voices of God in our life, discipline every bit as strenuous as exegesis."[80]

Sometimes our failure to notice may be self-protective. We fail to notice certain scenes because they are painful to face. Attentiveness requires daring and courage because it requires empathy, a form of imagination that can be very painful. Many novelists feel that the empathy to imagine others' lives is the genesis of fiction writing, that novelists create their characters by first becoming them. In relation to preaching, this is known as "empathic imagination." It marks the difference between preaching at and preaching for our congregation. It is an exercise in imagining what it is like to be individual members of our congregations and tailoring our messages to their needs for comfort and challenge.[81] The scene might be:

> Concertgoers scattering, seeking shelter at the Harvest Music Festival, October 1, 2017
>
> Nightclub goers at the Pulse nightclub in Orlando, Florida, huddling in terror as they were picked off by a shooter, June 16, 2016
>
> A toddler boy, face down in the surf on the Turkish shore near the resort town of Bodrum, September 2, 2015

The preacher shares with the artist the obligation to notice and open ourselves to the pain of others and the injustices of life. Attentiveness is a habit that requires not only discipline but also daring and courage. Pulitzer Prize winning fiction writer Robert Olen Butler aptly says:

> The great Japanese film director Akira Kurosawa said that to be an artist means never to avert your eyes. And that's the hardest thing because we want to flinch. The artist must go into the white hot center of himself, and our impulse when we get there is to look away and avert our eyes.[82]

Bringing scenes they'd rather not see to the attention of our congregations is an obligation of our calling to preach. The way we do it requires the exercise of wisdom. How much detail? How many scenes in one sermon? What balance between show and tell? Have I shown scenes of sorrow vividly enough to awaken the congregation's conscience? Have I shown so much that I have squelched their hope? As homiletician O. Wesley Allen points out in his book *Preaching and the Human Condition*,

"No preacher ever brought the gospel to bear on the lives of those in the pews in a way that was truly salvific while wearing floaties and standing in the baby pool of life."[83]

At the same time, he warns preachers to "resist the temptation to so thoroughly expose the congregation to trial or horrors of the human condition that it overwhelms them to the point that in the time frame of a single sermon they cannot hear any good news proclaimed."[84] Allen recommends that preachers keep their eyes on the long game, realizing that preaching is the work of more than one week, introducing an aspect of the human condition in each sermon, always to be met by God's inexorable will for justice and mercy.

Recently, more and more voices in the homiletical literature are criticizing the inadequacy of "prosperity preaching" from the "baby pool of life" in whatever cultural context it manifests itself. Luke Powery, in his book *Dem Dry Bones: Preaching, Death, and Hope* calls it "'Candy' theology"[85] and turns to African American spirituals as a resource for facing the reality of death in a context of hope.[86]

It's possible to avert our eyes, not just from the negative, but also from positive events within us and around us. We need to ask ourselves, in relation to any one sermon and to our cumulative preaching over time, "Have I *shown* the bad news and only *told about* the good news?" Then we need the reminder that the preacher's vocation is also to notice and proclaim the good news in her or his inner life, the Scriptures, and the world.[87]

Sometimes our failure to notice such scenes is due to depression, fatigue, or pessimism. We fail to discern hopeful scenes around us, places God is at work repairing the world, what the rabbis called *Tikkun Olam*.[88] Roman Catholic theologian Mary Catherine Hilkert points out that the preacher's vocation is, not only to name "ungrace," places of brutality and injustice in life and Scripture, but also to "name grace" in those same places.[89]

When we are naming grace, we notice:

> A young woman whose father and stepfather have been jealous of each other for years, but both men walking her down the aisle together at her wedding.
>
> A fifteen-year-old boy, his boat loaded with Pedialyte®, diapers, and water bottles, ferrying supplies to stranded neighbors in a South Carolina town flooded by rains in September 2015.

> Friends and family of nine people killed by a hate-filled young man on June 17, 2015, at Emmanuel African Methodist Episcopal Church in Charleston, South Carolina, gathering in a courtroom and speak words of forgiveness to him.

> A firefighter carrying a woman and her infant to safety from the waters of Hurricane Harvey in Houston, August 2017.

When God told Solomon that "no one like you has ever been before and no one like you will ever be again" (1 Kgs. 3:12), God was commissioning Solomon to activate his unique voice, not just his physical vocal chords, but his unique perspective on the world. I mentioned earlier that one's Voice, one's unique contribution in preaching, is the sum total of what one notices. If the preacher's Voice is muted, it could be because of fear: she notices plenty of things she'd like to talk about but is afraid to bring them up in the pulpit because of memories of past retaliation or fear of future consequences. If the preacher's Voice is muted it may be because of fatigue: he is too tired to notice much of anything. If the preacher's Voice is muted it may be because he or she, having preached many sermons and observed little visible change, has succumbed to a sense of futility.

I don't know for certain, but I imagine that every one of the preachers before whose portraits we have stood in our gallery experienced those same impediments to the use of their unique, incisive Voices. We have God to thank for providing them with a faith more than equal to their fear, with energy more than equal to their fatigue, and with a purpose more than powerful enough to banish any sense of futility. We have them to thank for responding to God by activating their knack for noticing, continually on high alert to where God is at work in their inner lives, their scriptural texts, and their congregational, cultural contexts.

We can walk through the marketplace in Constantinople because John Chrysostom trained his HD knack for noticing every detail of his physical surroundings.

We can sit in a cathedral as the words of a language we neither read nor understand roll over us, our eyes reflecting the jewel-tone panes of the windows that surround us, because medieval artists noticed that images can touch our minds and hearts, to teach and inspire.

We can close our eyes and see a vision of God as a nurturing mother because Julian of Norwich applied her listening heart, her knack for noticing to the literature of her day, and her own inner experience of God.

We can stand next to the manger with Martin Luther, listening to the sounds of carousing from the inn waft across the yard, because he knew how to pay a biblical scene the attention it deserves: respecting nuances of setting, plot, characters, conflict, and imagery.

We can slog through the Slough of Despond with Christian because John Bunyan kept his eyes open on the way to church and thought about what it would be like to fall into Squitch Fen and never make it out. He knew when a scene from the landscape of his own life was crying out to be connected to the struggles of the human spirit.

We can participate in a smackdown with the devil in Bethesda Chapel in 1860 because Catherine Booth knew that if she didn't grab onto and record that scene, it would slip away. So she wrote it down where it still serves as an invitation and inspiration for future preachers.

And we can look over the shoulder of Martin Luther King Jr. as he unfolds a letter written in a childish hand, and he begins to smile because he knew how to paint a wide-lens, panoramic metanarrative about justice and peace and opportunity for every child of God. But he also knew how to zoom in and show us a poignant, palm-size scene of one young girl's gesture of kindness.

Chapter Three

Making a Scene in Scripture

Scene One: The Gift of Creation—God's Knack for Noticing

There is that moment in the theater, when the house lights have been turned off but the curtain has not yet risen, when you sit expectantly in the dark. Then the curtain rises and the first scene of the play begins. In the account of creation in Genesis, which probably dates from the sixth century BCE, God is portrayed as the One who both creates something for us to notice and models the knack for noticing it. God is the first and foremost playwright—the creator, out of nothing but God's Word—of the first scene, complete with setting, characters, plot, and divine voiceover. The process of creation is fueled by the divine knack for noticing. God's repeated recognition that what God has created is good punctuates the process of Creation.[1]

> In the beginning when God created the heavens and the earth, the earth was a formless void and darkness covered the face of the deep. . . . Then God said "Let there be light"; and there was light. And God *saw* that the light was good. (Gen. 1:1–4, emphasis added)

In case we didn't catch the theme, it is repeated after each bright, lush, gleaming, rustling feature of Creation that God speaks into being: light, land, sea, sun, moon, stars, birds, beasts, and fish (Gen. 1:10, 18, 21, 25). And finally,

> So God created humankind in his image,
> in the image of God he created them;
> male and female he created them.
> 1:27

57

We hear the refrain one more time, to cap off the scene: "God *saw* everything that he had made, and indeed, it was very good" (Gen. 1:31, emphasis added).

These words "And God saw . . . that it was good" occur seven times in chapter 1. They function as an "approval formula." God, like a master craftsman who has completed a work, looks at it and finds that it is a success or judges that it is good. In the Old Testament, events are in community. They have no meaning unless they happen for something or someone. So God's judgment is that creation is good for the community.[2]

Once creation is completed, the responsibility for the ongoing noticing of its goodness is shared with the creation itself. The praise of the creator is a continuation of the recognition by the creator. Since creation is good, we are now to take up the task of praising its Creator.[3] The theme of praise is prominent in the Psalms. The Hebrew title of the Psalter is *tehillim*, "praises":[4]

> The heavens are telling the glory of God
> and the firmament proclaims his handiwork.
> Ps. 19:1

> O Lord, our Sovereign,
> how majestic is your name in all the earth!
> . . . .
> When I look at your heavens, the work of your fingers,
> the moon and the stars that you have established;
> what are human beings that you are mindful of them,
> mortals that you care for them?
> Ps. 8:1–4

Exercising our knack for noticing God's goodness in creation and offering our praises is an expression of what it means to be made in the image of God, the original *noticer*!

God's knack for noticing continues after creation. It is a golden thematic thread that unifies the ongoing scenes of Scripture. It is expressed throughout Scripture in anthropomorphic terms as the exercise of divine seeing and hearing. Are we glad God has such excellent vision and hearing? That all depends on what we are found to be doing and saying when the divine spotlight rests upon us. For throughout Scripture God reveals a knack for noticing human sin as well as human goodness. In the scene from the garden, God notices that humans have been disobedient. We aren't told how God knows this. Whether God notices an apple missing or some fig leaves torn off the tree doesn't matter. What matters is that God takes a walk in the garden, pretending (if you ask me) not to know where Adam and Eve are hiding.

After Cain's murder of Abel, Cain is standing out in the middle of the field looking down at his hands. They are cramping from the effort it took to strangle Abel, or maybe snap his neck or bash in his head with a rock, who knows? God says to Cain, "What have you done? Listen; your brother's blood is crying out to me from the ground" (Gen. 4:10)!

Genesis 6:11 paints a scene that leads to God sending a flood to destroy the earth. God surveys the world God has created, concluding that "the earth was corrupt in God's sight, and the earth was filled with violence." It is time for a do-over.

The prophets continually remind the nation of the divine knack for noticing sin.

Wild-haired, haggard Amos walks through town crying out, "The eyes of the Lord GOD are upon the sinful kingdom" (Amos 9:8).

Jeremiah stands in the town square offering a multiple-choice test to the people on God's behalf, a barrage of rapid-fire rhetorical questions: "Am I a God near by, says the LORD, and not a God far off? Who can hide in secret places so that I cannot see them? says the Lord. Do I not fill heaven and earth" (Jer. 23:23–24)? The answer code is yes, no one, and yes.

Along with scenes of God's knack for noticing human sin, there are scenes in which God notices human suffering. As Moses stands by the burning bush, sandals in hand, we hear this poignant divine address:

> Then the LORD said, "I have observed the misery of my people who are in Egypt; I have heard their cry on account of their taskmasters. Indeed, I know their sufferings, and I have come down to deliver them from the Egyptians." (Exod. 3:7–8)

The psalmists, whether tossing and turning in their beds or surrounded by enemies on the battlefield, speak of a God who notices human sufferings and comes to our assistance.

> Why do the wicked renounce God,
>   and say in their hearts, "You will not call us to account?"
> But you do see! Indeed you note trouble and grief,
>   that you may take it into your hands;

the helpless commit themselves to you;
  you have been the helper of the orphan.

Ps. 10:13–14

In the Hebrew Scriptures, God is portrayed as attentive through the metaphors of human sight and hearing; by contrast, the idols of other nations are dumb as posts. They have no ability to notice anything.

The idols of the nations are silver and gold,
  the work of human hands.
They have mouths, but they do not speak;
  they have eyes, but they do not see;
they have ears, but they do not hear,
  and there is no breath in their mouths.
Those who make them
  and all who trust them
  shall become like them.

Ps. 135:15–18

We exercise our knack for noticing as an expression of our being made in the image of a God who is alive and alert.

And that is the end of scene 1. We will now take a ten-minute break. There are refreshments in the lobby.

Scene Two: The Gift of Wisdom—Our Knack for Noticing

The curtain is back up for scene 2. In this scene, we get to meet Someone we may not have noticed in scene 1, but who was present and played an active role. In Proverbs 8, she introduces herself to us:

The LORD created me at the beginning of his work,
  the first of his acts of long ago.
Ages ago I was set up,
  at the first, before the beginning of the earth.
When there were no depths I was brought forth,
  when there were no springs abounding with water.
. . . .
  then I was beside him, like a master worker;
and I was daily his delight,
  rejoicing before him always,

rejoicing in his inhabited world
and delighting in the human race.
Prov. 8:22–24, 30–31

And in Proverbs 3, we learn that

The LORD by wisdom founded the earth;
by understanding he established the heavens;
by his knowledge the deeps broke open,
and the clouds drop down the dew.
Prov. 3:19–20

Woman Wisdom expresses an aspect of the character of God at work in the world. Wisdom is the gift of God's ordering Presence at work in the multiple scenes of our daily lives and the natural world. What good is a gift if we can't discern and appreciate it? So along with this gift of Wisdom has come the knack for noticing it. The sages of Israel believed this knack was a divinely created gift. "The hearing ear and the seeing eye— / the LORD has made them both" (Prov. 20:12). We recall from the scene of Solomon at Gibeon in 1 Kings 3 that the *lev shomea*, the "discerning mind" or the "listening heart," is the gift Solomon requests from God. "For the LORD gives wisdom; / from his mouth come knowledge and understanding" (Prov. 2:6).

When I was in the fifth grade, my mother took me to an eye doctor for a checkup. The teacher had suggested it. "Alyce does well with reading. But when we do math problems, I have to put her on the front row, because I don't think she can see the board."

The eye doctor informed my mother, "Your daughter is severely myopic, and she has astigmatism in her right eye." I still remember the feeling when, at age ten, I put on my new glasses, and, for the first time, I saw that the world had shape and sharpness. I had assumed that, beyond the radius of a foot or two, it was a blur for everyone. I am sorry to report, however, that my math grades showed no noticeable improvement.

When our son Matthew was three years old, I took him along on my annual eye checkup. I sat in the big padded chair. He stood beside me, looking around with wide-eyed interest at the grapefruit-sized plastic replica of the human eye on the counter and the eye chart on the wall. At the doctor's request, I took off my glasses and began to read the lowest row I could. "A E B . . . and that is, well, I'm not sure what that one is. It could be a D or it could be an O." At that point, I heard an earnest little voice in my ear, "Mommy," he said, "It's an O!" I looked down into his worried little face and read his thoughts. "My future is in the hands of a woman who does not even know the alphabet!" "Son," I said, "I can read, I just can't see. That's what the glasses are for."

That's what wisdom is for. We are given wisdom to discern Wisdom. We are to train our knack for noticing on our inner lives, our scriptural traditions, and our surroundings to discern where God's Wisdom is at work in the world. We are to watch and to listen.

> [D]o not let these [insights] escape from your sight:
>   keep sound wisdom and prudence,
> . . . .
> Then you will walk on your way securely
>   and your foot will not stumble.
>
> Prov. 3:21–23

> "And now my children, listen to me:
> . . . .
> Happy is the one who listens to me,
>   watching daily at my gates,
>   waiting beside my doors."
>
> Prov. 8:32–34[5]

Biblical Wisdom's description of foolishness is being "wise in one's own eyes."[6] It's as if to say, "I don't need to seek God's Wisdom to watch or listen for where God is at work in the world because my own opinions are all I need."

> A fool takes no pleasure in understanding,
>   but only in expressing personal opinion.
>
> Prov. 18:2

It would be the equivalent of my saying to the eye doctor: I don't need your knowledge or experience. The problem is that the world is blurry, not that my eyesight is poor.

Proverbs recommends the fear of the Lord as the antidote to being wise in our own eyes.

> Do not be wise in your own eyes;
>   fear the LORD, and turn away from evil.

> It will be a healing for your flesh
>> and a refreshment for your body.
>>> Prov. 3:7–8

The "fear of the LORD" is not, "Be afraid, because God's gonna get-cha!" On the contrary, Proverbs 1:7 tells us that "the fear of the LORD is the beginning of knowledge."

The fear of the Lord is biblical Wisdom's code word for faith. In its broad canonical context, it consists of a mix of trembling before God's transcendence, trusting in God's faithfulness, and being willing to take directions from God.[7] It is the one fear we are to spend our lives cultivating, the fear to end all lesser fears. The fear of the Lord fuels the knack for noticing, the listening heart, that posture of grateful attentiveness to God whose fruit is wise and scenic teaching and preaching.

That marks the end of scene two. Don't go far. You will not want to miss the next scene.

Scene Three: The Gift of Wisdom in Person—the Word Made Flesh

In the first scene of our play, God appeared to be alone on the stage. In the second scene, we discovered that Woman Wisdom had been present as well. And now, in this third act, we are told that the Word (*Logos*) was also involved. This certainly qualifies as a pileup of protagonists! To say that their interrelationships are complex is a ludicrous understatement. Are Sophia (Woman Wisdom) and Jesus the Word (Logos) the same entity? Or does he steal her identity and delete her name from the script? Or do they coexist, moving forward into future scenes as Son and Holy Spirit?[8] The prologue to the Gospel of John borrows the qualities and job description of Woman Wisdom from Proverbs 8 and attributes them to the Word (*Logos*). John wasn't the first to make this connection. A century earlier, the Hellenistic Jewish philosopher Philo identified the feminine-gendered Jewish Wisdom with the masculine-gendered Greek Logos. So John introduces Jesus as the only begotten Son of the Father rather than the Son of Divine Sophia.[9] Fast forward past the prologue, and we find most early church writers following John's and Philo's lead and identifying Wisdom with the Logos, the divine in Jesus Christ.[10] The unfortunate result was that the tradition of the Divine Feminine was suppressed by the trinitarian and christological disputes of the early church.[11] Divine Wisdom has played a significant role in Orthodox theology but less so in modern Western theology. An exception is the work of feminists, especially Catholics, who have explored her appearances in what are called the "apocryphal" or "deuterocanonical" books.[12]

In Greek drama, the tent (*skene*, the origin of the word *scene*) was where the actors changed in between acts of a play. In the eloquent prologue to the Gospel of John, we are told that God came to earth as chief protagonist and brought his own tent, his incarnate human body. "The Word became flesh and lived among us" (John 1:14). The Greek verb *skenoun* ("make a dwelling or pitch a tent") is related to *skene*, the word for tent. The verse's literal meaning is "And the Word became flesh and 'made a dwelling' or 'pitched a tent' among us."[13] This majestic yet intimate assurance has Old Testament resonance. In Exodus 25:8–9, Israel is told to make a tent (the tabernacle, *skene*) so that God can dwell among God's people. The tabernacle becomes God's localized presence on earth. In the traumas of exile, God promises, in better days to come, to "reside among the people of Israel forever" (Ezek. 43:7).[14] Not only in the Pentateuch and the prophets, but also in the wisdom literature from the intertestamental period, we find the theme of God's tenting with us. In The Wisdom of Jesus Ben Sirach 24:8, Wisdom sings: "The Creator of all . . . / chose the spot for my tent, / saying, In Jacob make your dwelling (*kataskenoun*), / in Israel your inheritance."[15] In rabbinic theology, *shekinah*, whose root in Hebrew resembles the Greek verb "to tent," became a technical term for God's presence dwelling among God's people.[16]

The Incarnation is God coming into our earthly scene to make a scene with us. God doesn't follow the advice, "Don't make a scene. Don't draw others into our drama." God voluntarily allowed Godself to be drawn into the human drama, whose initial, delightful plotline had long since veered into dangerous, devious paths. God allowed Godself to be drawn into the arena of the world God created as good, with human beings made in the divine image, but in which sin now flourished alongside goodness.

New Testament scholar Ben Witherington characterizes Jesus as, "Wisdom in Person."[17] The name is quite appropriate, given that the seven "I am" sayings of John's Gospel echo the gifts promised by Woman Wisdom in the book of Proverbs.[18] There are also multiple texts in the Synoptic Gospels that identify Jesus as Wisdom.[19]

Proverbs 1:7 tells us that "the fear of the LORD is the beginning of wisdom." The New Testament tells us that faith in Jesus Christ as the Word and Wisdom of God is the beginning of wisdom. This Wisdom is a gift, but it is a gift that calls for disciplined pursuit. It requires that we be doers, not just hearers of the Word (see Matt. 7:21; Jas. 1:22). In this we are not alone. For Wisdom has come in person to demonstrate the divine knack for noticing both human sin and human suffering, to call us to repentance, and to offer us divine grace

Or, as my grandson Graham would say, "Jesus is walking by the seashore telling people that he loves them."[20] We are now to walk along with him, activating our knack for noticing in the scenes of our everyday lives.

This Jesus has an almost uncanny ability to discern the negative, self-centered thoughts, of both his enemies and his disciples. In Matthew 9, Jesus has just healed a paralytic with an assurance of the forgiveness of his sins (9:2). We can almost hear the inner murmurings of the scribes hovering in the air: "'This man is blaspheming.' But Jesus, perceiving their thoughts, said, 'Why do you think evil in your hearts'" (Matt. 9:3–4)?

Likewise, when his disciples argue among themselves as to which one of them was the greatest, "Jesus, aware of their inner thoughts, took a little child and put it by his side, and said to them, . . . the least among all of you is the greatest" (Luke 9:46–48; see also Mark 9:33–37).

Jesus mirrors the divine attentiveness not only to human sin but also to human need.

Jesus is portrayed in scene after scene, in both John's Gospel and the Synoptic Gospels, as acutely attentive and perceptive when it comes to human thoughts and impulses. John's Gospel recounts several encounters with troubled people stuck in their circumstances. Jesus discerns both their deepest dreads and their hearts' desires and invites them to break free of their barriers to enter into community and wholeness.[21]

In the Synoptic Gospels, we are told that "Jesus went about all the cities and villages, teaching in their synagogues, and proclaiming the good news of the kingdom, and curing every disease and every sickness" (Matt. 9:35; see also Mark 6:34).

His motivation was attentiveness to the sufferings of God's children. "When he saw the crowds, he had compassion for them, because they were harassed and helpless, like sheep without a shepherd" (Matt. 9:36).

Jesus notices the plight of those on the bottom rungs of society of the day: the poor, the disabled and chronically ill, those forced into roles in which they have no control over their bodies, those the Roman Empire refers to as "the expendables." New Testament scholar Stephen J. Patterson describes their condition in his book *The God of Jesus: The Historical Jesus and the Search for Meaning.*

> They are expendable because they have nothing to offer the culture that might be considered of value. They are the beggars and the homeless. These are persons who might do those jobs no one else

would do, like tax collecting. These are persons whose person counts for nothing, like prostitutes. . . . There is no savings account put away for a rainy day. When it rains, you beg or starve. For a peasant living at a subsistence level, expendability is only one day away.[22]

Not only is Jesus attentive to their plight, but he invites them into his table fellowship. He honors children in the presence of his self-important disciples.[23] He honors women in the presence of their judgmental detractors, for example: John 8:1–11 (woman caught in adultery); Mark 14:3–9 (woman who anointed Jesus at Bethany); John 4 (woman at well). He includes women as his followers.

Matthew 20:32 depicts two blind men calling to Jesus when he is leaving Jericho. Even through the din of the crowd Jesus hears their cries. "Jesus stood still and called them, saying, 'What do you want me to do for you?'"

A similar account appears in Mark 10, in the story of the healing of blind Bartimaeus. The phrase "Jesus stood still" (v. 49) appears to have embedded itself in the memories of the evangelists as epitomizing Jesus' hyper-attentiveness to the sufferings of others.

Jesus enjoins his followers to exercise their own knack for noticing. "Let anyone with ears, listen" (Matt. 11:15; Mark 4:9)!

Not only in his life but also in his teachings, Jesus demonstrates his knack for noticing. In his scenic preaching, he is indebted to the sages of Israel, masters of proverb and story.

I want to give them their due before turning to Jesus' own scenic preaching.

The Sages of Proverbs Make a Scene

I mentioned in chapter 2 my first encounter with scenes from Proverbs in graduate school. After writing that first paper, I was drawn into the study of the scenes of Proverbs with no more will than a speck of lint being sucked into an Oreck® Commercial Triple Brush Push Power Sweeper. So strong was the appeal of the scenes in Proverbs that, after my initial experience with them, I found myself drawn into scenes from Old Testament wisdom literature beyond Proverbs, scenes painted by the authors of Job and Ecclesiastes. I eventually wrote a dissertation entitled "Subversive Sages: Preaching on the Proverbial Sayings of Proverbs, Qoheleth and the Synoptic Jesus," with the wise guidance of Thomas G. Long and C. Leong Seow. It resulted in a book entitled *Preaching Proverbs: Wisdom for the Pulpit. Proverbs* are what I call "freeze dried stories," drawn from the sages' observations of repeated cause-effect patterns in the realms of nature and human relationships: "Like clouds and wind without rain, / so is one who boasts of a gift never given" (Prov. 25:14); "A soft answer turns away wrath, / but a harsh word stirs up anger" (15:1). Proverbs draw the reader/hearer into a scene and send that reader out with it as a sort of ethical flashlight, to shine its light on those scenes in life with which it is an "apt fit," a wise word.[24]

A proverb compels us to look back. Spanish novelist, playwright, and poet Miguel de Cervantes (1547–1616) defined a *proverb* as "a short sentence drawn from long experience, containing a truth."[25] A proverb compels us to look forward; this gave rise to another, even more eloquent definition of a *proverb* as "a winged word, outliving the fleeting moment."[26]

Its *scenes* are intended to foster *hokma* (wisdom),[27] skill in deciphering life in specific scenarios.[28] The words *hakam* (wise) and *hokma* (wisdom, in Greek *sophia*) occur much more frequently in Proverbs, Job, and Ecclesiastes than they do in other parts of the Hebrew Bible; hence their designation as wisdom books.

After the book of Proverbs, the next step in my scenic journey was to encounter the book of Job. I entered into the series of scenes that make up the drama of Job, one scene after another. The nation, with postexilic, post-traumatic stress syndrome, was striving to come to terms with innocent suffering. Scenes move from wily Satan in the heavenly council, to the wind collapsing the house and crushing his children, to the well-meaning but worthless advice of his friends, to his whirlwind encounter with God.

The Sages of Ecclesiastes Make a Scene

From there it was onto the scenes observed and imagined by the melancholy yet strangely serene Qoheleth, the name given to the sage(s) responsible for the book of Ecclesiastes. The name *Qoheleth* probably comes from the Hebrew verb *qahal*, to gather. It could be a reference to the activity of gathering students or gathering proverbs.[29]

Qoheleth reminds me of the wisdom of a contemporary website, Demotivators®. They produce posters that, at first glance, look like the positive messages about confidence, teamwork, and perseverance seen on many office walls. But a closer look at the scene of the guy jumping off a cliff in a hang glider reveals the caption, "Believe in yourself, because the rest of us think you're an idiot." A closer look at the poster with the big bright letters *AMBITION* shows a salmon leaping into the jaws of a waiting bear, with the caption, "The journey of a thousand miles sometimes ends very, very badly."[30]

Qoheleth trains his knack for noticing largely on scenes from the shadow side of life for a reason. He is out to undercut traditional wisdom's optimistic assumption that wise actions invariably lead to positive outcomes. He does so by close attention to the harsh realities he observes in the everyday scenes around him. If he had stayed in his office reading the book of Proverbs, he perhaps could have maintained a sunnier view of life. But he had to walk around and observe scenes and draw disappointed conclusions. The wise die just like the fools (see Eccl. 2:14–17). Amassing wealth does not ensure it will be wisely spent after one's death, so accumulating wisdom is also futile (see 6:1–3).

After painting a rather positive scene, in which a poor wise man delivers a city from an enemy siege (9:13–17), he concludes, "Wisdom is better than weapons of war, / but one bungler destroys much good" (v. 18).

After making what sounds like a positive comment about the superiority of wisdom over folly—"The wise have eyes in their heads, / but fools walk in darkness"—he comments, "Yet I perceived that the same fate befalls all of them" (2:14).

After describing a scene in which a slave is being beaten by a master in a field, he observes,

> Again I saw all the oppressions that are practiced under the sun. Look, the tears of the oppressed—with no one to comfort them! And I thought the dead, who have already died, more fortunate than the living, who are still alive; but better than both is the one who has not yet been, and has not seen the evil deeds that are done under the sun. (Eccl. 4:1–3)

He calls this constant experience of disappointment *hebel*, which means "breath or breeze." It is his way of expressing the fleeting nature of life. He uses it to refer to the ephemerality of life (6:12; 7:15; 9:9), to joy (2:1), to human accomplishments (2:11; 4:4), and to youth and the prime of life (11:10).

Qoheleth's vision, while shadowed, does allow a ray of light or two. For him, the precarious quality of human life makes each moment of joy and pleasure all the more precious.

> Go, eat your bread with enjoyment, and drink your wine with a merry heart; for God has long ago approved what you do. . . . Enjoy

life with the wife whom you love, all the days of your vain life that are given you under the sun, because that is your portion in life and in your toil at which you toil under the sun. (9:7–9)

Those somewhat upbeat verses end with this thought: "Whatever your hand finds to do, do with your might; for there is no work or thought or knowledge or wisdom in Sheol, to which you are going" (9:10).

I intend to imitate Qoheleth's skill at scene painting, even if it is accompanied by music in a minor key! "No one can anticipate the time of disaster. Like fish taken in a cruel net, and like birds caught in a snare, so mortals are snared at a time of calamity, when it suddenly falls upon them" (9:12).

"Remember your creator in the days of your youth," he advises, and then launches into a description of the physical conditions of old age, a description that is so eloquent an outpouring of vivid metaphors it almost makes you wish you were already old . . . almost (12:1–8).

I plan to borrow Qoheleth's method of scene painting but not all aspects of his message. I respect his subversive spirit, his refusal to avert his eyes from scenes that contradict the easy assurances of "live wisely and all will be well." We need to acknowledge them in our preaching. But you won't hear me preaching his message that God is distant (5:2), the giver of good fortune and misfortune alike (7:13–14), that unjust suffering is a shame, but there isn't anything we can do about it, and that death is the end (9:10).

Jesus Makes a Scene

Jesus' Aphorisms

Like Qoheleth, Jesus is edgy, out to subvert the assumptions of the status quo. His short sayings employ vivid scenes that challenge the entrenched attitudes and actions of religious tradition. But there the similarity between them stops. Jesus' sayings don't stop at subverting the status quo; they prepare the way for the inbreaking of a more just and merciful human community, the kingdom of God. Jesus is evidence that God is immanent, not just transcendent and distant. He offers the opportunity for eternal life to those who trust in him and his Father.

Accepting that opportunity requires a radical change in our habitual actions and attitudes. New Testament scholar Robert Tannehill, in his classic work *The Sword of His Mouth*, directs our attention to subversive scenes he calls "focal instances":

- "If your hand or foot or eye causes you to stumble . . ." (Matt. 18:8; Mark 9:43–48).
- "No one sews a piece of unshrunken cloth on an old cloak. . . . No one puts new wine into old wineskins . . ." (Matt. 9:17; Mark 2:22).
- "It is easier for a camel to go through the eye of a needle than for someone who is rich to enter the kingdom of God (Matt. 19:24; Mark 10:25; Luke 18:25).[31]

These scenes provoke the hearer/reader to picture a variety of extreme and highly improbable scenes.[32] For a moment, I observe the world from the outside looking in. I recognize the deficiencies of traditional norms, and I question the given world. Literary critic Wolfgang Iser says they "defamiliarize us" to our habitual social assumptions.[33]

Jesus' Parables

The next stop in my scenic journey was to meet the proverb's first cousin, a longer narrative genre: parable. Several years ago, Donald McKim, theologian and editor at Westminster John Knox Press, called me and asked me to write a volume in their "For Today" series. These are a series of scholarly, yet accessible study guides to various genres of Scripture. "You can write on either the psalms or on parables," he told me. Later that evening, I remember seeing an interview between Barbara Walters and the comedian Billy Crystal: "How do you decide what projects to say yes to?" asked Barbara Walters. Crystal replied, "I always go toward those I fear the most. That is the place of energy and growth for me."

So I chose to write a book called *The Parables for Today* because there are quite a few of them that make me, if not exactly afraid, at least very uncomfortable! Parables and proverbs share the same family name, *mashal*, and the same family traits; hence the heading *Meshalim*, the plural of *mashal*, for the book of Proverbs. Both proverbs and parables are brief, close to the ground, often metaphorical genres of wisdom teaching. *Mashal* is Hebrew for "to be like"; the Greek rendering, *parabole*, means "to set alongside." Both proverbs and parables offer the reader or listener the same invitation: set the short sentence or the slightly longer narrative alongside scenes from daily life and determine how it is like or unlike those scenes. We recall that Jesus, in introducing a parable, very often said, "The kingdom of God is like . . ." before he launched into a seemingly innocuous story whose subversive sting slowly gets under the listener's skin. A parable is, according to C. H. Dodd's definition from 1935, "a metaphor or simile drawn from nature or common life arresting the hearer by its vividness or strangeness leaving the mind in sufficient doubt as to its precise application as to tease the mind into active thought."[34]

At first glance, Jesus' parables are a series of harmless scenes from first-century village life. But do a double-take, and we discern that they are actually status-quo subverting scenes whose effect is to offend people in power. A tax collector is praised for his prayer, and a respected Pharisee is rebuked for his. A good Samaritan is the hero of a roadside rescue tale. A poor woman is portrayed as the heroine in an encounter with an influential judge whom she pesters until she receives her fair share of justice. A banquet hall is filled with rabble because the invited guests make one excuse after another not to attend. A miraculous harvest comes from carelessly sown seeds. A shepherd leaves ninety-nine sheep to find one. Laborers who work one hour receive as much as those who work all day.

Jesus' parables do not boil down to a single moral lesson that sounds like something you would find in a fortune cookie, which was the view of a former era of interpretation:[35]

- Go out of your way to help your neighbor (good Samaritan).
- Use your abilities, don't bury them (parable of the talents).
- Be humble when you pray (Pharisee and tax collector).
- Don't squander your youth and resources, and don't disrespect your elders (prodigal son).

In the words of Amy-Jill Levine, in her book *Short Stories Jesus Tells*,

> What makes the parables . . . difficult is that they challenge us to look into the hidden aspects of our own values, our own lives. They bring to the surface unasked questions, and they reveal the answers we have always known, but refuse to acknowledge. For our own comfort we may want to foreclose the meaning rather than allow the parable to open into multiple interpretations. We are probably more comfortable proclaiming a creed than prompting a conversation or pursuing a call.[36]

At the close of a recent workshop, a pastor came up to me. I had mentioned that the parables were not as innocent as they appear at first, but deep study reveals their subversive power.

She had an intense, almost pained expression on her face. "I would like to tell you something I don't want to share with the whole group," she said.

She had my full attention. Who doesn't like privileged information?

"I think the parables are manipulative, and I think the parables are cruel. That Jesus would deliberately use them so people would not understand is cruel. I don't understand it. All I can do is accept it."

I thought I knew the verses that were the problem for her. I couldn't quote them word for word, but I remembered they were from Mark 4:

> And he said to them, "To you has been given the secret of the kingdom of God, but for those outside, everything comes in parables, in order that
> 'they may look but not perceive,
>   and may indeed listen, but not understand;
>   so that they may not turn again and be forgiven.'" (Mark 4:11–12)

What else could I do but attempt singlehandedly to redeem the parables?

First I mentioned that the phrase "in order that" could actually better be rendered "with the result that."

Her facial expression showed she wasn't buying that.

I continued, with renewed zeal, to point out that Jesus is not saying he uses parables deliberately so some will be excluded, but is acknowledging that some will see and hear, but will not, at a deeper level, understand and take his words to heart.

Her body language (arms folded across chest) was not promising.

I persevered. "So these verses are not a statement of divine intention that some not hear, but a description of the mixed reception of any prophet's life and teaching, whether those of Isaiah, which these verses cite, or of Jesus."[37]

She patted my arm. "Thank you for trying," she said. "But the parables are manipulative, and the parables are cruel. I don't understand them. I just have to accept them. I'm not blaming you for them."

She wasn't, but her words caused a flashback to a similar incident in my life. Some years ago, I was leading a workshop on the parables of Jesus as part of the Perkins School of Theology's annual Perkins Theological School for the Laity, held every March. We were engaged in what I thought was an energetic discussion of what, for a lot of people, is their least favorite parable: the parable of the dishonest steward from Luke 16:1–10. Several people had contributed ideas. Looking back, maybe I should have stuck with the parable of the good Samaritan. And maybe I shouldn't have used the word *polyvalent* to describe parables when a more down-to-earth description would have sufficed. But hindsight is 20/20.

For whatever reason, in the midst of our discussion, a man of mature years raised his hand. He was sitting by the door. He had come prepared to learn, with his backpack, notebook, and a cup of Starbucks® coffee. Pointing a finger at me, he said, "Well, all I can say is that I feel sorry for the original disciples if the parables are as complicated as *you* are making them!"

I responded the way any wise teacher would: "What an interesting comment! Let's pursue it after our break!"

The only trouble was that after the break, his seat was empty. His coffee cup was in the trashcan beside the door. His notebook and backpack were nowhere to be seen. He had tossed his coffee cup, shouldered his backpack, and continued his life pilgrimage without appropriating the polyvalent parable of the dishonest steward for the scenes of his everyday life. All I could conclude is that not everyone, in C. H. Dodd's words, wants to "have their minds teased into active thought."

I felt downcast, but really, I can't be held personally responsible for people's responses to Jesus' preaching. It's his fault. He's the one who preached in scenes. I've always thought that, if he had preached in three points and a poem, he would have lived a lot longer.

That is probably not the best segue into chapter 4, "Making a Scene in the Pulpit," but so be it.

Chapter Four

Making a Scene in the Sermon

Drawn into the Drama

The word *drama* comes from the Greek "to do." Drama is about action. Preaching in scenes draws people into the action. The people who sit before the preacher in the pews in a traditional service, on folding chairs in a contemporary service, or on couches in a home-church setting, have come from scenes in their daily lives into the scene of the service. They will go from the service into some of the same scenes from which they came to it: family meals, rushed mornings, conflictual workspaces, solitary nights in front of the TV. Scenic sermons acknowledge the scenes from which they have come and send them out to play their part in future scenes with more integrity, courage, and serenity, and with a sharpened knack for noticing God at work in their worlds.

My homiletical agenda finds a theological ally in Kevin M. Vanhoozer's theological project, which he sets forth in his book *The Drama of Doctrine*.[1] He is seeking to shift our understanding of doctrine and Scripture in a way that parallels my vision of scenic sermons. He seeks to shift our understanding from theology as a spectator sport to theology as theater, a dramatic production "into which we are grafted as participants with speaking and acting parts."[2] Doctrines resemble "stage directions for the church's performance of the gospel."[3] At the same time, he seeks a shift from viewing the Bible narrowly as data to a more dynamic relationship to the Bible understood as drama. To draw people into the drama of doctrine, for Vanhoozer, is to change their definition of *theology* as theoretical knowledge to *theology* as wisdom, knowledge which is gained, not just by talking but by walking.[4]

For Vanhoozer, "At the heart of Christianity lies a series of vividly striking events that together make up the gospel of Jesus Christ. The gospel, God's gracious self-communication in Jesus Christ, is intrinsically dramatic."[5]

> The church now lives between . . . the acts of a divine drama of redemption. Each act of the play is set in motion by an act of God. The first act is creation (Genesis 1–3), the setting for everything that follows. Act 2 (beginning from Genesis 12 and running through the rest of the Old Testament) concerns God's election, rejection, and restoration of Israel. The third, pivotal and climactic act is Jesus: God's definitive Word/Act. Act 4 begins with the risen Christ sending his Spirit to create the church. The fifth and final act is the eschaton, the consummation of all things, and the consummation of God's relationship with Israel and the church. The church lives at present between the definitive event of Jesus and the concluding event of the eschaton, poised between memory and hope.[6]

For Vanhoozer, the wisdom metaphor of "the Way," from both Old and New Testaments, expresses the dynamic quality of Scripture, doctrine, and the life of faith.

> *Jesus Christ is the word and wisdom of God, the revealer and the redeemer: the way, the truth, and the life.*[7]

The term "the way" refers to the path of wise living in Proverbs, to Jesus himself (John 14:6), and to the path of Jesus' followers, whose gate is narrow and whose way is hard (Matt. 7:14). "The Way" was a common designation for the early Christian movement. The Christian way is not something we contemplate with our minds only; it is fundamentally dramatic, involving speech and action on behalf of Jesus' truth and life.[8] "The proper end of the drama of doctrine is wisdom: lived knowledge, a performance of the truth."[9]

Vanhoozer sets forth new metaphors for theology as dramaturgy:

- Scripture (script that calls for faithful yet creative performance)
- Theological understanding (performance)
- Church (company)

- Pastor (director)
- "Doctrine . . . serves the church by directing its members in the project of wise living, to the glory of God."[10]

For him, the theater metaphor is dynamic and active, not static and passive. A theater audience is not disinterested. "There is . . . a degree of emotional and imaginative investment in the kind of beholding that takes place in the theater that goes beyond the disinterested speculation of theorists."[11]

By the same token, theology is not a spectator sport. Its main purpose is to "equip Christians to understand and participate in the action of the principal players (namely, Father, Son and Spirit). . . . [Theology] insists on audience participation."[12]

So does preaching in scenes.

What Is a Scene?

According to novelist Sandra Scofield, "Scenes are those passages in narrative when we slow down and focus on an event in the story so that we are 'in the moment' with characters in action."[13] They are powerful because the reader is emotionally involved, left with images and a memory of the action.[14] A scene is a segment of story told in detail, the opposite of summarizing. "Scene is event: something happening. It is not description or information or rumination alone, although any of those things may be a part of it."[15] Scenes are compressions of real life rather than imitations. That is why dialogue in scenes is shorter and sharper than real talk, with its "uhs" and "wells" and "so's." Dialogue in a scene has to accomplish something; it must move the story forward.

Screenwriter Christopher Keane defines the scene as "'an event in a screenplay that occupies time and space.' Any change of setting or time marks a new scene."[16] So it is important to let the reader or viewer know where the characters are and what time of day it is.

"A scene has to have a beginning, middle, and end, and . . . it must be sharply focused. . . . [A] scene sequence must be connected by a 'single idea.' . . . [T]here is a single driving force throughout the scenes in a sequence, and . . . an idea or force connecting the sequences into the larger idea of the film or story or novel or play" (and I would add, sermon).[17] Several scenes combine to form an act of a play. Several acts combine to form the total play.

Four Characteristics of Effective Scenes

Pulse

A scene has a *pulse*, which is the product of the interaction of event and the characters' emotions.

In a scene, characters do things and feel things. They act and react. The pulse is the active energy between action and emotion; it is the "underlying source of the scene's anxiety or excitement, a thread that is pulled through the scene by the action."[18] For example, in the scene, "the man behind the pillar" in my sermon "The Yellow Backpack," the pulse is the power of the Word preached as it encounters the desperate unhappiness of the man behind the pillar (see chap. 5). In the scene in which a bear paces his now nonexistent cage, from the sermon "Locked in a Room with Open Doors," the pulse is the tension between the bear's perceived captivity and his actual freedom.

Summaries may play a role in movies, novels, plays, and sermons. The sermons in chapter 5 all contain summary sections in which information is offered to deepen and unify the sermon. But it is in the scene that you capture the hearts and imagination of readers/viewers.

Purpose

A scene has a *purpose*, a function in the narrative (sermon).

"There is a reason a passage is rendered in detail rather than summarized. There is a reason why it appears where it does in the sequence of events. It accomplishes something for the story. It changes something. It makes *now* different from *the past*."[19]

Potential purposes can be to:

- Introduce new plot elements,
- Reveal something about a character,
- Set up a situation that will be important in a later scene,[20]
- Offer information needed to move the plot forward.

Plot

A scene has a *plot* or structure: a beginning, middle, and end.

There is a situation at the beginning, a line of action, and a new situation at the end. The scene establishes each of these three parts.[21]

Point of View

Listeners need to know from whose perspective they are experiencing a scene: the preacher's or one of the characters in the scene? It is best to keep a single *point of view* in a scene, though throughout a sequence of scenes, the point of view can change.[22]

Preachers need to be on the lookout for scenarios, experiential wisps and glimmers, that could be developed into fuller scenes. These grow out of the preacher's mulling over the characters and conflicts of those around her or him (landscape), in the context of what is going on within her or him (inscape). As Fred Craddock puts it, "Effective preaching reflects the minister's open receptivity to those life scenes which are noticeably emotional in flavor."[23] Life is a lot more interesting when we take time to notice the scenes all around us. So are sermons.[24]

Twenty-First Century Scenic Preaching

When my children, now grown, were younger, I made every effort to show a lively interest in their educations. Every afternoon I would greet them at the door with questions: "How was school today? What did you do today? What are you learning about now?" So one afternoon, when our son Matt, now in his late twenties, was in Mrs. Houseman's second-grade class, he came home prepared:

"What are you learning in school now?" I asked brightly.

"We are doing a unit called Sex Is Interesting," he replied with a studious expression on his face.

"Oh," I began, attempting to reconcile this educational approach with my mental image of Mrs. Houseman. I thought for a long moment and then said, "All right, well, I guess this makes sense; though it seems awfully soon to introduce this topic."

But he wasn't done yet. He continued, "Our homework for tonight is to make a collage of pictures of naked people from magazines." His deadpan was so good that I actually began mentally going through our magazine subscription list: *Women's Day, Time, Business Week, Christian Century*.

Then I spied his little grin, and he said "Gotcha!"[25]

When you think back on this book, hear my voice in your head, asking brightly, "What did you learn from my book?" "What are you taking away from having read my book?"

You have your reply ready: "Scenes are interesting."

And now, let's do our homework together. Let's gather a collage of options for using scenes in sermons to reach the potential listeners in our homiletical mission field.

What I suggest are three sermon shapes that use scenes. You will recognize some familiar friends, retrofitted to emphasize the power of scenes for today's listeners. These shapes are meant to suggest evocative possibilities rather than serve as sermon blueprints.

Preaching to the Biblically and Theologically Untutored: The Deductive Sermon That Opens with a Scene

An expert in his or her field stands on a stage and speaks, often without notes, to a receptive audience. First the expert makes a proposal, then substantiates it with data and arguments, and then spells out the difference it makes for our attitudes and behavior. Sounds like a sermon, right? Statement of theme, exegesis, application; no, it's a TED talk. It might be radio host Celeste Headlee talking about "How to Have a Better Conversation" through conscious-listening. Or psychology professor Andrew Solomon on "Depression: The Secret We Share." Or research sociologist Brené Brown on "The Power of Vulnerability." Or model Cameron Russell on "Looks Aren't Everything: Believe Me, I'm a Model." Or social entrepreneur and human-rights activist Vivek Maru on "How to Put the Power of Law Back into People's Hands."[26]

TED talks are eighteen-minute talks on a variety of subjects, from science to communication to popular culture to health to global issues. Their form is often proposal-demonstration, much like our old deductive, propositional friend, "three points and a poem." The speaker offers a proposal, illustrates it with scenes and stories, backs it up with data and argument, and then shows how it enhances our daily attitudes and actions in the world. Homiletician Sally Brown interprets the immense popularity of TED talks as a sign that "propositions, as such, are not the communicational problem for contemporary listeners, whether in the pew or anywhere else, that New Homileticians sometimes suppose them to be."[27] It's all in how they are used:

> The problem occurs when propositions function like hammers instead of keys that can open doors. Hammer-like propositions, instead of offering proposals for listeners to consider and demonstrating why they are worthy of assent, *demand* submission on the basis of the speaker's personal authority or the authority of a source

that cannot be questioned. Keys, on the other hand, are entrusted to the listener. They can become valuable tools that listeners use to explore their world.[28]

TED talk speakers offer the implications of an important, clear idea to listeners. The authority of the speaker comes, in part, from their research specialty, but also from road testing their proposal on the highways of life. The speaker is personable, and the talk is practical. They offer a key, not a hammer, to use Brown's language. They are saying, "Take this insight and see how helpful it can be in your daily life."[29]

There is still room for the deductive sermon that begins with a general claim and illustrates it with particulars. It can be an effective conveyor of biblical, theological teaching, which is something that was not particularly emphasized by the New Homiletic. Over the past few decades, in response to concern about a lack of biblical knowledge, there has been a resurgence of didactic, propositional preaching: "the teaching sermon," a contemporary version of the three points and a poem. Thomas Long calls this "six points and a video clip."[30] I have concerns about the form, the purpose, and the impact of such sermons.

With regard to form, such sermons can go on for forty-five (or more) minutes with informational slides, video clips, and visuals behind the preacher. When done effectively, such a sermon resembles a stimulating lecture. But the central message may be dispersed into so many points that listeners have a hard time identifying it. What will be remembered is the most vivid scene or story of the sermon, whether or not it is connected in listeners' minds with the central point. This format runs the risk of losing the invitational quality of preaching in the barrage of information.

Over time, such preaching runs the risk of casting the preacher as answer giver, and listeners as graspers at disparate straws of meaning and information. Long warns that it may "reinforce the worst tendencies of an episodic culture, encouraging people to grasp disconnected principles and rules and insight, provided by an authority figure from the outside, in order to survive in the chaotic whirlwind of life."[31]

I suggest that deductive preaching has ongoing value when it remembers the best lessons of the New Homiletic for the teaching function of preaching: the use of imaginative, scenic elements to teach creatively. Paul Scott Wilson recommends that we create a picture in words of the biblical scene before discussing the text, put theological thoughts into a character's head, utilize biblical images to teach theological truths, and paint pictures of specific social ills.[32] While keeping God and a strong theological message at the heart of preaching, he recommends we approach preaching like movie making, using one dominant image per sermon, employing the senses, and creating experiences for listeners rather than just reporting them.[33]

Deductive preaching these days can take TED talks as a reminder of some of its own time-honored homiletical principles. Present one great, clear idea. Set a time limit (in TED it is eighteen minutes). Deliver, don't read. Use stories that draw people into caring about the topic. Begin your talk with a relatable experience or intriguing idea. Get right to the topic. Don't meander around with preliminaries. Show how the idea makes a difference. Have a clear but unobtrusive structure. Stay planted. Don't purposelessly perambulate.[34]

When you rent a car, you have to state who the primary driver will be for insurance purposes. We make a similar decision when we craft a sermon. Who will be the primary driver? Will it be logical argument, image, or narrative? Deductive sermons are driven by logical argument.[35] Over the past several years, when I have chosen to preach an argument-fueled sermon, I have begun with a scene before moving to the points, either a relatable scene from daily life or a scene painted from the scriptural context. In these distractible days, sermon openings need to have sharper hooks than ever before. We need to take more care than ever that our three points are three aspects of a central point, not three separate sermons. We need to work harder than ever to tie illustrative segments so tightly to their conceptual points that they will be remembered together. The sermon "Finding Faith amid Our Fears," in chapter 5, begins with a scene from my classroom. It identifies the fear of the Lord as the fear we are to spend our lives cultivating and then explores two strands of the concept in the Hebrew Bible. Scenes and anecdotes illustrate each point. Sermons can touch emotions and shape imaginations even as they convey robust teaching content. An effective approach is to start with a scene, image, or metaphor that has been drawn from Scripture or life. Out of that scene, the preacher develops a conceptual thread (focus) that unifies the sermon from start to finish.[36]

Preaching to Serial Taskers: The Multi-Scene Sermon

In 1964, just as the Beatles were launching their invasion of America's airwaves, Marshall McLuhan published *Understanding Media: The Extensions of Man* in which he coined the phrase "the medium is the message."

A popular medium molds what we see and how we see it; eventually, if we use it enough, it changes who we are as individuals and as a society. "The effects of technology do not occur at the level of opinions or concepts," wrote McLuhan. Rather, they alter "patterns of perception steadily and without any resistance."[37]

Nicholas Carr's work *The Shallows: How the Internet Is Affecting Our Brains* suggests that our minds have become our medium. Elsewhere, he writes, "Consider yourself as you enter keywords into Google's search box and begin following a trail of links. What you see is a mind consumed with a medium."[38]

Due to our rapid, online hunting of information, "many of us are developing neural circuitry that is customized for rapid and incisive spurts of directed attention."[39] We are losing the neurons for concentration and meditation, those "that support calm, linear thought—the ones we use in traversing a lengthy narrative or an involved argument, the ones we draw on when we reflect on our experiences or contemplate an outward or inward phenomenon."[40]

According to Carr, "Intensive multitaskers are 'suckers for irrelevancy.'"[41] As Thomas Merton puts it, "Our minds are like crows. They pick up everything that glitters, no matter how uncomfortable our nests get with all that metal in them."[42] Says Carr, borrowing a phrase from T. S. Eliot's "Four Quartets," "the Net" encourages a state in which we are "distracted from distraction by distraction."[43]

According to a prominent neuroscientist,

> The constant shifting of our attention when we're online may make our brains more nimble when it comes to multitasking, but improving our ability to multitask actually hampers our ability to think deeply and creatively. . . . 'The more you multitask, the less deliberative you become; the less able to think and reason out a problem.' You become . . . more likely to rely on conventional ideas and solutions rather than challenging them with original lines of thought.[44]

[. . . I'm sorry, but somehow I just got temporarily sidetracked from my line of thought by click bait, a slideshow of "Celebrities You Didn't Realize Were Dead," and then I saw a pop-up ad for Stitchfix, an online personal shopping service that features some really good-looking blazers, and then I had to watch a video posted by a friend on Facebook of "Old Ladies Argue in Car" on YouTube. I'm back now, and please don't judge me. The sustained thinking it takes to write a book is getting harder and harder.]

Anyway, as I was saying, we think we are multitaskers, but we are actually serial taskers. Rather than engaging in simultaneous tasks, we, in fact, shift from one task to another to another in rapid succession.

What serial taskers need is to have their attention grabbed and to be invited to follow a sustained line of reflection that touches both emotions and mind.

Qualities of the Multi-Scene Sermon

Be Clear

Designed for people whose narrative connective skills may be rusty, the multi-scene sermon is, first and foremost, clear. It is not to be mistaken for a series of stories strung together. It is, rather, a sequence of scenes, punctuated with informative summary, unified by means of a single, profound theme—what screenwriters call a *throughline*. Homileticians have long advocated the importance of a clear, central theme in a sermon. The multi-scene sermon, with its variety of sermon sequences, offers models for how listeners can use a theme to connect the episodes or scenes of their daily lives with those of Scripture.

Clarity and unity of theme are more important now than ever. Screenwriter Blake Snyder gives screenwriters advice we can appropriate for sermons:

> Forget all about your screenplay for now, the cool scenes that are bursting forth in your imagination, the soundtrack and the stars you KNOW would be interested in being in it. Forget all that. And concentrate on writing one sentence. One line. Be able to answer the question "What is it?"[45]

The theme of a screenplay is also called the one-line, the log-line or the throughline. In Snyder's book *Save the Cat*, chapter 1 is entitled "What Is It?" Snyder draws a scene of a group of friends trying to decide on a movie to see together on a Saturday night and failing to find one with a clear one-line.[46]

We can look at a few descriptions of movies to see what Snyder means.

- Gandalf and Aragorn lead the World of Men against Sauron's army to draw his gaze from Frodo and Sam as they approach Mount Doom with the One Ring. (*Lord of the Rings*)

- Two teenagers from rival New York City gangs fall in love, but tensions between their respective friends build toward tragedy. (*West Side Story*)
- An ex-prize fighter turned longshoreman struggles to stand up to his corrupt union bosses. (*On the Waterfront*)
- A snobbish phonetics professor agrees to a wager that he can take a flower girl and make her presentable in high society. (*My Fair Lady*)
- Three World War II veterans return home to small-town America to discover that they and their families have been irreparably changed. (*The Best Years of Our Lives*)
- Two astronauts work together to survive after an accident leaves them stranded in space. (*Gravity*)
- A team of female African American mathematicians serve a vital role in NASA during the early years of the US Space program. (*Hidden Figures*)

Says Lisa Cron in *Wired for Story*:

> Stories that lack focus often aren't about anything at all. . . . I can't tell you how many manuscripts I've read where if someone asked, "What's it about?" my only answer would be, "It's about three hundred pages." . . . If you can't summarize your book [sermon] in a few sentences [or one] rewrite *the book* [sermon] until you can.[47]

I went to Topeka, Kansas, a few years ago to lead a preaching workshop with a group of pastors. When the workshop was over and it was time to head to the airport, I got in my rental car and began the trip. I turned at all the places Google Maps GPS told me to turn. At last, I saw a sign with a little airplane logo on it. I breathed a sigh of relief. But then came mile after lonely mile with no little airplane signs. Was this still the right road? Had I made a wrong turn? Then there was one. This time my anxious heart leapt with relief. Then mile after mile of nothing.

Sermon listeners today need more little airplane signs. Build a hand rail; drop a trail of breadcrumbs; put up luminaries along the sermonic path. Pick whatever metaphor you like, but keep my distractible, restless mind on track with you. Keep gathering up where we've been as we move toward our destination. Do it with terse transitions and savvy segues. Excessive verbiage is not required, but keep me knowing I'm on the right road to the airport.

A few months ago, I sat in a conference room with a group of laypeople at First United Methodist Church in Allen, Texas, where I live. They had agreed to be "The People's Preaching Lab," and to be trained as sermon listeners for my students who preached at the 11:00 a.m. service in the chapel every week. I was presenting my sermon feedback sheet, which, admittedly, is two single-spaced pages long. "Could we streamline this?" asked one of the group members.

So they worked together to identify what was most important to them in listening to sermons. They identified authenticity of the preacher, biblical knowledge, relatable examples, and communicating not reading. But first and foremost these laypeople craved clarity of theme. "We want to know what the sermon is about, and we want the ending to reinforce the theme."

I want our deductive preaching to be more inductive, to start off with a scene. And I want our inductive, multi-scene preaching to be a tad more deductive, to have a high-definition throughline.

O. Wesley Allen Jr., in his *The Homiletic of All Believers: A Conversational Approach*, points out that:

> If we are honest, we must recognize that human thought constantly mixes deductive and inductive reasoning. Indeed, in real life, the two form a reasoning circle (not necessarily circular reasoning) in which conclusions reached through inductive reasoning become the starting point for deductive reasoning. And, likewise, implications derived deductively from strongly held truth claims become the building blocks of inductive reasoning that leads to new conclusions. Thus, to be true to the full range of human experience, preachers should be able and willing to use both inductive and deductive approaches in sermons.[48]

Be Compelling

Some sermons have bursts of insight and emotion but in the end are a blur, sporadically compelling but not clear. And others are clear but not compelling. In these days of diffuse attention, we must have both. The word *compel* is from the Latin *compellere*, a combination of *com* (together) and *pellere* (drive). Imagine a Google search in which we have a clear question we are investigating, and we single-mindedly pursue it, eschewing all click-bait and pop-up distractions to find an answer. Most of my Google searches have a lot more rabbit trails than that. Imagine a forward moving journey together with our listeners.

A play or movie is compelling if it progresses as a sequence of scenes, each with a specific purpose and sequence.[49] At key junctures, scenes are interspersed with summary. Each scene contains sensory cues to invite listeners in, and each scene has a purpose, a reason for being. The sequence of scenes has forward motion, and there are no extraneous scenes. Skip Press, author of *The Complete Idiot's Guide to Screenwriting*, offers two questions for us to ponder with regard to crafting compelling scene sequences.

- How does the end of this scene propel us into the next one?
- Is this scene memorable apart from the overall movie?[50]

Karl Iglesias, scriptwriting consultant, challenges screenwriters to "Think of your script as a house of cards, each scene a card. If you can remove a scene, and the house still stands, in other words, if the story still works without it, that scene doesn't belong in your script."[51]

Try thinking about the progression of portions of your sermons as a fiction writer would, as scenes. In some, you might do some teaching in the framework of a setting, dialogue, or image. Others might take the shape of an anecdote or first-person experience.

Novelist and screenwriter Raymond Obstfeld recommends that once we've written a scene, we reread it and complete four focus sentences:

- The purpose of this scene is to _____.
- When the reader finishes this scene, he [or she] should feel _____.
- When the reader finishes this scene, he [or she] should think _____.
- When the reader finishes this scene, he [or she] should wonder _____.[52]

I have, for years, trained my Introduction to Preaching students how to think intentionally about the purpose of an entire sermon and be able to express it in one sentence. The beauty of preaching in scenes is that it forces us to think about the purpose of each smaller segment of the sermon as well.

This might lead to some painful but helpful insights: This lengthy opening story has nothing to do with the text, but it shows people I'm approachable and that I love animals. This extended, exegetical lecturette contains information not pertinent to my sermon's theme, but since I put in all that time researching the text, I'm going to share everything I learned; plus it is important for people to know that their preacher knows some Greek and Hebrew words.

Every semester I invite acting professor Kevin Paul Hofeditz to coach my new preaching students. The first thing he tells them is this: "Most people think that an actor is someone who pretends to be someone else. But an actor is someone who gives himself or herself over fully to the objective of the play. And she or he does this, scene by scene, reflecting on the objective of each scene. If an actor asks a director, 'What emotions am I supposed to show in this scene?' the director will probably say, 'What is the objective of the scene?' If you know that, you don't have to overthink what emotions to show in your portrayal of your character." His advice is helpful for us preachers, who have to not only perform our sermons but also, before that, write the script!

Raymond Obstfeld advises his students to think of each scene in their work as an inner tube designed to keep the larger work afloat. "The more memorable scenes there are, the more we see the entire structure floating in front of us and, therefore, the more we appreciate the whole work. The fewer memorable scenes there are, the quicker that work sinks to the depths of mediocrity."[53]

Traditional deductive preaching was criticized for not having any "moves." The points could be interchanged, and the sermon would never feel it. The multi-scene sermon has to have a plot that requires the sequence of its scenes. But it is free to pick and choose from the New Homiletics' plots to sequence its scenes or to create fresh sequences. I present numerous contemporary options in chapter 5 of *Novel Preaching: Tips from Top Writers on Crafting Creative Sermons*. Eugene Lowry's "Lowry Loop" is a narrative plot form that moves from problem to resolution in a five-part sequence: oops, ugh, aha, whee, and yeah. Fred Craddock's inductive journey form invites the congregation along on the whitewater rafting trip of exegetical discovery with the preacher. David Buttrick offers a series of rhetorical units (moves) unified by a logical thread that form a pattern of understanding in consciousness using images from Scripture and contemporary life. Frank Thomas and Henry Mitchell lead listeners on a journey from identification of false beliefs to celebration of the truth of the gospel. Paul Scott Wilson's *Four Pages of the Sermon* moves from trouble in the text and world to divine grace in the text and world. Patricia Wilson-Kastner models the sermon sequence on the process of Ignatian prayer, setting an intention, seeking insight, and receiving renewed energy for discipleship. Mike

Graves depicts the sermon as a series of vignettes sewn together in quilt like fashion.[54]

Thomas Long, in his book *Preaching and the Literary Forms of the Bible*, suggests that one crucial option is shaping sermons like the biblical texts on which they are based, whether proverb, epistle, narrative, psalm or apocalyptic text. As one example, Long's suggestion means that, when preaching on a parable, sometimes ending with a question and inviting listeners to answer it for themselves is the best option. For example, at the end of a sermon on the parable of the prodigal son, end with the questions, "Will the older son go into the party and eat and drink with family friends? Or will he head back out to plow the lower forty, while the sounds of the party echo in his ears?"

The multi-scene sermon can take many forms. And, in my view, the multi-scene sermon *should* take many forms over the weeks, months, and years. People living from episode to episode without developed connective skills need models for connecting the scenes of their daily lives. And they need more than one. Because sermon form shapes faith, and faith is not as simple as some of the preaching I've heard (and probably done) would suggest. No one form deserves the right to be front and center every week. If I preach deductive sermons, heavy on information, every week, it conveys to the congregation that faith is a matter of accepting the preacher's propositions about God. If I preach complication-resolution sermons every week, it conveys to the congregation that faith means believing that God exists to solve my problems. If every week I preach inductive sermons that make assumptions of biblical, theological knowledge the congregation does not possess—that leave it all up to the listener to apply the theme to their everyday lives—I convey to the congregation that faith is something they should have but, inexplicably, lack. If I end every sermon with a "honey-do" list, however laudable, I convey to the congregation that faith boils down to helping clear debris from the Habitat for Humanity lot next Saturday, giving up television for Lent, or becoming a foster parent.

The New Homiletician most intentional about how form shapes the faith, not just of individuals, but of communities, is David Buttrick in his *Homiletic: Moves and Structures*.[55] Buttrick is not a fan of propositional, point-driven sermons that place story and metaphor in a subordinate position to the concepts they are called on to illustrate. Buttrick prescribes sermons that are shaped by the logical progression of biblical texts, unfolding, not as static points, but as a series of five to six "moves," language modules of three to four minutes in length. He trusts the logical connection between his "moves" to serve as transitions and gives meta-phor, imagery, and story a central role in preaching. His "moves" are connected by interrelated images that occur from move to move. The careful placement of moves result in an "image grid" intended to have a specific impact on the congregation.[56] Buttrick would be in favor of my emphasis on restoring scenes and imagery to a central place in the pulpit, but he would want them to follow the flow of biblical texts, not partake of New Homiletic plots.

Homiletician, poet, and musician Thomas H. Troeger has long been a creative proponent of the use of imagery in sermons. In several books written over the past thirty years, he has lifted up the power of imagery to reach diverse learning styles in our media-steeped congregations.[57] Among his suggestions are to play with an image, write the sermon as a movie script, use a flashback, create a parable, and assume there is more to the story. Troeger's sermon, "Scenes from a Marriage," speculates about the couple's life after the wedding at Cana as, year by year, they enjoy more of the wine Jesus multiplied for them and live into their memories of him.[58]

The approach he suggests that is most like the scenic sermon is the sermon as a movement of images. The images flow from one to another with a minimum of explanation from the preacher. The congregation enters into the image world of the text with all five senses. Images impact the congregation in a holistic way, at the levels of mind, heart, and will. The result is that, when the community leaves the world of the image, they can perceive their everyday world from the perspective of the image world. The movement of images could be organized in a wide variety of ways. Barbara K. Lundblad's "Standing Still and Moving On" (the disciples on the road to Emmaus in Luke 24:13–35) is a sermon whose images follow the flow of a biblical text.[59] My own practice with regard to images has become to make the throughline that unites the scenes more obvious and to be more directive with regard to avenues of response to the sermon.

Respect Complexity

One of the reasons contemporary people are not buying our metanarra-tive is because the plot is too facile, too close to sounding like easy answers and clichéd solutions. We need to respect our listeners' experience of chaos by not presenting false hopes and easy answers in our sermons. One of my favorite pieces of wisdom from a novelist is Edith Wharton's advice to choose a subject worthy of your audience. Says Wharton,

> There are subjects trivial in appearance, and subjects trivial to the core; and the novelist ought to be able to discern at a glance between the two. . . . The novelist . . . learns . . . to resist surface attractions, and probe his story to the depths before he begins to tell it.[60]

The same applies to scene sequences. We need to choose scene sequences for our sermons across the weeks, months, and years that are worthy of our audience's experience of the ambiguities of life and the complexities of Scripture. Most of the plots of the New Homiletic move from an aspect of the human condition to God's initiative on our behalf to the transformed identity and life that can result. This is well and good, if not presented as an easy passage, neat and tidy.

Our congregations know that complication doesn't always lead to resolution, and that itch doesn't always lead to scratch. If we are faithful to the gospel in our preaching, we will admit that the good news doesn't always simplify our lives and make us more functional. Sometimes it pours itching powder all over us.

How about a four-part sequence of scenes that goes like this: Here is the good news. Here is how we live. What is it about the good news that we aren't getting? Here is the good news again.

What about, sprinkled in here and there throughout the year, a multi-scene sermon that begins with resolution and then complicates it? Here is our neat, tidy life. Here is the gospel. Here is our messy, overturned life. In what way could this possibly be a good thing for us and the world?

Nora Tisdale, in her book *Prophetic Preaching: A Pastoral Approach*, suggests several sermon sequences for prophetic preaching that lend themselves to multi-scene sermons. One she calls "Upsetting the Equilibrium (Moving from Ease to Dis-Ease)." She points out that in his book, *The Homiletical Plot*, Eugene Lowry sets forth a narrative model for preaching in which the preacher moves from upsetting the equilibrium to some sort of resolution of the sermon's initial tension. Says Tisdale,

> However, sometimes in prophetic preaching, the movement in a sermon may be all about upsetting the equilibrium—and leaving it that way. The prophet's role is to shake us out of our "ease" and into a state of "dis-ease" so that we see ourselves and our calling in Christ differently.[61]

She uses as an example a sermon by Brian K. Blount called "God on the Loose" (based on Mark 1:9–11). Here is the sequence of scenes:

- "God Breaks into the World and Is 'On the Loose' through the Baptism of Jesus"
- "The Troubling Call to Us: To Be Leaders Who Welcome God on the Loose"
- "The Good News in the Midst of the Troubling News." We can tap into the boundary-breaking power God loosed in Jesus to change the world we live in.[62]

Yet another sequence Tisdale suggests for prophetic preaching is "Invitation to Lament." She offers the example of a sermon preached by biblical scholar and homiletician Carolyn Sharp two weeks after Hurricane Katrina devastated the Gulf Coast, which invites us to lament and calls for justice, refusing to offer easy hope. Sharp ends by quoting Matthew 2:18b: "Rachel weeping for her children; / she refused to be consoled, because they are no more." She charges listeners to "refuse to be consoled, but to offer to God the sacrifice of our passion for justice and compassion for those who suffer." Here is the sequence of scenes:

- Hearing the Lament of the World
- Acknowledging Our Complicity in the Suffering
- Invitation to Lament[63]

Types of Multi-Scene Sermons:

The Multi-Scene Sermon That Begins with a Biblical Scene

The multi-scene sermon can begin with a scene from the inscape, textscape, or landscape of the preacher's knack for noticing. It can begin with a scene from the Bible, from a historical incident, a contemporary or personal scene. Often a guiding image and refrain grow out of the initial scene. As the preacher moves through the sermon, she or he verbally gathers up the thematic essence of each scene as the sermon moves forward to the next scene, to imprint it on the memory of our serial-tasking audience. This multi-scene sermon model provides an extra dollop of deduction into the inductive scene sequence. Whatever sequence it chooses to take, the sermon highlights its throughline in High Definition (HD).

The sermon "Paul's Pack List" (see chap. 5) begins with a scene of Paul in prison making a list of what the Philippians will need on their journey of faith; it unfolds from there as it explores false notions of humility and biblical notions of humility. It is inspired by Philippians 2, with scenes exemplifying the compassion and courage of which the virtue of humility, a divine gift, is composed.

The Multi-Scene Sermon That Begins with a Personal Scene

The "Yellow Backpack" (see chap. 5), a sermon on the healing of Bartimaeus in Mark 10:46–52, is an example of a multi-scene sermon that begins with a personal scene: me leaving my card in an ATM machine, and a woman chasing me down to return it. It moves on to things we have lost that we don't get back. Then it moves to Bartimaeus, what he had lost (sight, community, dignity) and what he had not lost (a single shred of stubborn faith). It delves into our own losses and challenges, and finally, it has us stand before Jesus responding for ourselves to the question, "What do you want me to do for you?" Other multi-scene sermons in chapter 5 that begin with contemporary scenes are "Foresight is 20/20," and "Peel off the Plastic." The sermon "A Friend at Midnight" could be viewed as a multi-scene sermon that shifts from front porch to front porch, or as a single-scene sermon that stays on the same porch in front of the same door, bringing new characters onto it as the sermon progresses.

Preaching to People with Continuous Partial Attention: The Single-Scene Sermon

The multi-scene sermon is like a play in which the curtain comes down between scenes. The single-scene sermon is like a one-act play. The basic stage setting and characters stay in place while others come onstage to take part in the ongoing action.[64]

I was having lunch with a colleague at Perkins and a student who had asked to meet with us regarding forming a ministry peer group in Houston. We sat in the red leather booth of a Mexican restaurant near campus, me on one side, the two of them across. My mind drifted from the conversation when I saw a text come in. I placed my phone under the table to read it. It was a very appealing invitation to speak at . . . "Alyce, are you on your phone?" my colleague demanded. I assumed my most innocent facial expression.

"Please, be *here!*" she said. She's my friend. She can say things like that to me! Besides, I was busted. I was caught in the act of Continuous Partial Attention (CPA).

Educator Linda Stone coined the term "continuous partial attention, or CPA." It is "the increasing inability and undesire to pay full attention to just one task, item, or person and instead continually scan for other opportunities . . . while waiting for the next interruption."[65] Two thousand years ago the Roman philosopher Seneca put it best: "To be everywhere is to be nowhere."[66]

Nicholas Carr, in *The Shallows: What the Internet Is Doing to Our Brains*, offers some rather ominous observations about attention. "One thing that sets us apart from other animals is the command we have been granted over our attention. . . . To give up that control is to be left with "the constant gnawing sense of having had and lost some infinite thing."[67]

Millennial Episcopal priest Adam Thomas, in *Digital Disciple*, suggests that, "The classification *Homo sapiens* is becoming less and less accurate. As I store more of both my memory and my capacity to solve problems outside my own mind, the 'wisdom' (*sapiens*), which marks me as a member of the human race, withers and dies."[68] He continues,

> For many people today, especially Millennials like me, employing the Tech to store information and to solve problems seems as natural as breathing. But this outsourcing of the mind diminishes the brain's capacity to do the things God created it to do. We can find answers to questions using the Internet, but the ability to question, the willingness to think critically, the desire to expand the mind and engage the cognitive process—these fundamental human characteristics are approaching their expiration dates.
>
> As these characteristics of *Homo sapiens* come to the end of their shelf lives, the facility and yearning to engage the mind with the heart and spirit in contemplation of the Divine are the next things to go. Truly, the more we outsource our capacity to think and remember, the less capable we are of discerning God's call in our lives. We spend our entire lives sifting through the torrents of external stimuli, so how do we continue to pay attention to the still, small voice of God within each of us?[69]

Neurologist Daniel Siegel, who specializes in teenage brain development, observes that youth accustomed to high levels of stimulus-bound attention flit from one activity to another, with little time for self-reflection or interpersonal connection of the direct, face-to-face sort that the brain needs for proper development. "Little today in our hectic lives provides for opportunities to attune with one another."[70] This would seem to make the preacher as sage all the more important a role. Someone needs to practice the knack for noticing one's inscape and connecting it to one's landscape and textscape!

The single-scene sermon is directed at those who experience CPA. It is like my colleague, tapping on the table and saying, "Be Here!" You invite people into one scene and stay there. Think about the sermon experience from the point of view of the listeners. Every week they come to the worship service, the scene of the sermon, from scenes in their own lives. Maybe the young couple on the front row just came from a blow-out fight, complete with expletives. Maybe the college student at the back is flushed with shame over the scenes from last night that flash through his or her mind. Maybe the social worker is plagued by scenes from the life of a child she was too late to help. Thomas Merton observed that "Our minds are like crows. They pick up everything that glitters, no matter how uncomfortable our nests get with all that metal in them."[71] When we preach, there are crows flying all around the sanctuary, flying back to collect scenes from the remembered past and forward to gather scenes from an imagined future.

Our sermon is the nest. In the single-scene sermon, you invite listeners to bring all their gritty, glittery scenes into one palm-sized scene. It can be from the preacher's personal experience. It can be from something the preacher has read, either historical or contemporary. It can be from Scripture. It can be a scene from a current event. If it is a biblical scene, you invite people in and, once they are there, you use the features of that scene to connect to their personal and communal lives, guided by the theme you have decided to highlight. If it is a scene from personal experience, historical or contemporary life, you invite people in and, once they are there, you use the features of that scene to connect their daily lives to Scripture, guided by your theme. In single-scene sermons, you invite people into one scene and do everything you can to keep them there. You explore aspects of setting, plot, character, conflict, imagery, and themes from within the scene, inviting connections from the wider world to join you in the scene. Paint a biblical scene and invite listeners to tromp around in it, ask questions, and make connections with their own lives and the world around them. Paint a contemporary scene and invite the biblical characters to tromp around in it. Paint a historical scene and invite the biblical characters to tromp around in it.

Types of Single-Scene Sermons

Single-Scene Sermon with a Biblical Scene as Its Home Screen

My sermon in chapter 5, entitled "Locked in a Room with Open Doors" (John 20:19–23), is an example of a single-scene sermon with a biblical scene as its home screen. It begins and ends with me standing outside the room in which the disciples have locked themselves. I invite my own memories (of a bear at the zoo) and the congregation to join me there. Eventually we notice Jesus there with us, and we observe his entry and the outcome.

Listeners are invited to stand next to the preacher, looking in at the disciples locked inside their fears, to draw to the scene memories and scenarios from the lives of the preacher and the congregation. The concern for clarity and a High Definition (HD) throughline shows up in the repetition of the sequence: "What an entrance . . . What a greeting . . . What a gift . . . What an exit." The sermon ends by coming back around to the memory the preacher shared at the beginning of the sermon.

Single-Scene Sermon with an Historical Scene as Its Home Screen

I know some would say that opening with an historical scene will fall flat because people don't care about history. The website Ancestry.com would beg to differ, and so would my own experience of preaching. It all depends on how well you tell the story.

Several years ago, Ken Loyer—then a graduate student in the systematic theology track in the Graduate Program in Religious Studies at Southern Methodist University—went to Moscow to teach a course on the theology of John Wesley.[72] He had a translator, but he also took along a scene. It was a print of George Washington Brownlow's *John Wesley Preaching from His Father's Tomb at Epworth*, with St. Andrew's in the background. Every morning, he put the picture up on an easel at the front of the classroom. The course proceeded along the lines of the narrative components of the scene. What scene preceded this one? Where is he? Why is he standing there? Who is he? Who are his listeners? What is his message? Why are they listening? What is going on around the scene? What is the next scene after this one?

When I heard about this, I began thinking about its application for a sermon. Perhaps one about *persistence* based on Philippians 3:12–16. The scene gives rise to any number of sermonic themes for a sermon that connects Scripture, historical heritage, and contemporary life.

Throughout a single-scene sermon, the setting stays the same. We stand listening to Mr. Wesley as he preaches from his father's grave. Others come to join us.

Here is the historical scene to go with the picture.

On Sunday June 6th 1742 John Wesley, the English Evangelist re-visited his home town, Epworth in Lincolnshire.

This was the town of his birth and his father had been the Pastor of the St. Andrew's Anglican Church there. The Wesley children had been raised there.

Prior to the Sunday service beginning Wesley offered to assist the Curate with the service, either by preaching or 'reading prayers' (from the Book of Common Prayer, then used by Anglicans).

[Says Wesley in his] Journal:

"[The curate] did not care to accept my assistance. . . .

"After the sermon, John Taylor stood in the church-yard, and gave notice, as the people were coming out, 'Mr. Wesley, not being permitted to preach in the church, designs to preach here at six o'clock.'

"Accordingly at six I came, and found such a congregation as I believe Epworth never saw before.

"I stood near the east end of the church, upon my father's tomb stone and cried, 'The kingdom of heaven is not meat and drink, but righteousness, and peace, and joy in the Holy Ghost.'"[73]

Single-Scene Sermon with a Literary Scene as Its Home Screen

André Dubus, the late novelist and short story writer, lost one leg and the use of the other in a 1986 accident. In an essay titled "Song of Pity" he tells of a cold winter afternoon years before his accident when he was a graduate student at the University of Iowa Writers' Workshop. He came upon a man in a wheelchair who was unable to continue up a steep incline, and Dubus pushed the man's chair the rest of the way. Years later, Dubus found himself in a wheelchair. He reflects back on that afternoon. "I lacked imagination. Or I lacked the compassion and courage to imagine someone else's suffering. I never thought of my friend making his bed, sitting on a toilet, sitting in a shower, dressing himself, preparing breakfast and washing the dishes, just to leave the house, to go out into the freezing air of Iowa."[74]

A sermon could begin with this scene and explore two questions: (1) What is it that empowers us to identify, at a deeply emotional level, with those experiencing losses, illnesses, sorrows we ourselves have never experienced? (2) What it is that keeps our hearts chilled and closed off to the sufferings of others?

Single-Scene Sermon with Scene from Preacher's Life as Its Home Screen

The sermon in chapter 5, "No Way?" after a brief circumstantial set up, places me in Germany, with impaired vision and limited German language skills, outside a medical building, unsure where to go for help, having been dropped off by a taxi driver. I envision others coming to join me: the people of John's church and John's Gospel, Thomas, and members of the congregation. We are all in the same boat. We envision Jesus standing there with us, offering us a lifeline. A memory of Alice Walker finding Zora Neale Hurston's grave in a field of brambles underscores that God can make a way out of no way. My cabdriver, Freeda, returns, having realized how lost I must feel. We affirm God's guidance of us even when we can't discern our way.

The Single-Scene Sermon with a Contemporary Scene as Its Home Screen
The sermon "A Friend at Midnight" in chapter 5 is a Communion sermon based on Luke's parable of the Friend at Midnight (Luke 11:1–11). It could be viewed as either a single-scene or multi-scene sermon. Its opening scene is a front porch, a setting listeners can visualize and personalize. The sermon maintains the image or metaphor of the front porch, but the porch changes, and the people on it change. Here is the succession of porches:

- The McKenzies' front porch,
- The villager in the parable's front porch
- The congregation's front porch
- Jesus' front porch in Luke's Gospel
- Ruby, my church member's, front porch
- Our front porch

Scene Surgery

Novelist Sandra Scofield, author of *The Scene Book* I referred to earlier, offers advice for novelists and screenwriters for analyzing the effectiveness of their scenes. She suggests that authors read through their work, place boxes around their scenes, and label each one. You will note my "scene labels" in the sermons in chapter 5. Then she suggests we ask each scene the questions of pulse, purpose, plot, and point of view.[75]

This exercise helps a preacher analyze where scenes can go wrong or fall short. Here are some questions that might identify aspects of a sermonic scene we need to work on:

- Pulse: Does the scene have emotional energy; is tension being built or resolved? Do you care about anyone in the scene?

- Purpose: If this scene were summarized or integrated into another scene, would the sequence suffer? Is this scene necessary?
- Plot: Is this the right place for this scene?
- Point of View: Does the scene have a clear, single point of view?[76]

Scene Checklist: Characteristics of Successful Scenes

Here is a checklist of successful scene characteristics. See appendix A for a list of questions to ask a sermon, questions that cover the following checklist.

Memorable Imagery

The imagination is the ability to experience that which is not immediately before us. Scenes, stories, and images are the product of imagination. Effective scenes feature powerful imagery. The power of imagery has been a staple of effective preaching for centuries. Says Henry Mitchell, speaking out of the legacy of African American preaching,

> The faith on which people bet their very lives comes *not* because one has heard and understood a great flow of logical persuasion, though the love of God demands that we understand all we can. Rather, it is the fruit of holistic encounter, with familiar images.[77]

Barbara Brown Taylor, a preacher and author gifted in both imagery and scene, confirms their crucial role in preaching:

> Preachers who wish to proclaim a lively word . . . will be fluent not only in the language of theology but also in the language of image, learning to paint pictures and tell stories as effectively as they compare ideas and organize thoughts. This is no new development in homiletics. Before there was Christian doctrine there was Christian story.[78]

Says Taylor, "For preachers, imagination is the ability to form images in the minds of their listeners that are not physically present to their senses, so that they find themselves in a wider world with new choices about who and how they will be."[79]

Patricia Wilson-Kastner, in her book *Imagery for Preaching*, reminds preachers that imagery is not limited to the sense of sight. Imagery is the whole sensory world of the text.[80]

Scenes provide a home for images, while images provide a clue to the interpretation of scenes. They focus listener or reader attention within the scene.[81] For example, in the sermon "A Friend at Midnight," there is a porch in every scene.

Images can itinerate from scene to scene in a sermon, providing a unifying theme and building in intensity. The images involved in baptism and Holy Communion illustrate this.[82] The visceral event of the exodus is a metaphor that has fortified the faith of marginalized people over the centuries. Scenes evoke images, and images evoke scenes.

Images that appear in the sermons in chapter 5 include: a customer service desk at which we return our fears, a training manual, a yellow backpack, a pack list, a front porch, a cage that no longer exists in which an old bear continues to pace, and a couch covered in plastic.

Sermons in chapter 5 feature both biblical and contemporary images. "The Yellow Backpack" and "Peel off the Plastic" are examples of images taken from contemporary life. "A Friend at Midnight" comes from Luke 11.

Frederick Buechner's sermon "A Sprig of Hope" refers to the olive branch the dove brought back to Noah (Gen. 8:11) as a sign of new life after the flood.[83] Anna Carter Florence uses the image of "At the River's Edge" (Exod. 2: 1–10) as a metaphor for the treatment of children in a society.[84]

Claudette Anderson Copeland uses the image of "Tamar's Torn Robe" (2 Sam. 13:1–20) for the anguish experienced by women who suffer abuse in communities that pride themselves on their righteousness.[85]

Homiletician Jennifer Lord offers a helpful exegetical process, focusing on discovering evocative imagery from text and contemporary context that she calls "Weekly Word Work." She guides preachers in brainstorming words and images that flesh out our theological jargon. She warns preachers not to rush to get to theological meaning or historical insight and pass over the words and images that inform them.[86] I've mentioned before the lack of knowledge of many contemporary people of Bible and theology. Talking in theological jargon is an efficient way to distance these would-be listeners. Use of imagery, metaphor, scene, and story fleshes out all those "tion" words: justification, sanctification, and transformation. Says David Buttrick, "Homiletical thinking is always a thinking of theology toward images.[87]

Concrete Significant Detail (CSD)

In 2012, I invited Janet Burroway to address the Academy of Homiletics at our annual meeting in Chicago. Janet has written seven novels, a book of poetry, and two manuals on writing: *Writing Fiction: A Guide to Narrative Craft* and *Imaginative Writing: The Elements of Craft*. The topic of her talk was *CSD*, which is not an abbreviation for a medical condition, but stands for the most important principle of storytelling for creative writers: Concrete Significant Detail. When telling a story, if there is too much insignificant detail, the theme and power of a scene are lost. At the other extreme, if there is not enough detail, if it is not concrete, I can't enter into the scene. I am left standing on the porch. That doesn't mean we have to drag every one of the five senses into every scene, which would exhaust our listeners. But we need to provide them with enough sensory detail to participate in the scene. Successful scenes have CSD.

> If those who have studied the art of writing are in accord on any one point, it is on this: the surest way to arouse and hold the attention of the reader is by being specific, definite and concrete. The greatest writers . . . are effective largely because they deal in particulars and report the details that matter.[88]

John Gardner, in *The Art of Fiction*, says, "[The novelist] gives us such details about the streets, stores, weather, politics, and concerns of Cleveland (or whatever the setting is) and such details about the looks, gestures, and experience of . . . characters that we cannot help believing that the story he [or she] tells us is true."[89]

A detail is "definite" and "concrete" when it appeals to the sense. It should focus the listener's or reader's attention, not diffuse it.[90]

Show, Don't Tell

Successful scenes show, they don't just tell. Show me characters' emotions through physical signs.

> Simply labeling a character's emotion as love or hatred will have little effect, for such abstractions operate solely on a vague, intellectual level; rather, emotion is the body's physical reaction to information the senses receive. The great Russian director Stanislavski, originator of realistic "Method" acting, urged his students to abandon the clichéd emotive postures of the nineteenth-century stage in favor of emotions evoked by the actors' recollection of sensory details connected with a personal past trauma. By recalling such details as the tingling of fingertips, the smell of singed hair and the tensing of calf

muscles an emotion such as anger might naturally be induced within the actors' body. . . .

[I]f the writer/speaker depicts the precise physical sensations experience by the character, a particular emotion may be triggered by the reader's own sense memory.[91]

If you have a scene, for example, in which a young man is experiencing anxiety because he is not accustomed to fine dining in elegant restaurants, don't tell us that. Have his hand hover over the array of three forks, waiting until his hostess picks hers up to lift his own from the table. In the sermon, show me characters' emotions through their actions and dialogue. In "Finding Faith amid Our Fears" (see chap. 5), in the scene of Mary McLeod Bethune and the KKK, we don't need to be told she is brave. We experience her decisive actions and brief instructions to others as the Klan approaches her school. In the sermon "No Way?" when Freeda comes back for me, we don't need to be told it was because she felt empathy for me. Her actions tell us that. In the scene from "The Yellow Backpack," I don't need to tell you that Matthew, the airline employee, thought I was a complete idiot. His eye rolling as he walked away told you that.

Biblical scholar Robert Alter observes that the Bible manages to "evoke . . . a sense of depth and complexity in its representation of character with . . . sparse, even rudimentary means." He refers to the "less is more" characterization of biblical prose as the "art of reticence."[92]

Dialogue

In summary portions of a sermon, it is appropriate to tell people things. But in a scene, whenever possible, put information in the form of dialogue. Put words in people's mouths. Rather than this, "Ben Franklin's Quaker friend told him that the general consensus around town was that he was arrogant"; say this, "Ben, people are saying that you're arrogant." Direct dialogue invites listeners one step closer to the scene.

Point of View

In general, choose one point of view and stick with it. In the sermon "Paul's Pack List" (chap. 5), I tell the story of two ships signaling back and forth. That seemed somewhat impersonal to me, so I rewrote it to be told from the point of view of the first captain, the one whose crew was almost dying of thirst. If I am telling a story from someone else's point of view, I stick with their point of view. In the story of Ruby, in the sermon "No Way?" I initially inserted more of my own feelings into the scenes. On reflection, I took them out and stuck with just reporting my actions rather than my feelings—because it was about her, not me. Sometimes we preachers give in to a narcissistic need to intrude into our stories about others. Remembering to stick with one point of view per scene is a helpful discipline!

Effective Openings

There are several ways to open, or "launch," a scene.

Image Launch

One way to open is to identify an image that is part of the setting of a contemporary or biblical scene.[93] Cleophus J. LaRue's sermon "Why Bother?" based on Acts 17:16–23 (Paul in Athens, in front of the Areopagus), begins with a contemporary image and quickly connects it with Scripture.

> Splattered across the front doors of a trendy restaurant in Palo Alto, California, were these words: "This is a bad place for a diet!" That most visible, in-your-face warning suggested to me that there are certain places where some requests are out of order and certain times where some appeals are in poor taste. No matter how noble, how worthy, how life-giving they are in and of themselves, there are certain times and certain places where it is simply unseemly to speak of some things. In like manner it appears to me to that we could splatter across the pages of our text this morning a similar warning: "This is a bad place for the gospel."[94]

Action Launch

Jordan Rosenfeld calls another way to launch a scene "the action launch." You jump right in, grabbing people's attention, filling in needed information as the action moves forward.[95] Listener interest is caught, wondering—Who? Where? What?—but it must be satisfied quickly, or they will just be confused. So be aware that this kind of launch works best as the opening of a sermon. And you don't want to overuse it, or it will become predictable, like any other rhetorical strategy.

I chose to begin my sermon "Finding Faith amid Our Fears" (chap. 5), which is basically a deductive sermon about the fear of the Lord as trembling and trust, in the middle of the scene of my students' first day in my Introduction to Preaching class at Perkins School of Theology.

Character Launch

This is a scene opening that gets the character into the scene as soon as possible by highlighting the most immediate desire of the character. The opening scene of "Paul's Pack List" (chap. 5) is a character launch scene. We feel Paul's sufferings and his urgent need to hand on advice to the Philippian church.[96]

Narrative Summary Launch

This is the scene opening that lays the groundwork and describes the scene.[97] The scene in which Leontine Kelly meets Mary McCleod Bethune features such an opening in the sermon "Finding Faith amid Our Fears." I describe who Leontine was and the occasion of their meeting to set the stage for the action for the scene. The opening scene of "Foresight is 20/20" is a narrative summary opening in which I explain why I was in Tupelo and how I came to be in the simulated worship service in the church where Elvis worshiped as a child (chap. 5).

Familiar Phrase Launch

Sandra Scofield suggests we sometimes open a scene with a word or phrase from an earlier scene to jog the reader's memory.[98] The refrain I use several times in "Training Day" meets this criterion: "Training is important. It helps us prepare ourselves for whatever a day may bring" (chap. 5).

In "Foresight Is 20/20," I begin the sermon with a scene from a reenactment of 1940s worship in Elvis Presley's birthplace, Tupelo, Mississippi: screens roll down and a surround-sound film begins. I transition from the opening scene to the transfiguration by referring back to the opening story. "On Transfiguration Day, the screens roll down from heaven for Peter, James, and John and they see the resurrected glory of Jesus" (chap. 5).

Setting Launch

This scene launch begins with a comment on some aspect of the setting or the event to set up the scene. Rosenfeld calls this a "setting launch."[99] (See chap. 5 for the following examples.)

In "Training Day," I set up a scene in which a popular commentator voices the lament we are all feeling: "Commentator Steve Hartman, in his CBS 'On the Road' segments, offers heartwarming stories of people he has met on the road around America. But Friday night, October 6, 2017, he just sat in a chair facing the camera and offered a lament."

In "Paul's Pack List," I set up the scene of Atticus Finch and Bob Ewell from *To Kill a Mockingbird* with a comment on our cultural setting. "Our culture defines humility as weakness. But in fact it is the conduit for the power of God, God's compassion, and God's courage."

In "The Yellow Backpack," having just concluded a scene in which Bartimaeus is portrayed as desperately shouting for Jesus' attention, I set up the next story—"The man behind the pillar"—in this way: "Now maybe you're not the shouting type. Maybe you're more private about your losses and your faith. Maybe you are the type who suffers in silence and doesn't want to draw Jesus' attention." The set-up both reaches back to what has just happened and points forward to the next scene.

Effective Endings

The end of a scene is a space for the readers to take a breath and digest all that they have just finished reading [hearing]. Endings linger in memory because they are where things finally begin to add up and make sense. At the end of a scene, if it has been done well, the reader will have a greater investment in the plot and characters, and feel more compelled to find out what happens next. In fact, you know you've done your work when the reader reaches the end of a scene and absolutely must press on.[100]

Summary Ending

The scene ends with a summary of what just happened in the scene at hand.[101]

The last scene of "Training Day" (chap. 5) is a summary of the lessons the sermon draws from Psalm 19 on how to train spiritually to face each day. "As Christians, we look up . . . we look within . . . we look around."

In "Paul's Pack List" (chap 5.), as I go through three false understanding of humility, I close each scene that illustrates one of them with a summary: "Humility is not low self-esteem. . . . Humility is not humiliation. . . . Humility is not a human achievement."

To summarize what has gone before with just a phrase or even one word is a strategy that highlights the throughline, helping listeners stay on track. I employ it in almost all of the sermons in chapter 5. Another example is in the repetition of the sequence of Jesus' actions in "No Way?" as Jesus passes through closed doors, greets the disciples, and breathes on them the Holy Spirit: "What an entrance! What a greeting! What a Gift!"

Dialogue Ending

Dialogue can be used to end a scene with intensity or surprise.[102] (See chap. 5 for the following examples.)

The sermon "A Friend at Midnight" ends with God speaking to us on our front porch. I don't often put words in God's mouth, but this time I took the risk, making sure they were faithful to a theme implied in the parable.

The first scene of "No Way?" ends with Freeda, my cabdriver, calling out "Good luck!" as she drives away; a parallel to Jesus' comment to the disciples: "Do not let your heart be troubled" (John 14:27).

Cliffhanger Ending

The first scene of "No Way?" is a cliffhanger ending[103] because it leaves me, sight-impaired and German-language deficient, in a difficult situation, standing in front of a medical building, and not knowing where to go for help.

Ending with a Question

In "Foresight Is 20/20" (chap. 5), I end a scene of my visit to a Sunday school class of widows with the question, "Do you know anybody who needs a dose of resurrection foresight?"

In "Finding Faith amid Our Fears" (chap. 5), I end the opening classroom scene, in which I asked students to write their greatest fear on an index card, with the question, "What would you write on your card?" I use the question to draw listeners into the scene that has just occurred.

Conclusive Ending

The conclusive ending[104] doesn't point to future scenes. It simply concludes something that has happened or ties up a plot point. In "Finding Faith amid Our Fears," after creating a degree of suspense about the identity of the fear that we are to spend our lives cultivating—listing several fears that are *not* the beginning of wisdom—I conclude with "You knew I'd get to it eventually. The fear of the Lord is the beginning of wisdom."

In that same sermon, the scene where Leontine Kelly meets Mary McCleod Bethune has a conclusive ending that reinforces the theme it was meant to serve and aims at connecting the scene to listeners. "I'm not a little girl. I'm a woman grown. But if someone asked me this question today, 'Who do you plan to be?' I would answer, 'I plan to become someone who fears the Lord and no one and nothing else'" (chap. 5).

The Benefits of Scenes

Teaching Power: Scene-ing Your Exegesis

Which is worse, a sermon that is boring but deep or one that is shallow but engaging? The answer is yes! Both are worse than what could be, which is a deep sermon—that is, one that offers profound biblical and theological insight—which is also "delightful"—engaging emotion and imagination and eliciting a faithful response.[105]

One of the most fruitful uses of scenes is what I call "Scene-ing your exegesis," or "Scene-ing your teaching."[106]

For example, in the sermon in chapter 5, "Finding Faith amid Our Fears," I was trying to get across the point that the fear of the Lord talked about in Proverbs 1:7 and 3:5–8 can overcome our fears. Rather than simply telling the congregation this truth, I had them imagine lying in bed at 3:27 a.m., staring at the ceiling as the "parade of fears" rolls down the main street of their minds, each fear with its own float. Then I ask them to imagine, coming down the street from the opposite direction on a collision course with their garden-variety fears, a float on which is the fear of the Lord, the fear that is the beginning of wisdom and that ends all fears. I did a litany of comforting Old Testament Scriptures that I said were "coming for their fears."

After the first service, a woman came up to me and said, "I'm going to be watching for the fear of the Lord float to crash into my fear of flying.

We are booked on a trip to England next month, and I'm not going to let it keep me from going." After the second service, a man came up and said, "I have decided that I am afraid of my addiction to alcohol and where it will lead me, and I want to seek out a support group. Do they have any that meet at this church?"

The scene I painted touched people's emotions more closely than a conceptual assurance of a scriptural truth would have. And it did so without dumbing down the truth. Rather, it embodied it in a scene into which listeners could enter and see themselves.

Another example, in a sermon on the parable of the unforgiving servant (Matt. 18:21–35), which is not included in this book, brings the congregational context of Matthew's Gospel to life in a scene:

> The folding chairs scrape against the floor as the worship attendees move them into two sections facing the front, with a wide center aisle between them. Gentile Christians are on one side; Jewish Christians on the other. As Matthew enters, he hears the whispered slurs, hissed from side to side. From the Jews, "God chose us first." From the Gentiles, "Yes, but God saved the best for last!"
>
> In this hot mess of a community, Matthew stands and offers the parable of the unforgiving servant that comes to us in Matthew 18.

In the sermon "Foresight is 20/20" (chap. 5), I wanted to teach the congregation about the situation in which Mark wrote his Gospel, the sense of helplessness and pessimism the community felt in a time of persecution. I first painted the scene of my being in the airport on my way home from Tupelo, and the postures of fellow passengers as we gathered around the flatscreen TV, listening to harsh news from Jordan. I then placed Mark's church in that same scene and compared their responses to their harsh conditions.

In "No Way?" (chap. 5), I want to teach the fact that, in John's Gospel, Jesus habitually offers a way forward to troubled people, offering them all they need for life's journey, as embodied in the seven "I Am" sayings of John. I place that teaching in a scene of Jesus standing at the edge of the pit that both we and John's troubled characters are in; Jesus is offering us a lifeline, as God in the Old Testament offered a lifeline to the Israelites.

Delivery Power

I jokingly tell my preaching students, "All that people want from us preachers today is the reality of careful preparation and the appearance of total spontaneity." That may actually be too true to be funny. Preaching in scenes makes it easier to internalize the message and preach it with minimal or no notes.[107] I still write out a manuscript, but I write it for the listening ear rather than the reading eye. That means employing all the strategies of oral communication that make a sermon easy to say and hard to forget: alliteration, rhyme, repetition, imagery, metaphor, story, and scene. In preliterate societies, what could not be remembered was forgotten. I remember as I preach that people can't turn the pages back and hear it again. It's like a one-time musical performance, an event in time.[108]

I'm not claiming that preaching without notes is some gold standard for sermon delivery. It is possible to preach from a manuscript and have excellent eye contact. I'm not claiming that the mere fact of having no notes makes a sermon somehow more "Spirit-filled." It is possible to preach with no notes and lead the congregation down a road called "Meandering Way." The Holy Spirit can hardly be blamed for lack of preparation or incoherence! Whatever our method, we need to keep in mind that preaching is an interactive event, not the delivery of a product that leaves no room for spontaneity or interactive energy. And we need to keep in mind that, however vividly we present our message, we still need to have a message, one that is worthy of both our congregation and Scripture, possessing biblical and theological depth and integrity.[109]

Preaching in scenes benefits to our performance of the sermon. Having a memorable sequence and picturing the message as you go makes for that beautiful moment in preaching where you pause while looking people in the eye and actually know what you are going to say next!

Preaching in scenes can eliminate three major pitfalls of sermon delivery: the pause-free sermon, the gesture-free sermon, and the passion-free sermon. More lively content leads to more lively delivery![110]

The following chapter contains nine sermons I've preached in various venues over the past few years. Even if I didn't indicate the date at the beginning of the sermon, you would be able to date most of them from current events they refer to. I believe that, as soon as we preach a sermon, it *should* sound dated. So I have made no effort to take out specific references and present these sermons as appropriate for any congregation anywhere. A checklist of questions to ask a scenic sermon appears in appendix A. I invite the reader to analyze mine and their own sermons by keeping in mind the characteristics of successful scenes.

I like coming around to where I began with a little more wisdom than I had at the outset. And so I end as I began, with a piece of advice we need to disregard in preaching these days: "Don't make a scene." This command is usually hissed through clenched teeth. Maybe spoken by a mom to a toddler at Target: "No, we're not buying that. Put it back. Don't make a scene." Maybe spoken by a man or woman to a date in an elegant restaurant: "Keep your voice down. We'll talk about this later. Don't make a scene!" Maybe spoken by a lawyer to her client on the way into the courtroom: "Let me do the talking when we get in there. Don't make a scene."

"Don't make a scene" means 'Don't draw bystanders into our drama." My advice to preachers these days is exactly the opposite: "Make a scene. Do everything you can to draw bystanders into our drama! For God's sake, make a scene in the pulpit!"

Chapter Five

Scenic Sermons

SCENIC SERMON 1: DEDUCTIVE SERMON THAT BEGINS WITH A SCENE

Sermon Title: "Finding Faith amid Our Fears"

Sermon Text: Proverbs 1:7; 3:5–7

Occasion: Ecumenical Community Worship Service, February 1, 2015

Location: Smith Chapel African Methodist Episcopal Church, Dallas, Texas

Reading of Proverbs 1:7; 3:5–7
Life in General, Mostly Dogs

I stand before the class of twelve students, the fluorescent lighting in the classroom accentuating the furrows on their foreheads. I begin handing out index cards and say, "Welcome to PR6300, Introduction to Preaching. Everyone take a card, and I'd like you to write some information on it that will help me tailor the class to your learning needs. Please put down your name, email, phone, denomination, church you are currently serving, amount of preaching experience, what you hope to learn from the class, and greatest fear."

I assume they understand that by *greatest fear*, I mean "about the class." That is, until I get home that evening and, after putting my children to bed, I start going through the cards. Under the "greatest fear" question, some had written things like standing in front of a group, being evaluated by my peers, not having anything to say, and being boring. These are all fears I can help them with. But then, near the bottom of the stack, next to *greatest fear*, somebody had written "aging.' Another student had written "death," and one poor soul, in a spurt of honesty, had written, "Life in general, mostly dogs."

What would be on your index card?

Returning Your Fears

You know that you can return your fears, right? Returning fears is the same process as returning anything else. You make an impulse purchase, online or in person. It arrives, or you get it home, and you think, "What was I thinking? I don't need this. It isn't in my budget. I bought it—because my brother-in-law has one, because I have always wished my feet were smaller, because I was having a bad day—choose one. But I don't need it. It doesn't fit. I'm returning it. You have to stuff it into the original package or box, print out the return label and take it to UPS. If you bought it at a bricks and mortar store, you have to find the receipt in an email or your wallet. You drive around for at least three weeks with the item on the backseat. You have to get in line at the customer service counter and wait your turn, wondering why all the people in front of you didn't have any more sense than to buy things they need, couldn't afford, and that didn't fit.

The Bible is always telling people to return their fears. All through the Bible, people on the brink of challenges are told by God or an angelic messenger, "Don't be afraid." Don't be afraid, Abraham, to set out at age seventy-five for an unknown land where you know no one. Don't be afraid, Moses, of speaking truth to power; it's only Pharaoh. Don't be afraid, Mary—everyone will think you're a woman of loose morals and eventually your heart will be pierced with pain—but don't be afraid. Don't be afraid, Paul, of being beaten, imprisoned, shipwrecked, and worse. Don't be afraid, we are told, over and over and over again.

The One Fear We Are to Cultivate

And yet throughout this same Bible, we are told that there is one fear that we are to spend our lives cultivating.

Proverbs 1:7 tells us that this one fear is the beginning (the first step) of wisdom. We are told later in Proverbs that this fear paves a path of wisdom beneath our feet and is the destination of the wise life (Prov. 2).

And here is a clue: This fear is not any of the fears that I'm carrying around in my backpack, purse, or backseat. Here are the fears we may have been chauffeuring around town:

- The fear that my cancer will return
- The fear that my children will move away
- The fear of losing my job
- The fear of losing my partner or spouse

These personal fears are legitimate. Many of you have experienced at least one of them; then you have gotten up from your bed of grief to live another day. But these are not the fears that lead to wisdom.

Beyond the personal, in the realm of our violent, hate-filled world, here are the fears many people are carrying around in their backpacks:

- The fear of mistreatment by the civil servants entrusted with the care of the community
- The fear of people of different race, religion, sexual orientation
- The fear of hate crimes by cruel minds
- The fear of being the victim of a terrorist attack

These fears are also real. We have to both protect ourselves and our loved ones and push back against the perpetrators of social injustice. These ugly truths may make us tremble with fear, but not with the fear that is the beginning of wisdom.

You knew I'd get to it eventually: The fear of the *Lord* is the beginning of wisdom! And it consists, Scripture tells us, of equal parts trembling and trust. The Bible tells us that our task is to spend our life cultivating the fear of the Lord, growing in faith. I don't know about you, but I've got nothing better to do!

Bishop Leontine Kelly Meets Mary McCleod Bethune: Who Do You Plan to Be?

Leontine Kelly (1920–2012) was the first African American woman ordained a bishop in The United Methodist Church. In 1984, she was the second woman and the first African American woman to become a bishop in any major Christian denomination in the world. In a phone conversation a few years before her death in 2012, she told me the story of when she was in third grade, growing up in Cincinnati. Her father was a pastor and community leader, her mother one of the founders of the Urban League of Cincinnati:

> One morning, as she was getting ready for school, there was a knock on the front door. Her parents were in the kitchen at the back of the house, so Leontine ran to the door, opened it, and there stood a distinguished, immaculately dressed woman who—without any "Good morning, little girl" or "Aren't you cute?"—simply said, "Little girl, who do you plan to be? You must be somebody."
>
> Leontine says, "I ran back to the kitchen and told my parents, "Momma, Daddy, Somebody is at the front door!
>
> When she asked me who I planned to be, well, my immediate plans were to be a third grader. But then I found out this was Mary McCleod Bethune, educator, civil rights leader and advisor to presidents on education. Born in 1875, the fifteenth child of South Carolina sharecroppers, she founded a school for African American girls in Daytona Beach, Florida. The school later became Bethune Cookman University. She became one of the first African American women to be a college president and was asked by President Franklin Delano Roosevelt to be a consultant in matters of national education. She came to be called "The First Lady of the Struggle." As I got older, as I learned more about the formidable woman who had stood on my porch, the more central the question she'd asked became for my identity: "Little girl, who do you plan to be?" And the more my answer became, "I plan to become like you."[1]

I'm not a little girl. I'm a woman grown. I'm not even middle-aged anymore, unless I live a life of biblical longevity! But if someone asked me this question, "Who do you plan to be?" I would answer, "I plan to become someone who fears the Lord and no one and nothing else."

The Fear of the Lord: The Bible's Code Word for Faith

A lot of people think the "fear of the Lord" means cringing in fear because God's gonna getcha! But the fear of the Lord is the Bible's code word for *faith*. It is a lifelong process of trembling before our Transcendent God and trusting our Faithful God.

The Fear of the Lord as Trembling

What do I mean by "trembling before our Transcendent God? Remember, this is not cringing because God's "gonna getcha"; it is falling to our knees in respect because God is God and we are not. I call that an awestruck attitude! The word for *fear* in Hebrew, *yireah*, means reverence, piety, and terror. Like *trembling*, *terror* is not because God's about to destroy you but because you are human and you suddenly realize the vast gap between you and God, and your knees tremble.

I am convinced that we have a whole lot of fears in this culture and not enough fear of the Lord. In today's world, many people are far more likely to live in fear of randomness, violence, and meaninglessness than in fear of the presence of God. When people live in these kinds of fear, they tend to find scapegoats: another religion, another race, another sexual orientation, another political party. Scapegoating leads to violence and retaliation. Haven't we had enough of that? Our culture is afraid of everything. It's time for us to show the world what it looks like to fear the Lord.

People in the Bible who don't have the sense God gave them, they don't tremble. Pharaoh is too arrogant to tremble and so brings destruction to many. Moses diagnosed his hardness of heart in this way: "But as for you and your officials, I know that you do not yet fear the LORD God" (Exod. 9:30). Oh, but they will . . . they will.

People with good sense in the Bible know to tremble before God.

- **Moses** at the burning bush obeys God's command to take off his shoes because he is standing on holy ground (Exod. 3:5).
- The **Israelites** on Mount Sinai (Exod. 19:16)
- **Isaiah**, when the temple shakes and he sees the Lord exalted on the throne (6:5)
- **Job**, when God speaks out of the whirlwind (Job 42:6)
- **Mary**, when she wakes up to find an angel standing at the foot of her bed (Luke 1:26)

The fear of the Lord means trembling before God and God alone. We realize in those moments that everything within us that is not of God must go. We gather up all those fears we have been about to make into a golden calf and fall down and worship. We take them to the divine customer service-desk and exchange them for the fear of the Lord, which is the Bible's code word for faith.

Faith Parade at 3:27 AM

I read a devotional writing a couple years ago. It is still vivid in my mind because it was my birthday and seemed that a word from God was speaking directly to me. The author said that, at 3:27 am or so, he often woke up and stared at the ceiling and couldn't fall back to sleep. There he observed the fear parade making its way down the main street of his mind, every fear with its own float. He said what he did then was to look down the street in the other direction, where he saw the faith parade coming down the street on a collision course with his 3:27-am fears. For me, the faith parade consists of one beautiful, biblical float after another.

Here comes Psalm 46:1–3:

> God is our refuge and strength,
>   a very present help in trouble.
> Therefore we will not fear, though the earth should change,
>   though the mountains should shake in the heart of the sea;
> though its waters roar and foam,
>   though the mountains tremble with its tumult."

Here comes Joshua 1:9:

> Be strong and courageous; do not be frightened or dismayed, for the Lord your God is with you wherever you go.

Here comes Psalm 118:5–6:

> Out of my distress I called on the Lord;
>   the Lord answered me and set me in a broad place.
> With the Lord on my side, I do not fear.
>   What can mortals do to me?

Here comes Psalm 23:4:

> Even though I walk through the darkest valley,
>   I fear no evil;
> for you are with me;
>   your rod and your staff—
> they comfort me.

On those floats, and many more, are the promises of a transcendent, trustworthy God. Those floats are on a collision course with your "3:27-am fears."

The Fear of the Lord as Trust

When we are able to turn and see the floats of God's faithfulness coming down the street toward our fears, *trembling* before our Transcendent God becomes *trust* in our Faithful God. When we embrace the fear of the Lord, we can relinquish lesser fears. "The fear of others lays a snare, / but the one who trusts in the Lord is secure" (Prov. 29:25). Deuteronomy 10:20 describes the covenant loyalty we need to cultivate in relationship to God: "You shall fear the Lord your God; him alone you shall worship; to him you shall hold fast, and by his name you shall swear." Proverbs 3:5–7 gives the same command to the wisdom student:

> Trust in the Lord with your whole heart,
>   And do not rely on your own insight.
> In all your ways acknowledge [God]
>   and [God] will make straight your paths.
> Do not be wise in your own eyes;
>   fear the Lord, and turn away from evil.

This does not mean that all will go well, or that the path will never twist and turn. It does meant that the path will be paved by the guiding, empowering Wisdom of God.

Mary McCleod Bethune: Trusting God's Faithfulness

One of the stories Leontine Kelly reported that she learned about Mary McCleod Bethune was this one, crafted by acclaimed storyteller Elisabeth Ellis in *Inviting the Wolf In: Thinking about Difficult Stories.*

> The Ku Klux Klan sent word to Mary McCleod Bethune that she better not try to vote. "Women haven't had the vote long enough for me to let a bunch of men in bedsheets keep me away from the polls." So she went and cast her ballot.
>   Then they sent word to her that she better not try to educate any more African American children. So she got in her buggy and drove down every back road begging parents and grandparents to

send their children to her school and had twice as many enrolled that fall as the year before. . . .

She was sitting at her desk one night, making out a test for the next day's lesson, when a little boy came thundering into the room. . . . [H]e gasped our, "They're coming!" She said, "Who's coming?" . . . He said, "Men with guns and clubs. My daddy says you can't be here when they get here."

. . . "You run home now. You tell your daddy I said thank you."

She walked out into the main room of her school and began to pull on a rope attached to an old bell. She could hear footsteps running from every direction. . . .

When everyone was gathered, [she] said to them, "The Klan is on its way to pay us a visit."

There was a murmur of fear that swept through the room. . . .

She said, "I want all you teachers to turn off all the lights. . . . When I clap my hands for the signal, I want you to turn on all the lights at once." . . .

Now you could look out the darkened windows and see thirty or forty pairs of headlights coming down the road.

She turned to the children, and said, "You little ones, stay where you are and try not to be afraid. You older ones, you come with me. We will go and meet them. Whatever I do, you do it too." . . .

She stood on the bottom step of the school. The children arranged themselves on the stairs behind her. By now the motorcade had reached the end of her driveway. She stood and waited. The first car stopped. A man got out in a long white robe and a tall pointed cap. He had a mask across his face. . . . He [directed] the entire motorcade [to] pass down her driveway. Still she stood and waited.

When the headlights of the first car flashed across her body, she clapped her hands for the signal. Every light behind her came on at once. Standing there with the bright light shining in front of and behind her, she looked like some tall, dark avenging angel.

She opened her mouth and began to sing. . . . "*When Israel was in Egypt land . . .*" And the children on the steps behind her answered back . . . "*Let my people go.*"

That first car kept edging past them. Mary McLeod Bethune's voice grew stronger. The children sang louder. The cars just kept inching past her. The men in the cars began to hunker down in their seats like it had finally dawned on them what it meant for a bunch of men to come, armed with guns and clubs, after an old woman and a school full of children. Not one stopped.[2]

Storyteller Elisabeth Ellis adds this realistic conclusion to the scene: "I wish I could tell you that Mary McCleod Bethune never had any more trouble with the Ku Klux Klan, but you and I both know that ignorance [and fear] takes a long time to die."[3]

Conclusion: Who Do We Plan to Be?

Who do you plan to be? We can—day by day, month by month, year by year—return our fears and exchange them for the fear of the Lord. This is the fear that is equal parts trembling at God's Transcendent Power—which is equal to all evil—and trusting God's Faithful Wisdom.

The God of Scripture, the sender of our Savior Jesus, stands on our doorstep today and asks us: "Who do you plan to be?" Let our answer be, "We plan to become like You."

Jesus knew what it was to fear the Lord, to tremble before no one and nothing less. He trusted God to be faithful to God's promises, even in the face of death. And he found that, in the end, God's word is true:

> Trust in the LORD with all your heart,
>   and do not rely on your own insights.
> In all your ways acknowledge [God],
>   and [God] will make straight your paths.
> Prov. 3:5–6

SCENIC SERMON 2: MULTI-SCENE SERMON THAT BEGINS WITH A BIBLICAL SCENE

Sermon Title: "Training Day!"

Sermon Texts: Psalm 19; John 1:1–5, 14, 18

Occasion: I serve as "Preacher in Residence," at Christ United Methodist Church in Plano, Texas. I preach there several times a year, and I hold a preaching workshop for their preaching staff one day a month. This was the sermon I preached the Sunday following the mass shooting on the Las Vegas strip, when a gunman opened fire on a crowd of concertgoers at a music festival, leaving fifty-eight people dead and at least five hundred twenty-seven injured.[4]

Location: Christ United Methodist Church, Plano, Texas

Introduction to John Reading

The prologue to the Gospel of John introduces us to Jesus as the Word of God. It affirms that God the Rock (God the Creator) is God the Redeemer (God the Son): "O Lord, my rock and my redeemer" (Ps. 19:14b). It assures us that the God who created light and human life will never allow that light to be overcome by darkness *(read John 1:1–5, 14, 18)*.

Introduction to Psalm Reading

Open the book of Psalms and you aren't just reading a collection of prayers. You've enrolled in a training course, a school of prayer in how to face whatever the day may hold. The title of Psalms in Hebrew is *Tehillim*, praises. The collection contains psalms of lament as well as psalms of praise. It helps us realize that lament without praise is despair, and praise without lament is shallow, hollow hallelujahs. The book of Psalms is a roller-coaster ride that, through all its ups and downs, stays on the track, and the track is God. It moves from confession ("Have mercy on me . . . / blot out my transgressions," Ps. 51:1), to lament ("By the rivers of Babylon— / there we sat down and there we wept," Ps. 137:1), to thanksgiving ("Make a joyful noise to the Lord, all the earth!" Ps. 100:1), to the very last line of all 150 psalms ("Let everything that breathes praise the Lord!" (Ps. 150:6).

Psalm 19 is our training-day psalm for this day, October 8, 2017. Psalm 19 begins with praise of God the Creator, comparing God's reliability to that of the sun. It moves to praising God's work within our lives, giving us clarity of vision to discern the needs of others and joy in the midst of sorrow *(read Ps. 19)*.

Plumbing Fiasco

One of my colleagues was attempting to do some home plumbing on a Saturday to unstop a sink in his kitchen. At the end of a stressful week at work, this was not how he had planned to spend his weekend. Stooped down under the kitchen sink, he unscrewed the pipe, and water began to gush out all over the kitchen floor. He closed his eyes and indulged in what I call an adult tantrum. That's when you briefly pretend to cry, and you feel better. He felt a pat on his shoulder and looked up into the face of his five-year-old daughter, who said, "It's okay. You're a really good daddy." Her unspoken message: "But you need some training to be a plumber!"

Hospital Visit

As I walk down the hall, the smell of ammonia and pine cleaner waft toward me. I hear the sound of hushed conversation at the nurses' station and the beeping of monitoring machines. I stop at the entrance of her room to take a deep breath. I think, "I'm just the summer ministry intern. I haven't even been to seminary yet. Shouldn't I have gone through some kind of training in how to talk to someone who has just received this diagnosis?"

Training is important. It prepares us to face the crises of daily life.

US Navy Chaplain's Training: Mara Morehouse Story

In my Introduction to Preaching Class one semester was a young woman named Mara Morehouse. After the first class of the fall, she came up to me and said, "I'm training to become a US Navy chaplain. The training conflicts with two of the classes for the semester. I know you're a stickler for attendance, but I have to go, and I promise to make up all the work." I wished her well and told her I'd like her to write up an account of the training to share with others when she got home. She was back in class in two weeks, with her usual excellent posture and sense of purpose. She wrote me this note to explain her experience:

Dear Dr. McKenzie:

I just finished the Direct Commission Officer Indoctrination Course in Newport, Rhode Island. During these two weeks, we were trained to do military, think military, live military. We were taught that every detail matters, from the way you lace your shoes, to the angle of your hand as you salute, whom to address as "sir," and whom to address as "petty officer," and how to respond to interrogation as a POW. As a chaplain, we are also trained in suicide prevention and how to conduct ourselves as non-combatants.

But it's not just training in facts. It's training in family. It's becoming part of a family with a very specific focus: to protect our nation and the "freedom of the seas."

First, I'm a sailor, a member of this family. Second, I'm an officer, a designated leader of this family. Third, I'm a chaplain, a servant to this family.

The training is mechanical, the development of muscle memory. It is also mental—you have to know what to do, then believe that, as a US Naval Officer, you can do it. It's stepping into a new identity. Thanks for the opportunity to share my story.
—Mara Morehouse.

Training is important. It prepares you for whatever crises, big or small, the day may hold.

Our Need for Training

The big crises are hitting the shore with numbing frequency. Another day, another hurricane, another earthquake, another massacre: Nice, France (July 2016); Pulse nightclub in Orlando, Florida (June 2016); Manchester, England, at an Ariana Grande concert (May 2017); almost a month ago, the tragedy here in Plano when an estranged husband killed his wife and seven others at a football watch party (September 2017).

Las Vegas, Nevada (October 1, 2017): with no apparent motivation, a person with a semi-automatic weapon—altered to fire like an automatic weapon—opened fire on a country music concert.[5]

I am open to any and all training experiences from all experts. Train me, child psychologists, in how to talk to my children and grandchildren. Train me, domestic violence counselors, in how to recognize the signs. Train me, first responders, in which way to run if shooting starts.

But before any of that, somebody train me in how to respond spiritually to a violent, chaotic world; some response other than moral paralysis, a shrug—"What can I do about it?"—or pessimism—"There is no good left in this world." Train me in prayer, in muscle-memory spiritual preparation, so it kicks in when tragedy strikes. Tell me the title of the training manual, and I'll order it. Oh, I already own it: the book of Psalms, in particular Psalm 19.

Psalm 19 as Our Training Manual in Lament

Psalm 19, though a psalm of praise, also trains us in lament. Verse 13 laments the many "insolent" people in this world. The Bible's definition of a *fool* is someone who is wise in his or her own eyes, in other words, insolent. These people are concerned with immediate self-gratification and have no concern for the consequences of their actions on others. Psalms 19 trains us to lament the pain they cause.

Let's lament together in the wake of the Las Vegas shooting. Can we, as a nation, work together to respect people's second-amendment rights while also placing restrictions on bump stocks, which allow semi-automatic weapons to deliver long bursts of bullets?

Normally, commentator Steve Hartman, in his CBS evening "On the Road" segment, offers heartwarming stories of people he has met on the road around America. But Friday night, October 6, 2017, he simply sat in a chair, faced the camera, and offered a lament and a challenge: "We are in a cycle of mourn, pray, and repeat. We can't stop it from happening again. But for God's sake, we ought to try."[6]

Psalm 19 as Our Training Manual in Praise

Psalm 19 trains us to not just lament but also praise in our prayers!

First, We Look Up!

The first six verses of the psalm are a hymn of praise to God's handiwork in the heavens, to God the Creator, who hung the sun. In the morning, when you wake up, no matter what awaits you in your life or on the news, go to a window and look up. It doesn't matter if it's cloudy. It's morning, and the sun has arisen with no assistance from you. At night, go outside and look up; admire the stars that have appeared in the night sky with absolutely no assistance from you. Listen as, without words, they proclaim the reliability of our Creator God.

Then We Look Out!

After you look up, look out. See the needs of those around you.

> The commandment of the LORD is clear,
>   enlightening the eyes.
>
> Ps. 19:8

I think back to the time I put on my first pair of glasses and could see, not just what concerned me in a two-foot radius from my face, but the faces of people further away from me. Some people have clear spiritual vision. They are concerned, not just with themselves, but with the good of the communities they serve. There are people who work to make a national priority of addressing gun violence in this country. There are people who lined up in Las Vegas to give blood, police officers who ran into danger rather than away from it, strangers who comforted the wounded and dying.

Closer to home, I see you, this group of Christians before me, leaders and congregation, who, in using your spiritual vision, have reached beyond your walls to help those in need. Your pastor Don Underwood says it this way.

> The image is burned indelibly into my brain. It was early September, 2005, and I was standing on the parking lot outside our newly constructed Sports & Rec Center. A bus pulled up, and people began to disembark. I had watched it all unfold on television: the flooding, the devastation, the fleeing, and the pictures of those who couldn't flee. Like everyone else, I had been gripped by the devastation and sheer tragedy of the storm. But this moment was different. It had suddenly become personal. Men and women, boys and girls, walked past me with faces that were expressionless. They had been traumatized and transported for so many days that they no longer showed emotion, neither sadness at what had happened, nor joy at the possibility of a good meal and a decent night of sleep. Some of them had come from the 9th Ward, and what I remember most distinctly—like an image from a bad nightmare—is the waterline stains mid-chest on their t-shirts. They were wearing the same clothes they had on when they escaped the flood waters days earlier.[7]

You opened your doors, offering sleeping quarters, sit-down meals, laundry service, and social services to traumatized men, women, and children. Said one church member, "I have been in church and Sunday school all my life, but I didn't get it. Now I do. This is what it means to follow Jesus." Senior Pastor Don Underwood summed up the impact of "Hotel Katrina" on his life and that of this congregation: "Whatever Christ United Methodist Church is today, our DNA has been radically altered by those who came into our lives and taught us what it means to love God by loving our neighbor."[8]

Then, We Look Within

After we look up and praise God, we look out to see the needs of others, and then we look within where we discover that "The law of the LORD is perfect, / reviving the soul" (Ps. 19:7).

Some days, even though the sun is shining, our inner weather is overcast. Our mood is downcast. On those days, our souls need to be revived, refreshed. The Hebrew word translated as "soul" is *nephesh*. Genesis 2:7 tells us, "Then the LORD God formed man from the dust of the ground, and breathed into his nostrils the breath of life; the man became a living being [a *nephesh*]" The *nephesh* is the "living inward being whose life resides in the breath and blood."[9] In other words, it is your unique identity, which depends, moment to moment, on the gift of God's presence.

On those days when your heart is heavy, it is God who refreshes your *nephesh*.

Young Mother of Stillborn Son

On August 17, 1960, at Seidel Memorial Hospital in Mechanicsburg, Pennsylvania, my mother gave birth to a healthy eight-pound baby boy. Her roommate on the other side of the curtain had given birth to a still-born boy. The next morning my mother awakened to see her roommate standing at the window, softly saying something over and over again. Listening very closely, my mother made out the words, "This is the day the Lord has made; I will rejoice and be glad in it. This is the day that the Lord has made; I will rejoice and be glad in it" (Ps.118:24).

My mother said, "How can you say that on today of all days?"

The young, grieving mother replied, "Why should today be any different from any other day?"

A person doesn't make that response to a tragic loss without a lot of prior training. If she is still living, that woman would be in her late eighties or early nineties. I picture her going home from that hospital room to practice her training in prayer every day from then on: Wake up and go to a window. Look up and see the sun. Praise God's reliable love. Look out and see the needs of others, and hear God's clear command to reach out to them in love. I picture her looking within on days when her *nephesh* is depressed and knowing God, the bringer of joy, is there, even on overcast days.

Conclusion: Training in Prayer

There is training in home plumbing. I saw a sign for it at the entrance to Home Depot. There is training in grief counseling for ministry interns. There is training for Naval chaplains. And there is training for you and for me each day of our unpredictable lives, training in prayer, lament in the context of praise:

As Christians, we look up and behold the face of Jesus Christ who helped God hang the sun. We look out and see the needs of a hurting world. We look within and find joy. We look around and see, in every tragic death and violent sorrow, the face of Jesus Christ who suffered the worst that humans can inflict on one another.

There is no suffering, no violation, no degradation, no sorrow that the God who hung the sun has not experienced through God's Son. That Son was crucified, dead, and buried, and on the third day he rose from the dead by the resurrecting power of God at work in every day, in every way.

I end this sermon with the words that form the exclamation point at the very end of our training manual in prayer, the book of Psalms:

> Let everything that breathes praise the LORD!
> Praise the LORD!
>
> > Ps. 150:6

SCENIC SERMON 3: MULTI-SCENE SERMON THAT BEGINS WITH A BIBLICAL SCENE

Sermon Title: "Paul's Pack List"

Sermon Text: Philippians 2:1–11

Occasion: Sunday Worship

Location: First United Methodist Church (FUMC), Colorado Springs

Greetings

I thank Kent[10] for his invitation to be your preacher on this special day, and for his gracious, complimentary introduction, which leaves me very eager to hear what I'm going to have to say! I have been here in Colorado since Wednesday night, leading a preaching workshop here at FUMC, and then driving north to visit my son Matthew in Broomfield and daughter Melissa in Longmont. Late yesterday afternoon, driving here from Broomfield, the sky darkened to navy blue and headlights on oncoming cars twinkled, with the mountains keeping their steady, majestic watch over it all. It reminded me of something a friend of mine says whenever she sees a scene of nature's beauty: "Well that's just God showin' off!" I'd say the whole state of Colorado is just God showin' off! And so I want to begin by thanking each of you personally for the natural beauty of your state.

Introduction to Philippians 2:1–11 Paul's Pack List

I do a lot of traveling, but Paul, writing to the Philippians from his first imprisonment in Rome in the early 60s CE, did a lot more traveling than I have. I've faced the inconvenience of canceled flights, lost luggage, and rushed meals in airport fast-food kiosks. But Paul faced beatings, imprisonments, and shipwrecks. I anticipate having a lot more journeys left in my life, but Paul had only one more journey to take, the one that would begin the morning a centurion appeared at his cell door and led him to the chopping block.

The prospect of imminent death tends to clarify a person's priorities. Philippians 2:1–11 is Paul's pack list for the Philippian church on their journey of faith. There is only one item on it. He never left this item behind in any of his journeys; he doesn't want the church to forget it either: Humility, the Mind of Christ (*read Phil. 2:1–11*).

My Tendency to Forget Vital Items on Trips

I always seem to forget something important when I travel. I went to Atlanta one time and forgot my thyroid medication. I began to wind down like a broken clock. Then I remember that my brother-in-law is an internist and could call in a prescription for me.

I went to Lincoln, Nebraska, and forgot to pack my laptop charger. I was sunk, until it occurred to me that there are stores in Lincoln where I could buy one.

I went to South Africa one August. It was ninety-eight degrees in Texas as I was packing. I left my boots behind. Who knew it would be winter in South Africa? Everyone else, apparently! Good thing they sell boots in Cape Town! It finally occurred to me that the way to avoid leaving something crucial behind is to make a pack list and check things off as you pack them.

Paul says to us this morning: You can leave behind your meds, your tech, and your boots. But make sure you take your humility with you on your journey.

What Humility Is Not

There are a lot of false notions of humility in our culture.

Low Self-Esteem

Here's one example. When I was a sophomore in high school, I had a painful crush on a junior I'll call Mike Bowman. There was just something about his personality I found appealing. He was an upbeat person, nice to everybody, a positive guy. It's just possible, thinking back, that he liked me too. But that, my friends, we will never know.

Mike played the saxophone in the marching band, and I played the clarinet. One day after band practice, he said, "Alyce, do you want to sit together at the game this Saturday?" I said, "Okay." Then I went home and thought about it. "He probably just asked me to sit with him because he feels sorry for me," I reasoned. So on Saturday, I sat one row down at the other side of the band from him, and did my best to avoid him until he graduated. Humility is not low self-esteem. That is not what we want to take on our life journeys.

Humiliation

For several years, my sister Susanna worked as a domestic-abuse counselor in the lovely rolling hills of Central Pennsylvania. More than once, she would work up PFA (Protection from Abuse) documents to help a woman and her children get free from an abusive situation, only to watch the woman return to the abuser, with her children. When she asked "Why?" often the answer was, "My pastor told me to go back. 'Stand by your man. This is your cross.'" It is never God's will that we be humiliated or that we use our power to humiliate others. Humility is not humiliation. That is not what we want to take on our life journeys.

A Human Achievement: Benjamin Franklin's Struggle to Attain Humility

Benjamin Franklin, a young up-and-comer in eighteenth-century Philadelphia, had a conversation with a Quaker friend, who observed that Franklin was widely considered to be proud and overbearing in his demeanor and conversation. I imagine he said something like, "Ben, people say you're arrogant!" After that criticism, Franklin, who had recently worked up a list of twelve virtues to attain, decided to add a thirteenth: humility. So Franklin embarked on a lifelong project to cultivate the virtue of humility. He became a better listener, with the result that people were more willing to listen to him. Still, after fifty-five years of struggling with pride, the seventy-eight-year-old Franklin remarked that it was perhaps a good thing that he had never conquered his pride, "If I could conceive that I had completely overcome it [pride], I should probably be *proud* of my *humility*."[11] *Humility is not virtue we can achieve on our own. That is not what we want to take on our life journeys.*

Humility as Divine Gift

What if humility is not a human achievement at all but a divine gift? Reading the New Revised Standard Version translation of Philippians 2:5— "Let the same mind be in you that was in Christ Jesus"—I used to think Paul meant we had to duplicate the mind of Christ on our own. Then I came across another translation in my Nestle-Aland *Greek-English New Testament* (emphasis added): "Have this mind among yourselves, which *is* yours in Christ Jesus." Right before my eyes, *humility* changed from an impossible human achievement to an accessible divine gift.

Humility: Least Respected Virtue in Our Culture

Humility is the least respected of all the virtues in our culture, because our culture defines *humility* as weakness. That's why so many leaders leave humility at home before they embark on their power trips. It seems as if every morning we wake up to a new mass shooting, a new allegation of sexual misconduct, another show of hatred for Muslims, Jews, and people of sexual orientations other than heterosexuality. We desperately need humility.

Humility: Most Important Virtue in the Bible

At the same time that humility is the least respected virtue in our culture, it is the most important virtue in the Bible for the journey of life.

Ask Moses: he was the only man with whom God spoke face to face. Why? Because he was the humblest man on the face of the earth (Exod. 12:3).

Ask the prophet Micah: "What does the Lord require of you / but to do justice, and to love kindness, / and to walk humbly with your God" (Mic. 6:8)?

Ask Mary: "Here am I, the servant of the Lord; let it be with me according to your word" (Luke 1:38).

Ask John the Baptist: "[O]ne who is more powerful than I is coming after me; I am not worthy to carry his sandals" (Matt. 3:11).

Ask Paul: "[I]t is no longer I who live, but it is Christ who lives in me" (Gal. 2:20).

Humility is not low self-esteem, not humiliation of or by others, not a human achievement; it is a gift already ours, if only we would access it—the mind of Christ.

Cast Down Your Buckets

Booker T. Washington, African American educator and orator, was fond of telling a story about how the captain of a vessel in the South Atlantic Ocean signalled for help from another vessel not far off: "Help! Save us, or we perish for lack of water!" The captain of the other vessel's reply was, "Cast down your buckets where you are." Supposing that the second captain had not gotten the message accurately, the captain of the troubled ship signalled yet again, "Help! Save us, or we perish for lack of water!" Again the nearby ship signaled back, "Cast down your buckets where you are!" This exchange went on until the captain of the first ship, in desperation, decided he had nothing to lose by following this outlandish advice. When his crew members cast down their buckets, they drew them up filled with clear, cool, sparkling water from the mouth of the Amazon. The captain had not realized that the powerful current of the Amazon River carried fresh water from the South American rain forests many miles out into the South Atlantic.[12]

Appropriating the Gift of Humility: The Philippians 2 Playbook

Here is how we appropriate this gift of humility, which is already ours, for our life journey.

Descent: Verses 6–8

> [Christ Jesus,] who, though he was in the form of God,
>   did not regard equality with God
>   as something to be exploited,
> but emptied himself,
>   taking the form of a slave,

> being born in human likeness.
> And being found in human form,
>   he humbled himself
>   and became obedient to the point of death—
>   even death on a cross. (Phil. 2:6–8)

We take a page out of Jesus' playbook. He "did not regard equality with God / as something to be exploited" (Phil. 2:6). One commentator suggests "ripped off" would be a good modern rendering for the word *exploited*.

In humility, Jesus does *not* divest himself of his divine identity or his *morphe* (Greek for "essence" or "form"). He *does* divest himself of his divine privilege.

He became "down to earth" in a literal sense. In complete identification with those on the bottom rungs of the human ladder, Jesus became a slave (*doulos*). He entered into the pain and suffering of the human condition, subject to all the limitations and injustices of a poor peasant in the Roman Empire.

In an episode of the show Undercover Boss, the CEO of a company works a week or two on the line or behind the counter, identifying with the employees. At the end of the episode, the boss gives some of the employees money for down payments or scholarships for their kids and then goes home to his or her mansion, filled with a sense of personal nobility. This is not what the incarnational journey of Jesus is about. Jesus was obedient unto death, even death by crucifixion, a death reserved for slaves; what New Testament scholar Morna Hooker calls "the nadir of humiliation."[13]

Christ emptied himself, served, and died without promise of reward. He acted on our behalf without hope of gain.

Flawed Funeral Bulletin: Promoting Ourselves above Our Paygrade

I heard the story of an Episcopal Church Communicators annual meeting at which, during the banquet, they give out a gag prize for "Miss-Communication Award of the Year." Recently, the prize went to a woman we'll call Susan. In the Episcopal Church, the liturgy for funerals is a set piece; only the names change. In Susan's church, a woman named Mary died. The next week, a man named Steve died. Susan did a straightforward "find and replace" on the names for the second funeral. The bulletin turned out beautifully, with artistic graphics and a great picture of Steve on the back cover. All was well until, during the service, the congregation earnestly began to recite the Apostle's Creed together: "We believe in God the Father Almighty, Maker of Heaven and Earth and in Jesus Christ his only Son our Lord, who was conceived by the Holy Spirit and born of the Virgin *Steve*."

We promote ourselves, but God promoted Jesus! Humility is the opposite of self-promotion beyond our paygrade.

Ascent: Verses 9–11

At verse 9, Philippians shifts our attention from what Jesus chose to do to what God did in response.

> Therefore God also highly exalted him
>> and gave him the name
>> that is above every name,
> so that at the name of Jesus
>> every knee should bend
>>> in heaven and on earth and under the earth,
> and every tongue should confess
>> that Jesus Christ is Lord,
>> to the glory of God the Father.
>>> Phil. 2:9–11

"Therefore" [what a strong word!] God has highly exalted him and given him "the name that is above every name." To give a name is to bestow status, authority, and power. The name *Jesus* is Hebrew for savior. Jesus chose to live down with us to live up to his name.

The phrase "every knee should bend" is not a reference to prayer, but to kneeling before the emperor, as was required. The only name before whom the Christian bows is Jesus. He is enthroned, and we kneel before him.

"In heaven and on earth and under the earth" reflects the Greek three-tiered picture of the world/the cosmos.

"Every tongue" means all nations, with tongue referring to language.

To "confess" is to admit openly, a risky act in Roman Philippi where Caesar is the only Lord in town; "that Jesus Christ is Lord": in Philippi, the title *Lord* (*kyrios*) is reserved for the Roman emperor and the Roman gods.

"To the glory of God the Father"—Christ's Lordship doesn't compete with God's sovereignty.[14]

Our culture defines humility as weakness. But, in fact, it is the conduit for the power of God, God's compassion and God's courage.

Humility, Not a Weakness, but a Conduit for Compassion:
Atticus Finch and Bob Ewell

Atticus Finch, the protagonist of Harper Lee's *To Kill a Mockingbird*, provides an excellent example of radical humility. Indeed, much of the book concerns his teaching this trait to his children, Scout and Jem. He has the courage to defend Tom Robinson, a black man in 1936 Jim Crow Alabama, against a false charge of the rape of a white woman named Mayella Ewell. Mayella's father waylays Atticus, spits in his face, and threatens him. Atticus just wipes his face and lets Bob Ewell rant. But Scout and Jem are frightened for their father, and they urge him to take some action. They are convinced that Bob Ewell means to harm or kill Atticus. Here is Atticus's response to them:

> "Jem, see if you can stand in Bob Ewell's shoes a minute. I destroyed his last shred of credibility at that trial, if he had any to begin with. The man had to have some kind of comeback, his kind always does. So if spitting in my face and threatening me saved Mayella Ewell one extra beating, that's something I'll gladly take. He had to take it out on somebody and I'd rather it be me than that houseful of children out there."[15]

Atticus' closing comment to his family on the incident is "I do wish Bob Ewell didn't chew tobacco."[16]

Humility is a conduit for compassion, but also for courage.

Humility, Not a Weakness, but a Conduit for Courage:
Testimony of a 9/11 Survivor

A few weeks ago, my husband, Murry, and I toured Ground Zero in New York City, the new buildings that have arisen in the place occupied by the World Trade Center Twin Towers. The memorial, with the names of all the nearly three thousand people who died that day, are inscribed in bronze plaques, backlit at night. The accounts of witnesses and survivors of the attack testify to the bravery and determination of the security personnel and fire fighters who remained calm and focused as emergency stairwells grew progressively warmer and sirens blared.

In the museum there is a picture of the evacuation of the North Tower. It shows a firefighter heading up the stairs with a calm, determined expression on his face.

Bruno Dellinger, an evacuee from the forty-seventh floor of the North Tower, recalling the firefighters in the stairwell in the oral archives of the museum, say this:

"In their eyes was exhausation and the realization of danger, but there was no panic . . . They were calm and focused. And I knew that I was walking down to live and they were going up to die."[17]

Conclusion

Thank you, God, for the divine gift of humility that is always accessible to us in our journeys. Thank you, Paul, for your pared down pack list:

"Have this mind among yourselves which is yours in Christ Jesus . . ."

SCENIC SERMON 4: MULTI-SCENE SERMON THAT BEGINS WITH A CONTEMPORARY SCENE

Sermon Title: "Foresight Is 20/20"
Sermon Text: Mark 9:2–8
Occasion: Transfiguration Day
Location: Christ United Methodist Church, Plano, Texas

Reading of Mark 9:2–8: Young Elvis

Last weekend I was in Tupelo, Mississippi, the birthplace of Elvis Presley, where he and his parents, Vernon and Gladys, lived until he was thirteen years old, before they moved to Memphis. I was invited to preach on Sunday morning at First United Methodist Church, Tupelo, and to do some Bible teaching Sunday night and Monday. I had Sunday afternoon free, so in the Sunday morning sermon, I dropped some big hints about how much I like Elvis. Sure enough, a couple from the church offered to take me on a tour that included not only the two-room shotgun house where Elvis was born, but also the one-room Assembly of God Church where he and his family worshiped when he was a young boy. It was here that Elvis was first exposed to the rich, Southern Gospel music that became a staple of his musical repertoire.

You go into the church and a docent greets you and then turns off the lights while huge screens roll down on three sides of the little sanctuary.

A video presentation featuring an acting troupe from Memphis reenacts what it would have been like to worship in a Pentecostal church in the mid-1940s in rural Mississippi. There was the young minister Brother Frank Smith, who first taught Elvis to play D, A, and E chords on the guitar. There were his young parents, Vernon and Gladys, struggling to keep food on the table and, sometimes, unable to pay the rent. There was young Elvis, invited up to sing "Jesus Loves Me." There was the Gospel quartet singing "In the Sweet By and By." And when Brother Smith invited everyone to stand and sing "Love Lifted Me," I forgot that it was 2015, and I was a tourist in a reenactment. I stood up and started singing. It was a little embarrassing, but I didn't care. I was transported into the past and fully part of that scene.

At the church potluck supper that evening, Jane Riley, one of the members of the church, now in her late seventies, told me that she had been a year behind Elvis in school. "What was he like?" I asked. "He was just one of boys in the class a year ahead of me. I used to see him strumming a guitar out under the tree in the play yard. He was from the wrong side of the Tupelo tracks. He wasn't a boy I would have ever have invited to one of my birthday parties . . . but if I had known then what I know now . . ." she said.

Yeah, what if, as ten-year-old Jane stood watching the boy play the guitar, three screens had rolled down from the sky, and she had seen a vision of the star that boy would become. I imagine she would have invited him to her birthday party then! But that's not how life works. The old saying is "hindsight is 20/20," as in, I wish I had known then what I know now. We never say "Foresight is 20/20."

Transfiguration Day

But on Transfiguration Day, Peter, James, and John could start saying it. The screens roll down from heaven for them, and they see the resurrected glory of Jesus just as they get ready to come down from the mountain and follow him to the cross. Yes, he'll be mistreated and killed. Yes, they will face sufferings with him. But yes! God will raise him from the dead and them along with him.

Now see the screens roll down in this sanctuary for us this Transfiguration Day 2015. Over there are two figures flickering on the wall: Elijah and Moses. They are talking with Jesus about his future resurrection glory. Moses is known for his humility (Num. 12:3), Elijah for his boldness. Both prophets endured suffering and found God faithful.

Both are considered by Jews as signs of the Messiah's arrival. Elijah would come first to point the way (i.e., John the Baptist). The Messiah would be a new Moses, the giver of a new law. And there is Jesus, dazzling with supernatural splendor. Shining white clothing is a sign of divinity throughout the Bible (e.g., God is "wrapped in light as with a garment," Ps. 104:2).

Over here we see Peter and hear him babbling about building three booths. Peter is a blurter who often speaks before he thinks. So who knows what is in his mind? He may be connecting this to the Jewish Feast of Tabernacles, when Jews make huts to remember the way God sheltered them in the wilderness. Or Peter may just think these three famous guys are too important to stand out in the open air. It's a moot point, because these blast-from-the-past visitors aren't staying long enough for Peter to build them a booth.

Now a cloud overshadows the scene and a voice speaks out of it, reminding us of God's glory in the cloud over Mount Sinai, and God's voice helping Moses gain the trust of the Israelites (Exod. 19:9). The divine means of communication authenticates the messenger in verse 7: "This is my Son, the Beloved; listen to him!"

Now the vision fades, and the three disciples are left alone with only Jesus for company. They have been given the gift of 20/20 Resurrection Foresight. They can take down the mountain with them their vision of Jesus' future resurrected glory as the lens through which they view every adversity they encounter. Do you know anyone who needs 20/20 Resurrection Foresight?

Highland Park Sunday School Class

A few years back, I was invited to teach on the parables at a Sunday school class at Highland Park UMC in Dallas. I arrived fifteen minutes ahead of the class start time. The room began to fill, mainly with women. I was greeted by one woman who told me her name also was Alice. Then another woman came in whose name was also Alice. So we were having a little Alice convention.

A woman stood off to the side, not talking to anyone, looking over the room. I invited her into our group (even though her name wasn't Alice, but Evelyn). "This class has been together quite a while, hasn't it?" I asked. "Yes," she said, "We started out as a couple's class in the 1950s. We are still called the 'Two by Two Class,' but maybe we should rename ourselves the 'One by One class.' Because now, all of us are old; and a lot of us are dead." Realizing how that sounded, she pasted a bright smile on her face and said "And we are so glad to have you join us this morning!"

All of us are old, and a lot of us are dead. Know anybody who needs a dose of 20/20 Resurrection Foresight?

Gate C10B

I was in the Memphis airport last Monday night, coming home from Tupelo, waiting for my flight to Dallas. Wolf Blitzer's *Situation Room* was on CNN. He was interviewing various international experts regarding the abduction of US aid worker Kayla Mueller. At that point, ISIS had published pictures of a building that they said was bombed by Jordan and in which she was killed. It was unclear if that was true. People around gate C10B stopped what they were doing, stood, or turned toward the wall screens, folded their arms, and shook their heads. It was as if they were saying, "Yes, we can read the future, and it's more of being at the mercy of this."

There are generally three gestures of response to this sense of helplessness:

- One is this head-shaking gesture, the response of pessimism.
- A second is the head-in-hands gesture, the response of anguish and sorrow. It is born of our empathy for those who suffer unjustly.
- A third gesture is the hands held up, protectively, against the face, the response of fear.

Mark's Community at Gate C10B

The community for whom Mark wrote were all waiting with me at Gate C10B. Mark's gospel was written for people who were experiencing all three of these responses. They were a small community, probably in Rome, facing persecution and destruction at the hands of the cruelest emperor of all, Nero (37–68 CE), who reigned 54–68 CE.

Mark rolls down the screens and shows the community how to be disciples in tough times. Here's a clue to the lesson: Act the opposite of the disciples in his Gospel. The old joke is that the disciples in Mark should really be called the "duh-ciples"; they just don't get it. Three times in chapters 8–10, Jesus foretells his death and resurrection. The disciples, as soon as they hear the word *death*, stop listening, and never hear "and be raised from the dead." So Peter, James, and John go down from the mountain trusting in appearances rather than in God. If it looks like death, it's death. If it looks like weakness, it's weakness. If it looks like failure, it's failure. Death has the last word on life.

Mark wants to rewind and have his community of faith walk down from the mountain with 20/20 Foresight; God's kingdom is already breaking in with Jesus' teachings, healings, miraculous feedings, and exorcisms. To the church, Mark is saying, "You're small but not unimportant. You are weak, but not without divine power. You have suffered loss, but God is at work in you bringing new life. Trust not in surface appearances but in God's resurrecting power that is at work in the worst of situations."

Maternal Theology Lesson

I did not, like Elvis, grow up in a Pentecostal, rural, southern Assemblies of God church.

I grew up in a small town on the Susquehanna River in New Cumberland, Pennsylvania, near the state capital of Harrisburg. We attended a Methodist church. It had dark oak paneling and was much smaller than the sanctuary here in Plano. As a little girl, I spent a lot of time standing on the pew, staring at the back wall of the church. You know how children turn around in a booth at a restaurant and stare at you with curiosity and no sense of what is socially appropriate? That was me. I was staring at the two men on the back wall, depicted side-by-side in huge stained-glass windows.

On the left was a sad man. He was kneeling. The background was dark. He had his hands together, propped on a big rock. On sunny Sundays, the sun would shine through the red tear on his face and glimmer like a ruby. I felt so sorry for him.

Beside him on the right was another man. His background was bright; he was wearing white, and he had bare feet. I wondered why he wasn't wearing sneakers. Then I noticed that his feet were about a foot off the ground! His arms were at his sides, and his face was serene and even a little bit happy. Sunday after Sunday, my mother would tug on my ruffled Sunday dress and say, "Alyce, turn around. Sit down. The sermon is about to start." Every week we had this struggle. Finally, one week she said in exasperation, "Why do you keep looking at those windows?"

"I'm wondering why that happy man won't help that sad man."

"Oh," she said, as if it were the most obvious thing in the world, "Well, they're the same man."

I tell my mother she was my first theology professor!

The bridge between Gethsemane and Jesus' victorious resurrection and ascension is the power of God to bring life out of senseless loss, to bring wisdom out of crushing disappointment, to bring community out of acts of violence, to bring honor out of humiliation, to bring new direction from a dead end, to make a way out of no way! The one who prays in the garden, about to experience the worst that human violence and prejudice can inflict, is the same one God raises from the dead on the third day. Because God's will be done. God's kingdom of justice and peace for everyone will come. God's purposes will be fulfilled. Isaiah 55:10–11 says that, just like the rain and snow return to heaven only after watering the earth,

> so shall my word be that goes out from my mouth;
>   it shall not return to me empty,
> but it shall accomplish that which I purpose,
>   and succeed in the thing for which I sent it.

"If only I had known then what I know now" is the cry of 20/20 hindsight. The 20/20 foresight of the resurrection says this: "Since we know now what we know now . . ."

Let us trust that God is ready and waiting in the most frightening and painful situations in our world—and in your life—to bring life from the forces of death.

Martin Luther King Jr., January 27, 1956

Do you know anyone who lives by 20/20 Foresight?

It is Friday night, January 27, 1956. A bold prophet of God slumps home, another long strategy session around the Montgomery bus boycott under his belt, and finds his wife asleep. He paces around his kitchen, his nerves still on edge. The phone rings, and a sneering voice on the other end says, "Leave Montgomery immediately if you have no wish to die." King's fear surges; he hangs up the phone and walks to his kitchen. With trembling hands, he puts on a pot of coffee and sinks into a chair at his kitchen table. He describes his experience in his book *Stride toward Freedom*, written in 1958:

> I was ready to give up. With my cup of coffee sitting untouched before me, I tried to think of a way to move out of the picture without

appearing a coward. In this state of exhaustion, when my courage had all but gone, I decided to take my problem to God. With my head in my hands, I bowed over the kitchen table and prayed aloud. The words I spoke to God that midnight are still vivid in my memory. "I am here taking a stand for what I believe is right. But now I am afraid. The people are looking to me for leadership, and if I stand before them without strength and courage, they too will falter. I am at the end of my powers. I have nothing left. I've come to the point where I can't face it alone."

At that moment, I experienced the presence of the Divine as I had never experienced Him before. It seemed as though I could hear the quiet assurance of an inner voice saying: "Stand up for righteousness, stand up for truth; and God will be at your side forever." Almost at once my fears began to go. My uncertainty disappeared. I was ready to face anything."[18]

Do you know anyone who lives by 20/20 Resurrection Foresight? That is the vision that brings us down the mountain with the faith to follow Jesus. His way leads to the cross, yes, but also to the resurrection!

SCENIC SERMON 5: MULTI-SCENE SERMON THAT BEGINS WITH A CONTEMPORARY SCENE

Sermon Title: "Peel Off the Plastic"

Sermon Texts: Psalm 23; Luke 15:1–7

Occasion: Annual "Sending Forth Service" in which we commission those graduating, retiring, and transitioning to new responsibilities in the community.

Location: Perkins Chapel, Perkins School of Theology

Introduction to Liturgical Occasion

So here we are together on a Thursday morning, approaching the Fourth Sunday of Eastertide, the day the Gospel lectionary readings transition from the resurrection appearances to reflections on the Risen Lord as our daily companion. It is traditionally known as Good Shepherd Sunday, because the Old Testament text is Psalm 23, and the theme of the Gospel reading, usually from John 10, is Jesus our Good Shepherd. I'm doing some bold lectionary off-roading today; I'm going to pair Psalm 23 with Luke 15:1–7, the parable of the lost sheep *(read the Scripture texts)*.

Psalm 23 as a Plastic-Covered Couch

I once heard an Italian comedian from New York City on TV, talking about his family. He said, "My grandma (Nonna in Italian) had a beautiful flowered couch in her parlor. I know it was beautiful because one time when I was seven or so I peeked under the plastic. So I asked her, 'Nonna, why is the pretty couch always covered in plastic?' 'I'm keeping it nice for when we have a really special occasion, or a really special visitor,' she said. As the years rolled by and the couch stayed covered, I realized she must have been waiting for a visit from the Pope, or better yet for Nonna, Frank Sinatra!"

Psalm 23 is like that beautiful couch covered in plastic. We save it for that really special occasion. And you know what that is: your funeral! It will be read with great solemnity to usher you from your death in this life to your life in the world to come. Memorize it now if you haven't already, because at the end of life, you are going to need a Shepherd.[19]

In my childhood, the picture of Jesus carrying the little lost lamb hung on the oak paneled wall of my Sunday school room. As far as I know, it hangs there still, visually memorized by generations of impressionable children, because, at the beginning of life, we all need a Shepherd.

A Shepherd back then; a Shepherd at the end. A Shepherd for when we are children; a Shepherd for the moment of our death. I don't know about you, but I need a Shepherd now!

Stuck in a Crevasse: We Need a Shepherd Now

Is there anyone else in the house who needs a Shepherd now? I look down into the crevasse in which the sheep is stuck, and I see the faces of people, people of Israel and Judah, "scattered sheep" the psalms and prophets call them (e.g., Ezek. 34:5). Earthly kings exploit rather than protect the vulnerable.[20] They need a Shepherd now.

Contemporary People

I see anxious faces in an Appalachian community, worried about their arts center; children who need more fiber and less salt in their lunches;

an elderly person who may not be able to get access to his medication; a student afraid to go to school; a woman, with gifts and grace to be a shepherd of the church, fearing that who she loves may preclude her from using those gifts as God has called her to use them. They need a Shepherd now.

Isaiah and His Exiles

Isaiah, stuck with his people in the crevasse, looked for God the Shepherd to come with might, to lead the people out of exile, to feed the flock, to gather the lambs in loving arms, to carry them in the divine bosom, gently leading the mother sheep (Isa. 40:11). We look for leaders who will be shepherds, not hired hands or thieves. We need a Shepherd now.

The "Expendables" of Jesus' Day

In that crevasse are the poor of Jesus' day, whom the Romans referred to as "the expendables." The sinners, the unclean, the shame–full need a Shepherd now. Jesus "had compassion for them, because they were harassed and helpless, like sheep without a shepherd" (Matt. 9:36).[21]

The Religious Leaders of Jesus' Day

With them are the religious leaders of Jesus' day, who are just as lost as those they disdain. They need a Shepherd now, whether or not they realize it, as they grumble about Jesus teaching and eating with these "expendables." They need a Shepherd now to help them to peel the plastic off their faith and value the *wholeness* of the community more than their shallow definition of *holiness*.

Religious Leaders of Today

The bishops of The United Methodist Church, the shepherds of the church, need a Shepherd now. They are down in that crevasse too, caught in a thicket of our denomination's deep divisions over the understanding of human sexuality, the interpretation of the Bible, and the definition of holiness. I hold and voice my own long-standing conviction that moving beyond heterosexism to the inclusion of all God's people is the way forward at the same time that I pray for these shepherds of the sheep in their discernment process.

It's getting pretty crowded in this biblical crevasse. But there is room for one more.

King David, the Flawed Shepherd

Toss in David, the shepherd king, gifted and flawed, the purported author of both Psalm 23 and Psalm 51. Literary critic and Hebrew Scriptures scholar Robert Alter, in his classic book *The Art of Biblical Narrative*, raises in our minds the questions: Was David an essentially noble person who did some ignoble things? Or was he essentially an attractive, charismatic opportunist who occasionally did some good things? I wonder if David the shepherd ever wondered the same thing about himself. I wonder if he yearned for the Shepherd to come and rescue him from himself.[22] Is there anyone in this house who needs a Shepherd now? If you have been waiting for a special occasion to peel off the plastic of Psalm 23, do it today as you go forth to scenes of retirement, new ministry, new roles, or the same settings with new challenges.

We Have a Shepherd Now

Who is the Shepherd who accompanies you now? You have a Shepherd who has gained a trusted name and acts with competence that conveys good character and reputation (Ps. 23:3).[23] Your Shepherd knows how to lead you to places where you can eat and rest and drink, not from a firehose, but from a slow flowing stream (v. 2). Your *nephesh* (your essential identity that resides in the breath and the blood, a gift from your Creator) is restored. Your Shepherd brings you back from your wandering, reinvigorated to serve another day. Your Shepherd will lead you in right paths (*derek hayashar*) that may not be straight, flat, and easy, but that are paved by the wisdom of God. Because the Shepherd is with you, you have no need to be afraid, even when you walk through the darkest valley (v. 4). This is not because nothing bad ever happens in this world, but because the Shepherd walks by your side. The Shepherd's rod and staff, wielded with confidence and attentiveness, are a discouragement to your enemies (v. 4)

Some commentators have assumed that the shepherd metaphor morphs into the metaphor of the banquet host in verse 5. But Old Testament scholar Samuel Terrein thinks it more likely that the shepherd metaphor continues to the very end of the psalm. The shepherd prepares a spread for the sheep. The shepherd goes ahead of the sheep and clears the meadow of vipers, scorpions, thorns, and poisonous plants so the sheep can feed in peace. Even the most competent shepherd cannot prevent all mishaps. So at the end of the day, your Shepherd will cover your scratches and wounds with oil. Your Shepherd will pour water or wine into your mouth from the Shepherd's own cup when you are too weak from recent exertions or attacks to lift your head. In the conflicts that await in your ministry, your Shepherd will honor you in the presence of those who would shame you (v. 5). Since famished animals often follow the flock to pick off those who lag behind, your Shepherd will relentlessly, not just follow, but pursue (*radap*) you with goodness and mercy to counteract the pursuit of death-dealing forces.[24] Day by day, guided by this Shepherd, you dwell in the house of the Lord, the presence of the Lord, your whole life long (v. 6).

Peel Off the Plastic

We have a Shepherd now! The parable of the lost sheep is more than a sentimental story for children, and Psalm 23 is more than a pretty poem to read at funerals or one fortune cookie we pull out of a whole bag. It has a contextual home in a collection of hymns/poems that John Calvin called an "anatomy of all the parts of the soul, with every human emotion reflected as in a mirror."[25] Psalms move like music, reflecting the complexity of the life of faith: praise that includes a minor key of lament and lament that resolves into a major key of praise and thanksgiving. Psalms represent our human response to the mysterious goodness of the God of creation and covenant in all the twists, turns, and trials of this unpredictable life.

Psalm 23, for example, is preceded by Psalm 21, a psalm of praise, and Psalm 22, which became the interpretive key to the passion of Christ among early Christians. Psalm 22 begins with the well-known words "My God, my God, why have you forsaken me?" and mutates into praise at verse 22, "in the midst of the congregation I will praise you," ending with the glorious confidence of verse 31, "he has done it." Psalm 23, a psalm of trust, follows.[26] Psalm 23 isn't a prettified denial of trauma and trouble; it grows out of it. Psalm scholar Denise Hopkins says Psalm 23 is rooted in "agitated memories of the exodus and the wilderness wanderings."[27] Its promises are echoes of the song of Moses from Exodus 15. Into these agitated memories strides God the Good Shepherd.

In his book *Deep Is the Hunger: Meditations for Apostles of Sensitiveness*, educator, activist, poet, and author Howard Thurman wrote words that have stayed with me since I read them years ago:

What is the source of your joy? . . . There are some whose joy is dependent on circumstances. . . . There are some whose joy is a matter of disposition and temperament. . . . [But] there are still others who find their joy deep in the heart of their religious experience. . . . It is primarily a discovery of the soul, when God makes known His presence, where there are no words, no outward song, only the Divine Movement. This is the joy that the world cannot give. . . . This is the joy that comforts and is the companion, as we walk through the valley of the shadow of death.[28]

Psalm 23 offers, not the false promise of protection, but the real presence of the Shepherd.

The good news is that we have a Shepherd now! And we have good news about this Shepherd to share with others. The parable of the lost sheep is more than a happily-ever-after story for children. Biblical scholar Amy-Jill Levine, in her book *Short Stories by Jesus*, chastises preachers for domesticating the parables. She seeks to recover their original offensive message. Jesus was killed for telling stories about a subversive Shepherd who sought out those whom the empire preferred to cast off and plow under. He was killed for enacting stories about eating with and elevating the expendables. There were no lengths to which he would not go—even death—to seek out and to save the lost sheep. He is the Good Shepherd, who, as John 10 tells us, lay down his life for the sheep by his own choice.

Brandon's Story

Some years ago, a student told me a story about a seven-year-old boy in her church named Brandon. He had an inoperable tumor and limited time to live. His parents began bringing him to church. He requested baptism. Normally, a child of his age would be asked to attend several classes during the Sunday school hour to learn about the Bible, worship, and baptism. My student told his parents she would waive that requirement in his case. "No," Brandon told them. "I want to come to the classes." So there he sat in his chair in the circle.

One Sunday, my student was using a flannel board to teach the parable of the lost sheep. She was employing the "I wonder" format, in which you tell a Bible story and then have the children ask "I wonder" questions. After she finished telling the the story, one boy put his hand up, "I wonder if any of the sheep got eaten while the shepherd was gone." Another said, "I wonder if the shepherd got in trouble for leaving the sheep."

Then Brandon put his hand up, "I wonder . . . if the sheep is stuck way down in the hole and is so tired and so weak that it can't move, will the shepherd come all the way down to get it?"

Her answer? "Absolutely, Brandon, absolutely."

If Psalm 23 Could Fly

Henry Ward Beecher, nineteenth-century social reformer and abolition-ist, paid tribute to Psalm 23 in a speech in 1856:

> It will go singing to your children and my children, and to their chil-dren, through all the generations of time; nor will it fold its wings till the last pilgrim is safe, and time is ended; and then it shall fly back to the bosom of God, whence it issued, and sound on, mingled with all those sounds of celestial joy which make heaven musical for ever.[29]

If Psalm 23 could fly, perhaps it hovered over the cross as the One sent to seek out and to save the lost breathed his last and commended his *nephesh* into the keeping of God the Good Shepherd, the God who had sent him. It can't be denied, Psalm 23 is a lovely textual choice for a funeral. But we have gathered this morning, not because someone we all love has died. We have gathered because someone we all love is alive! We have gathered to celebrate the good news that the Shepherd we need right now is with us right now. We go forth to new appointments and tasks to seek out and to save the lost in the Shepherd's name, to share the good news of our Shepherd's abiding, saving presence with a hurting world. Thanks be to God!

SCENIC SERMON 6: MULTI-SCENE SERMON THAT BEGINS WITH A PERSONAL SCENE

Sermon Title: "The Yellow Backpack"

Sermon Text: Mark 10:42–56

Occasion: Preaching Workshop for Clergy from the Connecticut, Rhode Island, and Massachusetts Conferences of the United Church of Christ

Location: Hull, Massachusetts

Introduction to Mark 10:42-56

Today Jesus is coming through Jericho. He is about to encounter a blind beggar named Bartimaeus.

Bartimaeus is not one of the original disciples. But he shows us what it looks like to be one. Right before this encounter, James and John argue over who is going to get to "ride shotgun" with Jesus in the world to come (Mark 10:35–37).

Right after this scene, Jesus enters Jerusalem to shouts of "Hosanna" (*Hoshiya na* in Hebrew), which means "Save us, please!"

The Palm Sunday parade will fade, and the disciples will scatter like cockroaches. So Mark places Bartimaeus's story here, just as Jesus heads toward Jerusalem and the cross, to say to us: "**This** is what it looks like to be a disciple" (*read Mark 10:42–56*).

ATM Card

A few years back, when our oldest daughter, Melissa, was getting married, I somehow thought I could perform the ceremony, host a houseful of out-of-town company, and help with wedding details—all without breaking a sweat. I thought I was doing pretty well until I overheard our middle daughter, Rebecca, say to her younger brother, Matt, "Just stay out of her way. She is in full freak-out mode."

So two days before the wedding, up bright and early, with my list in hand, I'm in my car and on a mission. Fill up with gas. Drive through car wash. Pick up non-wedding-party family suits and dresses at dry cleaners. Drop by florist and remind them of wedding day timeline. Grocery store—pick up deli trays for lunch at home before wedding; drugstore—buy sewing kits for bridesmaids' gift baskets in case of last minute wardrobe malfunctions. Get cash at ATM.

I drive through the bank lane; I put my card in; I pull out my fast cash; I peel out, heading toward home. I detest being tailgated. So when a minivan pulls right up behind me, and then beside me, and then the driver motions for me to pull over, here's what I'm thinking: "It's ten in the morning. You have two children in the car, and you're drunk!" That's when she holds up a small, rectangular, plastic card with my bank's name on it.

I wish life were like that; every time I lose something, I get it back. I wish that, every time I lose something, Jesus would ask me, "What do you want me to do for you, Alyce?" I would just say, "I want it back," and he would drive up in his minivan and hand it over into my car window.

What We Have Lost

The truth is, many things we lose in life we never get back:

1. I still remember the rejection letter I got when I was applying for teaching jobs. It said, "Dear Dr. McKenzie, while our search continues, it no longer includes you [not even *we appreciate your interest and value your gifts*]." Lost opportunity.

2. A pastor walks into the waiting room outside the obstetrics unit. There is her church member, a young man who had hoped to be father in a few months, rocking back and forth in his chair, asking "What did we do wrong? What did we do wrong?" Lost child.

3. A woman, almost eighty years old, enrolls her husband in a dementia unit at a facility near the apartment they've shared together since he retired. She says, "He is getting good care. But last night after I visited with him and came home, it hit for the first time: I'm alone now." Lost spouse.

Gabby Giffords, US Congressional Representative from Arizona (2007–2012), was shot in the head January 8, 2011, in a grocery store parking lot near Tucson. In the attack, eighteen others were injured, and six were killed. She lost her career, and her ability to walk, speak, read, and write. She has made progress in regaining many of her abilities, and she has great spirit, but she has lost some things that are not coming back.

What Bartimaeus Lost

Bartimaeus was born able to see, but through an accident or an illness he lost his sight.

That's not all he lost. When he lost his sight, he lost his community, his livelihood, his future. Why these losses? Because of the false belief of his time, that blindness, illness, and poverty were punishments from God for some sin the person had committed. He lost faith in himself as he began to believe that bad theology. His confidence leached away year by lonely year. Lost sight led to lost livelihood; lost community; lost faith in himself.

What Bartimaeus Did Not Lose: A Single Shred of Stubborn Faith

But there is something Bartimaeus did not lose: his faith in God. Have you got some faith? Sometimes we think that we don't have faith unless we feel joyful and peaceful all the time. Allow me to introduce you to the faith of Bartimaeus. His faith is based on more than feelings.

Here's his story: Bartimaeus, when he hears that Jesus of Nazareth was coming to town, gathers up the one thing he hasn't lost, his single shred of stubborn faith, and he goes and spreads out his beggar's cloak at the corner of "Desperate and Driven" and begins to call out Jesus' name. Every time the crowd tells him to shut up, he shouts out, even louder, "Jesus, Son of David, have mercy on me" (Mark 10:47)!

Bartimaeus held onto a single shred of stubborn faith. That kind of faith reminds me of the psalmists. They vent their anger and pain in the same breath that they stubbornly expect God to save them. Psalm 42 could have been written by Bartimaeus in those long years of his darkness and isolation:

> As a deer longs for flowing streams,
>   so my soul longs for you, O God.
> My soul thirsts for God,
>   for the living God.
> When shall I come and behold
>   the face of God?
> My tears have been my food
>   day and night,
> while people say to me continually,
>   "Where is your God?"
> . . . .
> I say to God, my rock,
>   "Why have you forgotten me?
> Why must I walk about mournfully
>   because the enemy oppresses me?"
> . . . .
> Why are you cast down, O my soul,
>   and why are you disquieted within me?
> Hope in God; for I shall again praise him,
>   my help and my God.
>   Ps. 42:1–3, 9, 11

It is in this tradition of faithful lament that Bartimaeus calls out to Jesus, the Son of the God addressed in the psalm, "Jesus, Son of David, have mercy upon me!"

The Man behind the Pillar

Now maybe you're not the shouting type. Maybe you're more private about your losses and your faith. Maybe you are the type who suffers in silence and doesn't want to draw yourself to Jesus' attention. Here is a story for you.

Dr. Theodore Parker Ferris, preacher, author, and preaching professor, served Trinity Episcopal Church in Boston, an old downtown church founded in1733, for thirty years (1942–1972). One Monday morning Dr. Ferris's administrative assistant came in and said, "Dr. Ferris, there is a man here who wants to see you." When the man was seated in Dr. Ferris's office, he leaned forward and said, "I'd like to thank you for saving my life."

"But I've never seen you before!" Dr. Ferris answered.

The man replied, "I have suffered from depression for some time. I was on my way to the Charles River, my pockets full of rocks, on a Sunday night. I saw the lights on and heard the music. For some reason I came in and sat in the gallery behind a pillar. What you said saved my life. I came to thank you."

"From that day on," said Dr. Ferris, "I always preach to the man behind the pillar."[30]

There is no hiding from Jesus behind the pillar. And Jesus is passing through this town this morning, about to embark on the road to Jerusalem. He is asking "Who's coming with me?" Like it or not, when he stands still, it's because he has noticed you. He is calling you, along with Bartimaeus, to stand before him. And he is asking you and me the same question, "What do you want me to do for you?"

Jesus' Question: What Do You Want Me to Do for You?

My Answer: Yellow Backpack Dream

How should I answer Jesus' question, "What do you want me to do for you?"

One night, I fell asleep mulling that over, and I had a dream. This was the kind of dream that makes me wonder if God thinks I'm a better listener when I'm asleep than when I'm awake.

In the dream, I was coming home from Europe after a long trip. I had this intense yearning to go home, to be home. I had checked my fifty-pound suitcase. I was at the gate. I was planning to take just two pieces of luggage on board: my rollerboard and my yellow backpack. I had a coat, which I had gone ahead and put on so I wouldn't have to carry it. I sat on the edge of my seat and double-checked that I had everything. With a sharp intake of breath I realized that I did not see my yellow backpack. I broke into a sweat under my heavy wool coat. I searched under the seat. I went to the counter and asked the attendant, Matt, "Has anyone turned in a yellow backpack?"

"No, ma'am," he said.

"But," I said, my voice rising with each word, "it has my passport, my driver's license, wallet, and my smartphone in it! I can't make it home without my yellow backpack!"

"Calm down, ma'am," said Matt, "We'll look around." He searched behind the desk, even in the closet where employees keep their stuff. There were yellow hats, yellow scarves, yellow shoes, but no yellow backpack. He announced to the waiting area that, if they had seen a yellow backpack, they should please bring it to the desk. He called over to the lost and found, and had them check; no, no yellow backpack. Then they began calling out all the categories of people who had better seats than I did: advantage platinum . . . advantage gold . . . one world emerald, sapphire, ruby, priority access. They were about to call group 1. I was beginning to panic, and then suddenly Matt put his arm around me and patted me on the back . . . several times. And then he said, "Ma'am, either you are a hunchback, or there is something under your coat." He helped me struggle out of my coat, and we both discovered that I was wearing my yellow backpack. He smiled, like they are trained to do, but ruined the effect a bit by rolling his eyes. And then I woke up.

"What do you want me to do for you?" Jesus asks. The best answer for me is, Lord, help me to remember that I have on me everything I need for the next leg of my journey. I don't need to get back everything I've lost in order to move forward with you. I don't need you to promise me that there will be no more losses in my life. I don't need to be cured of all of my physical pain and limitations. Help me to remember that I have everything I need to continue my journey home, because I make that journey with you.

Bartimaeus' Answer

Help me to take a page out of Bartimaeus' book. He doesn't say "Give me back the job, give me back the friends, give me back the years, give me back the tears." No, he says, "My teacher, let me see again" (Mark 10:51); not so I can go back, but so I can go forward and bless others as a follower of Yours. "Immediately he regained his sight and followed him on the way" (v. 52). In this brief exchange, Bartimaeus became the only person in the Gospels to follow Jesus immediately after Jesus heals him.

Our Answer

"What do you want me to do for you?" Lord, we do not ask you to restore all that we have lost. We ask that you remind us of what you have already done for us. What we already have by your presence, your love.

When I lost the opportunity to teach at the school that rejected me, God comforted me with the knowledge that God has accepted me. And God encouraged me to apply again somewhere else. And through the years, God has helped me encourage other young scholars at low points in their job searches.

When the young parents lost their baby, they still had the arms of God, who was embracing their child, also embracing them. God was encouraging them to embrace other couples in their losses and struggles with infertility and miscarriage.

When the woman whose husband had dementia, who no longer recognized her, walked into her empty apartment, she found that she was not alone. God, who knew her name, was there. And God turned her mind to dwell on the other lonely people in her building and how she might reach out to them.

When Gabby Giffords lost her career, her motor skills, her ability to speak and read and write, God was with her through her husband and many friends, encouraging her to press on. When terrible loss struck Sandy Hook Elementary School in Newton, Connecticut, December 4, 2012, I believe it was God who motivated Gabby and her husband, Mark Kelly, to visit the parents and grandparents of the children who were killed and offer them presence and comfort, which came from the depth of their own losses.

When the man hides behind the pillar, feeling all hope is lost because of guilt over his past, Jesus speaks a life-saving word of forgiveness to him, "Your life has meaning and purpose. It is not over yet."

Conclusion

For years, I have sung alto in our local church choir. My favorite anthem of all is called "Write Your Blessed Name" by K. Lee Scott. The words come from a poem by Thomas à Kempis, a German priest who lived in the 1400s. They are my answer to Jesus' question, "What do you want me to do for you?"

> Write your blessed name, O Lord,
> upon my heart,
> there to remain so indelibly engraven,
> that no prosperity,
> no adversity,
> shall ever move me from your love.[31]

SCENIC SERMON 7: SINGLE-SCENE SERMON THAT BEGINS WITH A CONTEMPORARY SCENE

Sermon Title: "A Friend at Midnight"

Sermon Text: Luke 11:1–11

   Occasion: Service of Word and Table; Communion Meditation

   Location: First United Methodist Church, Arlington, Texas

Introduction to Luke 11:1–11

The parable of the friend at midnight is one of several parables that appear only in Luke. The prodigal son and the good Samaritan are two others unique to Luke's Gospel. In Luke 11:1–4, we have the Lord's Prayer, which emphasizes Jesus' close, prayerful relationship with God. The parable of the friend at midnight is told in verses 5–8. In verses 9–11, Jesus exhorts the disciples to persevere in prayer to God. Bread is an important metaphor in this passage and throughout Luke's Gospel. "Give us each day our daily bread" (v. 3) is a reminder of the exodus, when God provided manna—bread—day by day for the Israelites wandering in the wilderness (Exod. 16). Bread stands for not only physical food but also spiritual food. We can count on God to sustain our spirits and bodies when we knock on God's door in prayer and ask for bread *(read Luke 11:1–11)*.

McKenzie's Front Door

If you came to my front door and rang the doorbell, you might not notice the tiny glass circle just above it. You might not realize that it's a door camera. Whenever someone rings the doorbell, the phone rings three times. We can then turn any of the televisions in the house to channel 17, see who is standing on the porch, and decide in advance whether to answer or not. This was the system several years ago, when landlines were not yet a thing of the past; now you can do all this on your smartphone.

Through the years, our door camera has not only saved us trips to the front door; it has also provided the kids and me with hours of entertainment. We have had our own personal reality show that we call "Front Porch."

> Man in red cap, holding a flat, square box. Dominoes!
>
> Handsome young man in a tuxedo, holding a corsage.
>
> Young girl, maybe eight years old, green dress with sash covered with badges, holding a clipboard.
>
> Two young men, black suits, I can see two bicycles at the curb.

You decide. Answer the door or not?

The Front Door in Luke 11

As a villager in first-century Palestine, you don't have a choice about answering the door. You have to put a smile on your face, get up, get the bread, and get the door. Hospitality is a primary value in this culture, a matter of honor. No matter what hour a visitor comes, you get up—with a smile—get the bread, and get the door. Houses are close together. Your neighbors can hear every ungracious grumble, and they will gossip the next day about what a grump you were. Everybody bakes bread in the common village oven, so they know who has fresh bread. That's why the friend has come to you. He's heard that you have the freshest bread. To grumble like the "friend" Jesus talks about in the parable would bring shame on your family and your village! You have no choice but to be a friend at midnight.

Your Front Door

Have a seat on my couch. I'll tune the TV to your "Front Door" It's your reality show. Who's going to be coming to your door in the days of Lent that lie ahead?

Maybe the florist will deliver flowers for your birthday. Maybe the UPS truck will bring something you ordered from Amazon.

Or it may be someone who needs something from you, who is asking for your support, your attention, your time, your sustenance. We can't say yes to everything and everyone, but there are times that we know we have to get up, put on a smile, get the bread, and get to the door. As Paul says so eloquently in his letter to the Galatians, "Bear one another's burdens, and in this way you will fulfill the law of Christ" (Gal. 6:2). Your young child wants to show you something when you're busy. Your grown child is in a crisis. Your parent needs help transitioning to assisted living. Your next door neighbor needs company after the death of her husband. Your neighbors need help recovering from a flood or tornado.

Somebody is at the door. They are calling, as in the parable, "I know you're in there. I see you through the window. I'm not going away until you come to the door."

People at Jesus' Door in Luke's Gospel

There was always someone at Jesus' door in Luke. Somebody was always knocking on the Lord's door, wanting bread, spiritual food to strengthen them for one more day: wanting healing, forgiveness, hope. When they felt overwhelmed by life, they knocked on the Lord's door: "Master, Master, we are perishing! (Luke 8:24, calming the storm). When they were staring death in the face, they knocked on the Lord's door: Jairus begs for help, "My twelve-year-old daughter is at the point of death" (see vv. 41–42). When they were suffering from chronic illness, they knocked on the Lord's door: The desperate woman in the crowd confesses, "I have suffered from a flow of blood for twelve years" (see vv. 43–48). When they were filled with guilt and shame about the past, they knocked on the Lord's door: The leper, ostracized for his illness, says "'Lord, if you choose, you can make me clean!' Then Jesus stretched out his hand, touched him, and said, 'I do choose. Be made clean'" (5:12–13)! Jesus was their friend at midnight, offering them bread.

The Disciples at Jesus' Door

One time, recounted here in Luke 11:1–4, several of the disciples knocked on Jesus' door with the request, "Lord, teach us to pray" (v. 1). What was their motivation? I wonder if it wasn't something like this: "We know how to be anxious, Lord. We know how to be disordered in our emotions, filled with nameless regret, dread, and guilt. Teach us to pray. We know what it is like for our tears to be our food day and night [see Ps. 42:3]. So fill us with the nourishing Bread of your presence, our spiritual food."

Me at God's Door in a Midnight Moment

The room was dark, except for a couple of candles burning. There was soft music. My mother had put Bach on the CD player. Bach had always been his favorite. She had strewn rose petals on his home hospital bed. I told her to go get some rest. The hospice saints would be back in several hours. The liver cancer wouldn't wait for long. But now it was almost midnight, and I kept a vigil at my father's deathbed. I had read to him from Psalm 121, "I lift up mine eyes to the hills— / from where will my help come? / My help comes from the LORD, / who made heaven and earth." I had read from the twenty-third Psalm, "The LORD is my shepherd. I shall not want." I had read Proverbs 3:5. "Trust in the LORD with all your heart, / and do not rely on your own insight." I had read 2 Corinthians 4:7, "We have this treasure in clay jars, so that it may be made clear that this extraordinary power belongs to God and does not come from us."

He was on morphine, so perhaps the reading was all for my benefit. At any rate, I was all read out. So I began to pray without thinking "Our father, who art in heaven . . ."

Jesus at God's Door

The prayer in Luke is a shorter version of that found in Matthew 6:9–13. It is Jesus' version of a daily prayer he had heard in the synagogue, the *Kaddish* (holy), a prayer of thanksgiving and praise to God.

> Exalted and hallowed be God's great name
> in the world which God created, according to plan.
>
> May God's majesty be revealed in the days of our lifetime
> and the life of all Israel, speedily, imminently, to which we say Amen.[32]

Jesus' prayer was a simpler, more direct, personal version of this prayer:

> "Father, hallowed be your name.
>   Your kingdom come.
> Give us each day our daily bread.
> And forgive us our sins,
>   For we ourselves forgive everyone indebted to us.
> And do not bring us to the time of trial."
>
> Luke 11:2–4

This prayer addresses a God who is honorable ("hallowed be your name"), accessible ("your kingdom come"), dependable ("give us each day our daily bread"), and merciful ("forgive us our sins . . . do not bring us to the time of trial"). This is the God to whom Jesus prayed and taught us to pray. This is the God to whom Jesus urges us to turn when we need bread at midnight.

This is the God from whom Jesus came and to whom he returned. This is the God with whom Jesus was one. This is the God whose character Jesus embodied and revealed to us in his earthly life. This is the God who nourished Jesus' spirit in times of prayer: early in the morning in a quiet place, late at night alone in the mountains, in a garden at twilight while others slept. The Son prayed, and God nourished him with courage, peace, and hope.

While praying his prayer, I take comfort that Jesus' advice about asking, seeking, and knocking came from his own experience in knocking on God's door at midnight and being fed by God: "So I say to you, Ask and it will be given you; search and you will find; knock and the door will be opened for you. For everyone who asks receives, and everyone who searches finds, and for everyone who knocks, the door will be opened" (Luke 11:9–10). He was speaking from personal experience of asking for bread—spiritual sustenance—from God, and being fed.

How else would he have found the courage at that final meal on that final night to break bread and offer it, saying, "This is my body which is given for you. Do this in remembrance of me" (Luke 22:19). He becomes, in that sacrament of the Lord's Supper, not just our friend at midnight, but our bread as well.

John Wesley spoke from his personal experience of being fed by God when he taught his followers that there are several means of grace: prayer (public and private), searching the Scriptures, acts of charity, worship, and the sacraments (baptism and Holy Communion).

In 1733, he wrote a sermon, "The Duty of Constant Communion," for his pupils at Oxford, in which he said that we ought to come to Christ's table whenever possible because this command was "his dying words to all his followers." We ought to come often to Christ's table "because the benefits of doing so are so great . . . the forgiveness of our past sins and the present strengthening and refreshing of our souls."

> As our bodies are strengthened by bread and wine, so are our souls by these tokens of the body and blood of Christ. This is the food of our souls: This gives strength to perform our duty, and leads us on to perfection. If . . . we desire the pardon of our sins, if we wish for strength to believe, to love and obey God, then we should neglect no opportunity of receiving the Lord's Supper; then we must never turn our backs on the feast which our Lord has prepared for us. . . .
>
> [T]hose who purpose to receive this . . . should prepare themselves for this solemn ordinance by self-examination and prayer.[33]

At Ruby's Door

Through this feast, we are strengthened by God in Christ to nourish others: to open the door with bread when they knock, or to go to them and stand on their doorsteps with the bread they need.

Years ago, when I was in seminary at Duke Divinity School, I served a little church in rural North Carolina as the summer student intern. The pastor gave me the task of going over the rolls and finding out who hadn't been to worship in a few months and going to see them and inviting them back. I noted that Ruby Shoffner had suddenly stopped attending about three months before and hadn't been to a UMW meeting either. That's how I came to be sitting in Ruby's living room, drinking sweet tea. "We sure miss you at church," I told her. "And I'm sure your friends in United Methodist Women (UMW) do too. She responded, "Well, I just don't have the clothes anymore, but I appreciate that you came out." The next day, when driving by her house, I saw her getting into her car to go to town. She was wearing an outfit that would have made any member of the UMW proud. I went back to see her in a few days, with the same pitch, "We sure do miss you, Ruby." She sighed, and then said, "Honey, you're young, and you're a Yankee, so I don't expect you to understand; but my husband's funeral was in the sanctuary three months ago, and since then, all I can think of when I go in there is death."

I took my leave and, over the next several days, I did two things: I stopped pestering Ruby, and I made a few phone calls.

Not long after, I was driving by her house around 7:00 pm one evening, on my way to a church meeting, I saw a group of ladies standing on her doorstep holding potluck offerings of casseroles, pies, and cakes. Driving back a few hours later on my way home, I saw her dining room lit up, and a circle of friends sitting around her table.

God at Our Door

I see on the Front Porch channel that there is someone on your front porch right now. I think you should answer the door. It's not a Girl Scout; it's not your daughter's prom date; it's not the pizza delivery person. Just go to the door and see who it is.

So you listen to me and you go to the door. And God is there! You chew on your lower lip and ask nervously, "How can I help you?"

God arches an eyebrow and says, "It's the other way around, or have you so soon forgotten what you said to me last night? I was listening. I certainly wasn't sleeping. And I distinctly remember," says God, "that precisely at midnight, as you lay in your bed—wide awake and staring at the ceiling—you said to me, 'Lord, I'm not sure what challenges and losses lie ahead, and there are many demands on me right now.' I clearly remember what you said next. You said, 'Lord, you are calling me to be a friend at midnight to others. Come to me now. Be my friend at midnight. I need some bread.'" God pauses and then asks, "Why do you look so surprised? Did you think I wouldn't come to the door? Well, here I am, as promised. Come and feast at my banquet!"

SCENIC SERMON 8: SINGLE-SCENE SERMON WITH A SCENE FROM THE PREACHER'S EXPERIENCE AS HOME SCREEN

Sermon Title: "No Way?"
Sermon Text: John 14:1–7[34]
  Occasion: Sunday Service, Sixth Sunday of Easter
  Location: St. John's United Methodist Church, Austin, Texas

Introduction to John 14:1–7

Do you remember the kindergarten game Show and Tell? The Gospel of John is the opposite kind of game; it's Tell and Show. In the prologue, John first tells us who Jesus is: He is "the Word [who] became flesh and lived among us . . . full of grace and truth" (John 1:14). He is the incarnate Wisdom of God who came from the Father to show us the way to the Father.

Throughout the rest of the Gospel, the evangelist John shows us who Jesus is in a series of encounters with people who are stuck in situations from which they cannot extricate themselves. All of them need to be shown the way:

- Nicodemus (John 3:1–21)
- The woman at the well (John 4:1–42)
- The man by the pool for thirty-eight years (John 5:1–15)
- The man born blind (John 9)
- And here, in John 14:1–7, Thomas

Our text from chapter 14 is part of Jesus' farewell discourse to his disciples, which begins after he washes their feet in chapter 13 and ends with chapter 17, just before his betrayal by Judas in chapter 18. Our text includes one of the seven "I am" sayings in John: bread, light, sheep gate, good shepherd, resurrection and the life, true vine. And the one you are about to hear: I am the way, and the truth, and the life (*read John 14:1–7*).

A Torn Retina

Several years ago, my husband, Murry, and I were in Germany, doing some touring before attending a preaching conference at Wittenberg, Germany, home of that great preacher Martin Luther.

We were in the charming medieval town of Rothenberg, staying at a bed and breakfast. That morning we decided to take a guided walking tour of the city. For a day or so, I had been bothered by the feeling that a dark curtain was partially blocking the vision in my right eye. I tried to ignore it. We were on vacation! Nothing bad can happen on vacation, right? During the walking tour, I noticed that the woman in front of me, wearing white slacks, had green flashing starbursts on her pants. It was either an interesting German fashion or something was seriously wrong with my vision. When we got back to the hotel I searched for my symptoms online and immediately went down to the lobby to ask the bed and breakfast proprietress, who fortunately spoke English, for the location of the nearest eye doctor. She called ahead and made an appointment. She then called her friend Freeda, who drove a cab, and asked her to come and get me. She told me, "Freeda has another pickup, but she will fit you in. You must be ready when she gets here, and do not keep her waiting." Murry stayed behind at the hotel, trying to find a cash machine to withdraw enough cash to pay for the doctor visit. He would follow shortly.

Freeda showed up. We drove, faster and bumpier than I would have liked, to the eye doctor some fifteen minutes away. There was no conversation between us; her English was as limited as my German. Let's just say that all the German I knew I had learned from Wayne Newton's 1963 version of *"Danke Shoen."* Freeda pulled up in front of a multi-storied medical building, pointed to it, gave what I assume were directions in rapid-fire German, and indicated that I was to get out of her cab. She peeled off, leaving me standing there with a troubled heart! I asked myself . . . Well, what would you be asking yourself in that situation? "How am I going to find my way?"

A Group Joins Me in Front of the Medical Building

At least I had some company huddled there with me. First came the members of John's church, a small church with a troubled heart in 90 CE. There were threats from without. They had been kicked out of the synagogue. They were facing persecution. There was strife within, internal wrangling over Jesus' identity. Some said, "Jesus is just a good teacher, nothing divine about him." Others said, "No, Jesus is completely divine, nothing human about him." They were in danger of disintegrating, unless someone could show them the way.

Also standing there with me were all the troubled hearts Jesus meets in John, trapped between no way and way. Nicodemus, a respected Jewish leader, comes to Jesus by night (John 3): "Part of me wants to follow you, but I am afraid of the fallout. I'm stuck. How am I going to find my way?"

The woman at the well (John 4): "I am so tired of coming here in the heat of the day to avoid my judgmental neighbors. I'm so tired of being looked down on by the community. How am I going to find my way?"

The man by the pool (John 5): "I have been stuck here for thirty-eight years, unable to get relief from my pain and this futile routine. But I don't know any other way."

And now here comes the disciple Thomas, joining me and the others in front of the medical building. I'm so happy to see him! If he spoke German, I'd be even happier. He looks as anxious as I feel. Neither of us can see the future. And both our guides have abandoned us or are about to.

I imagine Freeda probably called out "Good luck!" as she drove away. And Jesus says something to Thomas and the disciples that sounds just as glib, "I am leaving, but do not let your hearts be troubled."

Personal and Cosmic Anxiety

As I stood there, I experienced personal anxiety. You know what that's like, anxiety about your immediate future. There is also something I call "cosmic anxiety": anxiety for the world, anxiety because we each know that there are forces in the world that oppose God's *shalom*, God's will for peace and justice for the human community. There are forces of violence, exclusion, and cruelty, which sometimes act in the name of religion. Cosmic anxiety shows up in individual faces:

- A father digging a little boy out of the rubble of a bombed out hospital in Aleppo;
- A family that loses nine paychecks because the company where they've worked for years is moving where there is cheaper labor.
- Eight hundred-plus delegates of a mainline denomination at a big meeting in a time when they face declining numbers and internal strife over issues of polity and sexuality.

"Do not let your hearts be troubled," Jesus commands (John 14:1). But when you can't see clearly, and you don't know where you are going, how can one not be troubled, for oneself, for our world?

No Way? Jesus' Tough Love Challenge

As I stood there, I remembered how in pastoral-care classes in seminary they talked about how to help someone who has fallen into a pit. There is even a cartoon to illustrate how to do it. One side of the cartoon depicts one person in a pit and another person crawling down there with him. The other side shows someone in a pit and someone else standing at the edge of it, throwing down a lifeline.

For all of us standing outside the medical building, with impaired vision, not knowing our next step, Jesus throws us a lifeline. He shows us the way. As he does over and over again in John's Gospel, Jesus stands at the edge of the pit, and tosses a tough-love lifeline, a way out of no way situations: "Nicodemus, woman at the well, man by the pool—I represent the God who specializes in making a way out of no way. This is the God who charts a path through the Red Sea in the exodus. This is the God who makes streams in the desert and a way in the wilderness for people in exile (Isa. 43:19). This is the God who offers the way of wisdom to the foolish wanderer. I imagine Jesus saying something like, "Thomas, stop the excuses. 'Lord, I don't know the way. How can I know the way?'"

"You know the way, Thomas, that path from no way to way that is paved by the presence and power of God. Here I am. I am everything you need for the journey: the bread, the light, the path, the vine, the door, the shepherd, the living water, the resurrection and the life, the way forward through the adversities of life to the many rooms my Father has prepared for you."

Alice Walker: Make a Way Out of No Way

It's funny how, when you're in uncertain situations, your mind wanders to memories you haven't thought of in a long time. As I stood there outside the medical building, I remembered a story I heard several years before. In the August heat in 1973, future Pulitzer Prize winning novelist Alice Walker stood looking over an acre of waist-high brambles and uncut grass. She was searching for the grave of Zora Neale Hurston. Zora, a Barnard graduate, author of four novels, two books of folklore, and an autobiography, is considered the most important collector of Afro American folklore in America. One critic called her, "one of the most significant unread authors in America." In 1959, Zora was in poverty, living at the St. Lucie County welfare home. She died of a stroke at age fifty-nine and was buried in an unmarked grave in the neglected cemetery that lay before Alice Walker's eyes in 1973.

Alice's heart was troubled by the injustice of it all, and she had come to find Zora. Elderly folks in town had drawn for her the closest thing to a map they could from their foggy memories. Holding it in one hand, she called to mind the old saying, "God can make a way outta no way"; she set aside her fear of snakes and plunged into the waist-high grass and thorns.

"Zora!" Alice started fussing, "I'm not going to stand here all day with these snakes watching me and these ants biting my ankles, where *are* you?" After significant time tromping around—eyes peeled for snakes, brambles scratching her shins—her foot sank into a hole. She looked down and realized she was standing in a sunken rectangle about six feet long and three feet wide. Found her!

She drove into town, to the Merritt Monument Company, ordered a headstone, and had this epitaph carved on it:

> Zora Neale Hurston
> "A Genius of the South"
> Novelist, Folklorist, Anthropologist
> 1901–1960[35]

The Return of Freeda

And so I stood in front of the German medical building, sight-challenged, unsure of what to do or where to go. I closed my eyes for a moment, and then I heard the sound of tires on gravel and looked up to see Freeda climbing out of her car. She took me by the elbow and said gruffly in the best English she could muster, "You are lost. I come back."

To everyone with a troubled heart this morning—to everyone stuck, somehow afraid there is no path from no way to way—take heart. You know the way.

He is both the path and the companion on the way.

He is going away, but . . . he is back in the presence and power of the Holy Spirit to lead us home to God!

SCENIC SERMON 9: SINGLE-SCENE SERMON THAT USES A BIBLICAL SCENE AS ITS HOME SCREEN

Sermon Title: "Locked in a Room with Open Doors"

Sermon Text: John 20:19–23

> *Occasion:* Second Annual National Young Preachers' Festival, a gathering of high-school, college, and seminary students interested in exploring ministry as a vocation. The two-day event featured sermons, keynotes, and workshops related to preaching.

> *Location:* United Methodist Church of the Resurrection, Leawood, Kansas

Introduction to Scripture Reading

In 1969, Presbyterian preacher and author Ernst Campbell (1923–2010), then senior minister of Riverside Church in New York, preached a sermon titled "Locked in a Room with Open Doors."

Dr. Campbell began his sermon with a story about a family that had two brothers. The younger one, for whatever reason, had a fear of open doors. The older one would taunt the younger brother with this threat: "Someday I'm going to lock you up in a room with all the doors open."[36]

Dr. Campbell's sermon was based on Deuteronomy 30:19. Mine, today, is based on the events that happened Easter eve. But I give credit and thanks to Dr. Campbell for a great title (*read John 20:19–23*)!

Scene One: Me Looking into the Upper Room

They have boarded up the windows, but they missed a spot, and through it I can see that they are all in there, all but Thomas, who seems to be missing. I'd like to go in and talk with them about what happened earlier today, but the door is locked, and I can't get anyone's attention. Seems like it's time for them to get out and start spreading the news instead of hiding in a panic room. I wonder what is stopping them.

My Memory of a Bear Pacing His Nonexistent Cage

They remind me of something I saw years ago when my kids were little, and our family went with my older brother Wade and his family to the Philadelphia zoo. Wade is 6'5", with a shock of copper-colored hair, blue eyes, and the family nose. He and Sharon brought their two children. Murry and I brought ours. I opted out of the reptile house opportunity and wandered off on my own, in a reflective mood, toward the bears. There I saw the tall red-haired man standing at the rail and went and stood next to him, leaning against him in a sisterly way, my attention focused on the bears. Many zoos have moved away from cages and confinement to freer, open habitats. There were the younger bears, strutting around, being bears, enjoying their free and open space on a fresh Saturday afternoon. But back in the far corner, there was a lone bear, an old bear, a mangy bear, with tufts of fur missing. Even from a distance, I could see that he had an odd look in his eyes. And he was pacing in a strange way, over and over again: walk five paces to the right, shake a leg, turn, walk five paces to the left, do the weird leg shake, walk back to the right. We'll leave him pacing his nonexistent cage for now.

In the Upper Room with the Disciples

Come now and stand with me outside the upper room. What are you thinking as you look in at the disciples? I realize that, in a way, I've been locked in a room with open doors at several points in my life. I've paced plenty of cages.

A Cage of Vocational Doubts

Called to ministry in my teens, despite my introversion and dislike of public speaking, here I am, age twenty-one, sitting in a borrowed preaching robe in the unairconditioned sanctuary of Page Memorial UMC in Aberdeen, North Carolina. It's the summer before I start seminary at Duke Divinity School. I have not yet had a preaching course. I am looking out at the congregation, thinking, "Why me? Why not Mr. Hinson the pharmacist? Why not Ms. Davis, the reading specialist? You're both older and wiser than I am. Come up here and help me out!"

I thank God Christ came in and said, "Peace be with you," calling me to step out of the cage and step up to my vocation.

A Cage of "Never Enough"

I see myself in there with the disciples pacing the "never enough" cage. Am I a good enough wife, mother, pastor, teacher, author, preacher? Am I doing enough? Is it good enough?

I thank God Christ came in, and called, and said, "Peace be with you," calling me to step out of the cage of "never enough" and into the gift of the Holy Spirit's presence in every arena of life.

Congregational Cages

Are you in there with the disciples? We all have experienced some rooms in our lives with very heavy doors and very rusty hinges. It's not as easy as just opening the door and walking out into the sunshine when we are:

- Locked in an abusive relationship.
- Locked in an addiction.

- Locked in by physical disability, or mental deterioration, of someone we love. And you sit before your loved one, who you know is in there somewhere, even though she no longer recognizes you.
- Locked in loneliness that seems to know no bounds.
- Locked in by discrimination on the basis of race, sexual orientation, or gender.
- Locked in by poverty, with so much to offer and so little opportunity to offer it.

Some of these are heavy doors with rusty hinges. Lots of people are locked in. Who can break them out? Who can break us out?

Jesus at the Door

I just noticed him standing next to us, looking in at the disciples with us. I wonder if he's going to reenact that lovely painting by Warner Sallman, "Christ at Heart's Door." It's based on Revelation 3:20: "Listen! I am standing at the door, knocking; if you hear my voice and open the door, I will come in to you and eat with you, and you with me." The lesson I've heard in many sermons is that the door has no handle (as in the painting), and so we must open it to him from within. That is not the biblical scenario of John 20, however. First of all, the Jesus I see standing next to us, looking in at the disciples, doesn't resemble the Jesus of artist Warner Sallman's painting. He doesn't have shoulder-length auburn hair for one thing; he doesn't look patient for another. I wonder what he is thinking to himself as he stands there.

Now, I would never presume to know, but I can't help wondering if it was something like this: "How is huddling in a panic room an example of following my directions? In none of the Gospels did I or an angelic messenger instruct you to, 'Go find a safe house with a panic room and lock yourselves in for an indefinite period of time!' That's it, I do not have time to watch you pace your cages anymore."

Jesus Going In

And suddenly, he's not standing outside anymore. He's in the panic room with them. Look at the expressions on their faces!

What an entrance! Where did he learn to come to where people are hurting and break them out like that? Well, he is the Son of a Father who has lots of practice passing through locked doors and setting prisoners free:

- Joseph at the bottom of a pit (Gen. 37:24)
- Meshach, Shadrach, and Abednego in the furnace; God sends an angel to protect them (Dan. 3)
- Daniel in the lion's den; God's angel shuts the lions' mouths (Dan. 6)
- The Israelites in bondage in Egypt; God opens a way through the waters for them to pass through (Exod. 14)
- Hagar and Ishmael dying in the desert; God provides a well of water (Gen. 21:8–21)
- Elijah hiding from Jezebel in a cave; God calls him out with a still, small voice (1 Kgs. 19)
- Lazarus dead in the tomb, starting to stink; Jesus calls him forth to live again (John 11)
- Paul and Silas in jail in Philippi; God provides an earthquake to break them out (Acts 16:16–40)
- Jesus in a prison of pain, trapped on a cross; death does not have the last word

Today, It's Our Turn. Today Is Your Day!

Today the Risen Christ has found your safe house, has breached your panic room. *What an entrance!* He passes through locked doors and stands before you in

- your apartment
- your bedroom
- your breakroom
- your classroom
- your conference room
- your cubicle
- your hospital room
- your kitchen
- your living room
- your office
- your cell . . . wherever you have locked yourself in so you can pace your cage

What an entrance! And what a greeting! He stands before us, not with a "Hi, how ya doing?" or "Have a nice day." This is no ordinary greeting. This is not a wish. This is statement of fact: "Peace be with you" (John 20:21b). Jesus, through the power of God, is Peace in Person, here to still our storms.

What an entrance. What a greeting. And what a gift! This gift can come only from someone who is one with us in our sufferings and also one with God in presence and power. This One is fully divine; he can pass through walls. This One is fully human; he shows us his hands and his side. This One knows what it's like to be bullied; sexually humiliated; discriminated against for whom he loves and how he has loved them; tased face-down on the pavement, though he holds no weapon. This One, on a Friday not long ago, was torn up, nailed up, and torn down. This One stands before us and breathes on us the Holy Spirit. He told us he was leaving. He told us he would be back. Now he's back, breathing on us the forgiveness and power of the Holy Spirit, the assurance of his personal, pervasive, permanent presence in our midst.

What an entrance! What a greeting. What a gift. And now, what an exit! After the Risen Jesus offers the gift of peace, he says, "As the Father has sent me, so I send you" (v. 21c). Then he breathes on them and us the Holy Spirit.

And now it's time to exit the panic room, to unlock the doors from within, to realize our cage has no bars. Today is the day that he has come in to call us out, to go with him where he is going next: to scenes of suffering; places where his beloved children are locked in by addiction, loneliness, prejudice, and violence; to proclaim release to the captives and to let the oppressed go free.

Back to the Bear

Now back to the bear. I stood there mesmerized by his endless pacing in his nonexistent cage. I elbowed the tall, red-haired man against whom I was leaning, companionably, and pointed to the bear.

"He kind of reminds me of me," I said. And then I looked up at him.

Right hair, right height; wrong nose . . . green eyes . . .

"Yeah," he said, "I know what you mean. Don't you kind of wonder what will ever make him stop?"

An Interview with a Scenic Sermon

Be Clear
What strategies has the preacher used to enhance the conceptual clarity of the sermon?
What is the throughline, or thematic thread, of the sermon?

Be Compelling
Does the sermon have forward-moving momentum? Do any scenes/summaries seem out of sequence or extraneous?

Honor Complexity
How has the preacher honored the complexity and ambiguity of listeners' experience? How has she/he honored their ongoing struggles, and the challenges of life, rather than conveyed that faith is a simple matter, and the sermon is the solution?

Images
What images does the sermon use to engage and focus listener participation?

Dialogue
What examples of dialogue occur throughout the sermon?

Show, Don't Just Tell
What has the preacher left for listeners to figure out for ourselves about events or characters in a scene?

CSD: Concrete Significant Detail
What details in the sermon's scenes enhance their credibility and realism for listeners?

Scenic Exegesis/Teaching
Where has the preacher used a scene to convey exegetical, historical, or theological teaching?

Beginnings and Endings
Analyze how each scene begins and ends using the categories in chapter 4.

The Four Ps

Point of View
Analyze the point of view of scenes. From whose perspective is each one told?

Plot
If it is a multi-scene sermon, what is the plot created by this sequence of scenes?

Purpose
Does any scene seem unnecessary or better compressed into a summary?

Pulse
What is the driving desire, need, or question that runs through the sermon? What are the stakes for you?

Biblical Exegesis Guide for a Scenic Sermon

Setting, Plot, Character, A Theme: S-P-C-A

Prayer is always our first step in sermon preparation. Far more than that, prayer is a spiritual posture that permeates the preaching life. *Preaching is a spiritual discipline of the pastor.*

In this method, you consult the commentaries near the end of your process, not at the very beginning. Keep a running list of the thoughts, questions, and hunches that you will check out in your later commentary research.

Initial Read Through

Read the text, allowing emotions, thoughts, and image to surface freely. Jot down key words and images. Don't evaluate, just make notes. If the text is not a narrative that contains scenes, brainstorm about possible scenes behind the text.

What Is the Location of This Scene in Its Book?

- Place the scene in the context of the book in which it is located. What scenes precede this scene? For example, if it is part of an Old Testament narrative, what comes before it that we need to understand to enter into the scene?
- If it is a parable of Jesus, where does it come in the flow of the evangelist's (Matthew, Mark, or Luke) account of Jesus' life? How does that influence your view of this scene's significance?

- If it is a non-narrative text, where does it come in the plan of the book in which it is located?

Before and After: What Scenes Come Before and After This Scene?

What comes directly before and after this scene? How does that impact your interpretation of the scene? We'll think more about the significance of what comes after this scene when we get to formulating the impact we want the message to have on our listeners, closer to the end of this process.

- Where does the scene fit into your current life context?
- Where does this scene come in the flow of your life right now? How does it invite you in to find clarity, comfort, or challenge?
- Does this scene remind you of scenes from your own life? The lives of those around you? Scenes in the larger world? Are there historical scenes this reminds you of?

Setting

What is the setting?

- What can you taste, smell, touch, see, and hear? Visualize this biblical scene in a contemporary setting. How would biblical and contemporary settings differ? How would they be alike?
- What catches your attention in this scene?
- What seems odd or intriguing to you about the scene?
- What are you drawn to and respond to favorably? What do you dislike about the scene?
- Is there a feature of the scene that is striking to you, that you want to find out more about when you do research in the commentaries?
- Are there images from the text that would make for vivid preaching?

Plot

What is the plot?

- What is the conflict behind the scene, in the scene?
- Who has power, and who doesn't?
- What is at stake? Who wants what?

- Where do you see similar conflicts in life within and around you in your community and world?

Characters

What is the cast of characters?

- Which character do you identify with most? Which one(s) would your congregation identify with most? What are their motivations for the way they act in the scene?
- How is each character admirable or flawed? (How are we?) How do our own actions and motives seem similar to theirs?
- Whose voice seems absent in this scene?

The Theme in the Scene

There are, of course, many options as to theme in each text (biblical scene). But you need only one per sermon! What is your sense, at this point, of the theme you want to build your sermon around?

One way to get at this is to ask, "What is this scene trying to do?" (the question of genre). Imagine the scene as someone's attempt to answer a question for themselves and their community. What is the question?

Look at the scene as it is recounted in several translations. Are there differences? Does anything seem important to how you would interpret the scene in a sermon?

Find out if the scene has twins or cousins (similar versions of itself) elsewhere in the biblical canon. What differences are there? Does that sharpen your sense of the theme of this scene?

Look at key words and concepts. Is there anything you don't understand? What words and concepts do you need to explore to understand the theme more deeply? Make note of them to explore in the commentaries.

The Theology of the Scene

Think theologically:

- Who is God, as portrayed in this scene?
- Who are human beings?
- What change does God ask of us?

- What are we to believe and do as a result of entering into this scene?

Consult Commentaries on This Scene

Take your list of questions and hunches to the commentaries.

Behind the Scene

As part of your research, find out more about the agenda of the author and the audience to which the work was directed. What can you find out about the author's purpose and the community to which it was written?

The Theme of the Scene/Sermon (Focus)

What theme have you chosen for your sermon, or what theme has chosen you? Form it into one clear sentence.

Impact of Scene and Sermon

These questions help us to think about people taking the theme of our sermon into what comes next for them after they leave the worship space:

- What comes after the scene? What impact do you want the sermon to have?
- What is the next scene for the characters in the biblical book in which it is located?
- What scene comes next for you?
- What scene comes next for your listeners as they leave worship and reenter their world?

Notes

Introduction

1. Fred B. Craddock, "Story, Narrative, and Metanarrative," *What's the Shape of Narrative Preaching? Essays in Honor of Eugene L. Lowry*, eds. Mike Graves and David J. Schlafer (St. Louis, MO: Chalice Press, 2008), 88.
2. Eugene L. Lowry, *The Homiletical Beat: Why All Sermons Are Narrative* (Nashville: Abingdon Press, 2012), 12–13.
3. Eugene L. Lowry, *The Sermon: Dancing the Edge of Mystery* (Nashville: Abingdon Press, 1997), 58–59.
4. Eugene Lowry calls this a movement from "itch to scratch" (*The Homiletical Beat*, 24).
5. Robert McKee, *Story: Substance, Structure, Style and the Principles of Screenwriting* (New York: HarperCollins, 1997), 35.
6. Alyce McKenzie, *Novel Preaching, Tips from Top Writers on Crafting Creative Sermons* (Louisville, KY: Westminster John Knox, 2010), 7. Gerard Manley Hopkins, Romantic poet and Catholic priest, coined the term *inscape* to refer to the unique features of a particular landscape or natural phenomenon. His theological basis for it is that God doesn't repeat Godself (Margaret R. Ellsberg, ed., *The Gospel in Gerard Manley Hopkins, Selections from His Poems, Letters, Journals, and Spiritual Writings* [Walden, NY: Plough Publishing House, 2017]).

Chapter 1: Scene Is the New Story

1. Robert McKee, *Story: Substance, Structure, Style and the Principles of Screenwriting* (New York: HarperCollins, 1997), 35.
2. Ronald E. Osborn, *Folly of God: The Rise of Christian Preaching* (St. Louis, MO: Chalice Press, 1999), 58–59.
3. Alyce M. McKenzie, *Novel Preaching: Tips from Top Writers on Crafting Creative Sermons* (Louisville, KY: Westminster John Knox Press, 2010), 2–3.
4. For a concise description of the homiletical history that led to the rise of the New Homiletic, see O. Wesley Allen Jr.'s "The Pillars of the New Homiletic," introduction to *The Renewed Homiletic*, ed. O. Wesley Allen Jr. (Minneapolis, MN: Fortress Press, 2010), 1–18.

5. Ernst Fuchs and Gerhard Ebeling are scholars most commonly associated with the New Hermeneutic. Thomas G. Long, *Preaching and the Literary Forms of the Bible* (Philadelphia: Fortress Press, 1989), is a treatment of the rhetorical intentions of various biblical genres and their implications for preaching.

6. Stephen Crites, "The Narrative Quality of Experience," *Journal of the American Academy of Religion* 39, no. 3 (September 1971): 291–311.

7. Two works published in the late 1950s paved the way for Craddock to topple propositional preaching from its throne: Robert Eric Browne, *The Ministry of the Word* (London: SCM Press, 1976); H. Grady Davis, *Design for Preaching* (Philadelphia: Fortress Publishers: 1958).

8. *Listening to the Word: Studies in Honor of Fred B. Craddock*, edited by Gail R. O'Day and Thomas G. Long (Nashville: Abingdon Press, 1993), offers insights from Craddock's colleagues and students into the impact of his approach on the field of homiletics.

9. In *The Homiletical Plot: The Sermon as Narrative Art Form* (Atlanta: John Knox Press, 1980), Eugene Lowry, a jazz pianist as well as a homiletician, applied Aristotle's dramatic theory for twentieth-century preaching, moving from "oops, to ugh, to aha, to whee, to yeah!"

10. Henry Mitchell, *Black Preaching: The Recovery of Powerful Art* (Nashville: Abingdon Press, 1990) and *Celebration and Experience in Preaching*, rev. ed. (Nashville: Abingdon Press, 1990).

11. Frank A. Thomas, *They Like to Never Quit Praisin' God: The Role of Celebration in Preaching* (Cleveland, OH: United Church Press, 1997), 3, emphasis original.

12. David G. Buttrick's magisterial homiletical tome is entitled *Homiletic: Moves and Structures* (Philadelphia: Fortress Press, 1987).

13. Richard Lischer, "The Limits of Story," *Interpretation* 38, no. 1 (1984): 26.

14. Ibid., 20.

15. Ibid., 30.

16. Francesa Aran Murphy, *God Is Not a Story: Realism Revisited* (Oxford: Oxford University Press, 2007).

17. Pew Research Center, "America's Changing Religious Landscape" (Pew Research Center's Religion & Public Life Project, 2015), http://www.pewforum.org/2015/05/12/americas-changing-religious-landscape/.

18. In their book, *Unchristian: What a New Generation Really Thinks about Christianity . . . And Why It Matters* (Grand Rapids, MI: Baker Books, 2007), authors David Kinnaman and Gabe Lyons interview people in the U.S. born between 1984 and 2002 (Mosaics) as well as some born between 1965 and 1983 (Busters) who self-classified as "outsiders," people looking at Christianity from outside communities of faith. What emerges is a suspicion of "metanarratives," or universalized accounts of who human beings are and who we should be, who is included and who is excluded, who is blessed and who is cursed, on the grounds that theology arises from and needs to prove itself in local contexts and should be open to ongoing critique and conversation.

19. "Rolling Stone: 500 Greatest Albums of All Time: 2012 Edition," MusicBrainz, https://musicbrainz.org/series/8668518f-4a1e-4802-8b0d-81703ced6418.

20. Alyce M. McKenzie, "Imagine a Future Like the Kingdom of God," Patheos Progressive Christian Channel, July 29, 2015, http://www.patheos.com/topics/future-of-faith-in-america/progressive/progressive-christianity-alyce-mckenzie-07-29-2015#Bq8yu7AXL4vHCkM5.99

21. David J. Lose, *Preaching at the Crossroads: How the World and Our Preaching Is Changing* (Minneapolis: Fortress Press, 2013).
22. Steve Wilkens and Mark Sanford, *Hidden Worldviews: Eight Cultural Stories That Shape Our Lives* (Downers Grove, IL: InterVarsity Press, 2009), 13.
23. Lemony Snicket (penname for Daniel Handler) and Brett Helquist, *The Slippery Slope, A Series of Unfortunate Events, book 10* (New York: Scholastic Books, 2004), 21.
24. Galen Strawson, "Against Narrativity," *Ratio* (new series) 17, no. 4 (December 2004): 428–52.
25. Thomas G. Long, "Out of the Loop: The Changing Practice of Preaching," *What's the Shape of Narrative Preaching? Essays in Honor of Eugene L. Lowry*, eds. Mike Graves and David J. Schlafer (St. Louis: Chalice Press, 2008), 126. Long sees the contemporary trend toward preaching as instruction to be symptomatic of this episodic quality of daily life.
26. Gerald M. Edelman, *Second Nature: Brain Science and Human Knowledge* (New Haven: CT: Yale University Press, 2006).
27. Lisa Cron, *Wired for Story: The Writer's Guide for Using Brain Science to Hook Readers from the Very First Sentence* (Berkeley, CA: Ten Speed Press, 2012).
28. Jonathan Gottschall, *The Storytelling Animal: How Stories Make Us Human* (New York: Houghton Mifflin Harcourt, 2012), xv.
29. Ibid., 58. In this analysis of the social function story, Gottschall is drawing on the work of psychologist and novelist Keith Oatley.
30. "37 Mind Blowing YouTube Facts, Figures and Statistics—2018," MerchDope, July 22, 2018, https://merchdope.com/youtube-statistics.
31. https://www.youtube.com/channel/UCYsWPPZMhf19EddYpPe6CYw.
32. "Biblical wisdom in the Old Testament is concentrated in three books that are sandwiched between the end of the salvation history and the beginning of the Prophets: Proverbs, Job and Ecclesiastes. The mighty acts of God in Israel's history (the exodus, giving the law at Sinai, crossing the Red Sea) are never mentioned in these books. The wisdom writings are more concerned with the regularities of ordinary life. They deal with wisdom (*hokmah* in Hebrew, *sophia* in Greek), an attitude of mind that enables the observer to see patterns in human experience and compress them in scenic one-liners that can be taught and learned" (Alyce M. McKenzie, *Preaching Biblical Wisdom in a Self-Help Society* [Nashville: Abingdon Press, 2002], 20).
33. See my discussion of the current "divided identity" in preaching in the introduction to *Novel Preaching*, 1–8.
34. Buttrick, *Homiletic*, 11–12.

Chapter 2: The Preacher as Scene-Maker

1. In chapter 1 of his popular introductory preaching text, *The Witness of Preaching* (Louisville, KY: Westminster John Knox Press, 1989), 11–57, Thomas G. Long identifies four models for the preacher: herald, pastor, storyteller/poet, and witness. I seek to add the *sage* to the lineup. Two more editions of *The Witness* have been published in 2005 and 2016.
2. Elisabeth Schüssler Fiorenza, *Wisdom Ways: Introducing Feminist Biblical Interpretation* (Maryknoll, NY: Orbis Books, 2001), 23.
3. Kenyatta R. Gilbert, *The Journey and Promise of African American Preaching* (Minneapolis: Fortress Press, 2011), 14–15. Gilbert, in honoring all three roles of the

preacher—prophet, priest, and sage—calls for African American preaching to be "trivo-cal" (10).

4. Alyce M. McKenzie, *Novel Preaching: Tips from Top Writers on Crafting Creative Sermons* (Louisville, KY: Westminster John Knox Press, 2010), 14–15. C.W. Smith is professor emeritus at Southern Methodist University. He is the author of nine novels, a collection of short stories, and a memoir.

5. For more background on the role of sages in Israel's life, see Alyce M. McKenzie, *Hear and Be Wise: Becoming a Preacher and Teacher of Wisdom* (Nashville; Abingdon Press, 2004), 1–15.

6. The story is recounted by Frederick Buechner in his *The Gospel as Tragedy, Comedy and Fairytale* (New York: HarperCollins, 1977), 1.

7. Roland E. Murphy, *The Tree of Life: An Exploration of Biblical Wisdom Literature* (Grand Rapids, MI: William B. Eerdmans, 2002), 1.

8. "Out of the heart come evil intentions, murder, adultery, fornication, theft, false witness, slander. These are what defile a person, but to eat with unwashed hands does not defile" (Matt. 15:19–20).

9. After the death of Solomon, the Israelite people were split in two, the northern nation of Israel and the southern nation of Judah. The Assyrians invaded Samaria in the northern kingdom in 722 BCE. The Babylonians invaded Judah in 586 BCE, destroyed Jerusalem, and deported thousands of Judeans to Babylon (McKenzie, *Hear and Be Wise*, 3–4).

10. See Claudia V. Camp's *Wisdom and the Feminine in the Book of Proverbs* (Sheffield: Almond Press, 1988), 23–46, 209–31; see also Alyce M. McKenzie, *Preaching Biblical Wisdom in a Self-Help Society* (Nashville: Abingdon Press, 2002), 111–17.

11. Fools create chaos in the community that runs counter to God's moral order. James Crenshaw, in his book *Old Testament Wisdom: An Introduction* (Atlanta: John Knox Press, 1981), 7–10, points out that there are at least eight different Hebrew words in Proverbs that represent various nuances on the theme of the fool.

12. McKenzie, *Hear and Be Wise*, 4–5.

13. For a fuller treatment of Qoheleth's thought, see Alyce M. McKenzie, *Preaching Proverbs: Wisdom for the Pulpit* (Louisville, KY: Westminster John Knox Press, 1996), 41–58; see also McKenzie, *Preaching Biblical Wisdom*, 145–68.

14. Elizabeth Schüssler Fiorenza, as quoted in Sallie McFague, *Models of God: Theology for an Ecological, Nuclear Age* (Philadelphia: Fortress Press, 1987), 52, emphasis original.

15. Amy Jill Levine, in her *Short Stories by Jesus: The Enigmatic Parables of a Controversial Rabbi* (New York: HarperOne, 2014), calls for contemporary readers to "hear the parables as the people who first heard them, Jews in the Galilee and Judea, did and thus to recover as best as we can the original provocation" (11).

16. I have my colleague Dr. John C. Holbert to thank for this piece of wisdom. He regularly comforted his first-year students by reminding them of their sacred uniqueness. Dr. Holbert is the Lois Craddock Perkins Professor of Homiletics at Perkins School of Theology, Emeritus.

17. Nancy Lammers Gross, *Women's Voices and the Practice of Preaching* (Grand Rapids, MI: William B. Eerdmans, 2017), xix.

18. Lucy Lind Hogan, *Graceful Speech: An Invitation to Preaching* (Louisville, KY: Westminster John Knox Press, 2006), 111.

19. Paul Scott Wilson, *The Imagination of the Heart: New Understandings in Preaching* (Nashville: Abingdon Press, 1988), 15.

20. Barbara Brown Taylor, *The Preaching Life* (Cambridge, MA: Cowley Publications, 1993), 15.

21. William B. McClain, "African American Contexts of Narrative Preaching: The Audacity of Hope," in *What's the Shape of Narrative Preaching? Essays in Honor of Eugene L. Lowry*, eds. Mike Graves and David J. Schlafer (St. Louis, MO: Chalice Press, 2008), 56.

22. Frank A. Thomas, *How to Preach a Dangerous Sermon* (Nashville: Abingdon, 2018), xix.

23. Mary Catherine Hilkert, *Naming Grace: Preaching and the Sacramental Imagination* (New York: Bloomsbury Academic Press, 1997), 44–57.

24. Macrina Wiederkehr, *A Tree Full of Angels: Seeing the Holy in the Ordinary* (San Francisco: HarperSanFrancisco: 1990), xii–xiii.

25. Barbara Brown Taylor, "Preaching the Body," in *Listening to the Word: Studies in Honor of Fred B. Craddock*, eds. Gail R. O'Day and Thomas G. Long (Nashville: Abingdon Press, 1993), 212.

26. A prime example is Mark's allegory of the seeds (Mark 4:14–20), which clearly reflects the challenges to faith posed by persecution and wealth that characterized Mark's community.

27. David Dunn Wilson, *A Mirror for the Church: Preaching in the First Five Centuries* (Grand Rapids, MI: William B. Eerdmans, 2005), 109–10.

28. Christopher A. Hall, "Letters from a Lonely Exile," *Christian History* 13, no. 44 (1994): 30–32.

29. Miriam Gill, "Preaching and Image: Sermons and Wall Paintings in Later Medieval England," in *Preacher, Sermon and Audience in the Middle Ages*, ed. Carolyn Muessig (Leiden: The Netherlands: Brill, 2002), 155–80.

30. Henry H. Mitchell, *Celebration and Experience in Preaching*, rev. ed. (Nashville: Abingdon Press, 1990), 17.

31. Daniel R. Lesnick, *Preaching in Medieval Florence: The Social World of Franciscan and Dominican Spirituality* (Athens, GA: The University of Georgia Press, 1989), 36–37.

32. Michael Pasquarello III, *Sacred Rhetoric: Preaching as a Theological and Pastoral Practice of the Church* (Eugene, OR: Wipf and Stock, 2012), 64.

33. Kathryn Hurlock, *Wales and the Crusades 1091–1291* (Cardiff: University of Wales Press, 2011); see also Augustine Thompson, "Retrieving the Medieval Sermon as an Event" in Muessig, ed., *Preacher, Sermon and Audience in the Middle Ages*, 25.

34. Hughes Oliphant Old, *The Medieval Church, The Reading and Preaching of the Scriptures in the Worship of the Christian Church*, vol. 3 (Grand Rapids, MI: William B. Eerdmans, 1999), 433.

35. Hugh Latimer, "Sermon on the Plough," *Project Canterbury: Sermons* (New York: E. P. Dutton, 1906), http://anglicanhistory.org/reformation/latimer/sermons/plough.html.

36. Carolyn Muessig, "Prophecy and Song: Teaching and Preaching by Medieval Women," *Women Preachers and Prophets through Two Millennia of Christianity*, eds. Beverly Mayne Kienzle and Pamela J. Walker (Berkeley: University of California Press, 1998), 147.

37. See Anna Carter Florence, *Preaching as Testimony* (Louisville, KY: Westminster John Knox Press, 2007), 5–17.

38. The speech became widely known during the Civil War by the title "Ain't I a Woman?" It was a variation of the original speech rewritten by abolitionist and women's rights activist Frances Dana Barker. Gage used a stereotypical Southern dialect. Sojourner Truth was from New York and grew up speaking Dutch as her first language. The speech can be found in Elizabeth Cady Stanton, Matilda Joslyn Gage, and Ida Husted Harper, eds., *The History of Women Suffrage*, vol. 1 (Rochester, NY: Susan B. Anthony, 1887), 116.

39. Kienzle and Walker, eds., *Women Preachers and Prophets through Two Millennia of Christianity*, parts 3–4, 118–333.

40. An *anchoress* (female anchorite) was a religious hermit who lived in an enclosure attached to a church and followed a life of prayer and asceticism. The anchoritic life was one of the earliest forms of Christian monasticism, especially popular among women, from the twelfth through sixteenth centuries.

41. Eunjoo Mary Kim, *Women Preaching: Theology and Practice through the Ages* (Cleveland, OH: The Pilgrim Press, 2004), 65.

42. Julian, *Julian of Norwich: Showings, The Classics of Western Spirituality* (New York: Paulist Press, 1978), 295–98.These excerpts are from chapters 59 and 60 of the Long Text of *Showings*.

43. Kim, *Women Preaching*, 67.

44. The Reformers favored biblical exposition and catechetical instruction in their preaching. See Hughes Oliphant Old, *The Age of the Reformation, The Reading and Preaching of the Scriptures in the Worship of the Christian Church, vol. 4* (Grand Rapids, MI: William B. Eerdmans, 2002), 16.

45. Martin Luther, as quoted in John C. Holbert, *Telling the Whole Story: Reading and Preaching Old Testament Stories* (Eugene, OR: Cascade Books, 2013), 11.

46. Ibid., 12.

47. John Donne, *Devotions upon Emergent Occasions*, ed. Anthony Raspa (New York: Oxford University Press, 1987), 87.

48. Frank J. Warnke, *John Donne*, English Author Series (Woodbridge, CT: Twayne Publishers, 1987), 64.

49. Paul Scott Wilson, *A Concise History of Preaching* (Nashville: Abingdon Press, 1992), 112.

50. Monica Furlong, *Puritan's Progress: A Study of John Bunyan* (London: Hodder and Stoughton 1975), 52–53.

51. Ibid., 92.

52. This information was posted on a website run by historian and museum curator Arnold Clive (Elstow: Pilgrim House, 2008, Bunyan family tree), https://en.wikipedia.org/wiki/John_Bunyan

53. Furlong, *Puritan's Progress*, 53.

54. From Thomas H. Troeger, *Creating Fresh Images for Preaching: New Rungs for Jacob's Ladders* (Valley Forge, PA: Judson Press, 1982), 29. For additional background, see Augustine Thompson, "Retrieving the Medieval Sermon as an Event," *Preacher, Sermon and Audience in the Middle-Ages, A New History of the Sermon, vol. 3, ed. Carolyn Muessig* (Leiden, The Netherlands: Brill, 2002), 25.

55. John Brown, *Puritan Preaching in England: A Study of Past and Present* (New York: Charles Scribner's Sons, 1900), 162, emphasis original.

56. George Whitefield, *The Collected Sermons of George Whitefield* (1714–1770), ed. J. C. Ryle (Jawbone Digital, 2015), loc. 358, Kindle.

57. Ibid., loc. 345, Kindle.
58. Ibid., loc. 7842, Kindle.
59. "Christian History: George Whitefield," *Christianity Today*, http://www.christianity today.com/history/people/evangelistsandapologists/george-whitefield.html.
60. Albert J. Raboteau, *Slave Religion: The "Invisible Institution" in the Antebellum South* (New York: Oxford University Press, 1978), 232.
61. Ibid., 215.
62. Ibid., 235. "*The American Missionary* was a magazine on religious and missionary issues (including racial issues) published in the late nineteenth and early twentieth century by the American Missionary Association (and sometimes by various Congregational missionary societies). . . . The American Missionary began publication in 1846 . . . [and] ceased publication with the March 1934 issue" (The American Missionary, *The Online Books Page*, http://onlinebooks.library.upenn.edu/webbin/serial?id=amission).
63. Excerpt from *The American Missionary*, 12 (February, 1868): 29; cited in Raboteau, *Slave Religion*, 235, spelling original.
64. O. C. Edwards Jr., *A History of Preaching* (Nashville: Abingdon Press, 2004), 444.
65. Paul Wesley Chilcote, *John Wesley and the Women Preachers of Early Methodism* (London: Scarecrow Press, 1991), 238.
66. Ibid.,143–44.
67. Pamela J. Walker, "A Chaste and Fervid Eloquence: Catherine Booth and the Ministry of Women in the Salvation Army" in *Women Preachers and Prophets through Two Millennia of Christianity*, eds. Beverly Mayne Kienzle and Pamela J. Walker (Berkeley: University of California Press, 1998), 289.
68. https://www.bl.uk/collection-items/minutes-of-the-1803-methodist-conference.
69. Chilcote, *John Wesley and the Women Preachers*, 321–32.
70. William L. Andrews, ed., Introduction, *Sisters of the Spirit: Three Black Women's Autobiographies* (Bloomington: Indiana University Press, 1987), 5. This volume includes the autobiographies of three nineteenth-century African American female preachers: Jarena Lee, Zilpha Elaw, and Julia Foote.
71. Ibid, 5–6.
72. Lee, *Religious Experience and Journal of Mrs. Jarena Lee: Giving an Account of Her Call to Preach the Gospel* (Pantianos Classics, 2017; first published in Philadelphia, 1836), 14.
73. Ibid., 15.
74. Walker, "A Chaste and Fervid Eloquence," 288.
75. Ibid., 291. Catherine Booth's pamphlet was titled *Female Teaching: or the Rev. A.A. Rees versus Mrs. Palmer, being a Reply to a Pamphlet by the Above Names Gentleman on f the Sunderland Revival.*
76. Jewell Johnson, *365 Daily Devotions for Women: Inspiration from the Lives of Class Christian Women* (Barbour Publishing, 2007), day 74.
77. For more on Catherine Booth's preaching, see Paul Scott Wilson, *A Concise History of Preaching* (Abingdon Press, 1990), 147–53; see also http://womenofchristianity.com /preachers-wives/catherine-booth/.
78. Martin Luther King Jr., "I See the Promised Land," *I Have a Dream: Writings and Speeches That Changed the World* (HarperSanFrancisco: 1986), 201–202. This was Dr. King's last sermon, delivered April 3, 1968 at Mason Temple in Memphis.
79. Evelyn Underhill, as quoted in Frederic Brussat and Mary Ann Brussat, *Spiritual Literacy: Reading the Sacred in Everyday Life (New York: Scribner*, 1998), 52.

Originally published in Evelyn Underhill, *Evelyn Underhill: Modern Guide to the Ancient Quest for the Holy*, ed. Dana Greene (Albany: State University of New York Press, 1988), 75.

80. Thomas H. Troeger, *Creating Fresh Images for Preaching: New Rungs for Jacob's Ladder* (Valley Forge, PA: Judson Press, 1982), 12.

81. Mark Barger Elliott, *Creative Styles of Preaching* (Louisville, KY: Westminster John Knox Press, 2000), 148–49.

82. Janet Burroway with Susan Weinberg, *Writing Fiction: A Guide to Narrative Craft*, 6th ed. (New York: Longman, 2003), 9.

83. O. Wesley Allen Jr., *Preaching and the Human Condition: Loving God, Self, and Others* (Nashville: Abingdon Press, 2016), 3.

84. Ibid., 9.

85. Luke A. Powery, *Dem Dry Bones: Preaching, Death, and Hope* (Minneapolis, MN: Fortress Press, 2012), 2.

86. See Debra J. Mumford, *Exploring Prosperity Preaching: Biblical Health, Wealth, and Wisdom* (Valley Forge, PA: Judson Press, 2012), and Cleophus J. LaRue, *Rethinking Celebration: From Rhetoric to Praise in African American Preaching* (Louisville, KY: Westminster John Knox Press, 2016).

87. For more detail about the pain, precision, and fruits of the knack for noticing, see McKenzie, *Novel Preaching*, 11–26.

88. Rabbi Elliott N. Dorff, *The Way to Tikkun Olam (Repairing the World)* (Woodstock, VT: Jewish Lights Publishers, 2005).

89. Mary Katherine Hilkert, *Naming Grace: Preaching and the Sacramental Imagination* (New York: The Continuum Publishing Company, 1997), 44–57.

Chapter 3: Making a Scene in Scripture

1. This first account of creation (Gen. 1:1–2:3) likely comes from the Priestly Source, created by priestly families, during exile under Persian rule in the sixth century BCE. It refers to God with the generic name *Elohim* rather than *Yahweh*, as in the second creation account (Gen. 2:4–24). The account's purpose is to reinforce confidence in God's goodness and fidelity in a time of national chaos. See Claus Westermann, *Genesis 1–11: A Continental Commentary, trans. John J. Scullion* (Minneapolis: Augsburg Publishing House, 1984), 22. See also Lawrence Boadt, *Reading the Old Testament: An Introduction* (Nahwah, NJ: Paulist Press, 1984), 93, 104.

2. Brian C. Howell, *In the Eyes of God: A Contextual Approach to Biblical Anthropological Metaphors* (Eugene, OR: Pickwick Publications, 2013), 109–110.

3. Westermann, *Genesis 1–11*, 113.

4. Biblical scholar Denise Dombkowski Hopkins points out that "Calling the whole psalm collection 'praises' means that Israel considered everything in the psalms—the laments as well as the hymns, thanksgivings and wisdom psalms—to be praise of God" (Denise Dombkowski Hopkins, *Journey through the Psalms* [St. Louis, MO: Chalice Press, 2002], 38).

5. "Wisdom, while a gift from God (Prov. 2:6; Sir. 1:9–10, 26; 6:37; Wis. 7:7; 9:4) is associated with disciplined effort to obtain her (Prov. 4:10–27; 6:6; Sir. 4:17; 6:18–36; Wis. 1:5; 7:14)" (Ben Witherington III, *Jesus the Sage: The Pilgrimage of Wisdom* [Minneapolis, MN: Augsburg Fortress, 1994], 115).

6. Prov. 3:7; see also Isa. 5:21.

7. We are to tremble because we are human and God is God (Exod. 19:16; Isa. 6:5); we are to trust because God is faithful (Deut. 10:12–13); and we are to take directions because God is a reliable guide to the ups and downs of daily life (Prov. 1:7; 3:7). For a fuller treatment of the virtue of the fear of the Lord, see Alyce M. McKenzie, *Hear and Be Wise: Becoming a Teacher and Preacher of Wisdom* (Nashville: Abingdon Press, 2004), 17–41.

8. For further exploration, see Witherington, *Jesus the Sage*, and Elisabeth Schüssler Fiorenza, *Jesus, Miriam's Child, Sophia' Prophet: Critical Issues in Feminist Christology* (New York: Continuum, 1995).

9. Fiorenza, *Jesus, Miriam's Child, Sophia's Prophet*, 153.

10. Others, like Irenaeus of Lyons, identified her with the third person of the Trinity. The affirmation of Sophia as fully divine (Prov. 8:22–31) and consubstantial with the Father was crucial for Athanasius's claim that Jesus was begotten by God and not a creature with a beginning in time. See Leo D. Lefebure, "Sophia: Wisdom and Christian Theology," *Christian Century* (October 19, 1994): 953.

11. Fiorenza, *Jesus, Miriam's Child, Sophia's Prophet*, 158. More recent scholarship has sought to recover traces of Sophia's role and influence as she developed in the Intertestamental period, in the books of *The Wisdom of Solomon*, and *The Wisdom of Sirach* (also known as Ecclesiasticus), and in the first few centuries of the Christian era, in 1 Enoch, and 4 Ezra (also known as 2 Esdras).

12. These include Tobit, Judith, Wisdom of Solomon, Ecclesiasticus, Baruch, the books of the Maccabees, 1 Esdras, and the Prayer of Manasseh. See Elisabeth Schüssler Fiorenza, *Wisdom Ways: Introducing Feminist Biblical Interpretation* (Maryknoll, NY: Orbis Books, 2001), 22–23. These books are referred to as *apocryphal* or *deuterocanonical* and are usually printed in Protestant editions of the Bible in an appendix after the New Testament.

13. Raymond E. Brown, *The Gospel According to John, 1–XII*, vol. 29 of *The Anchor Bible* (Garden City, NY: Doubleday and Company, 1979), 13.

14. See also Joel 3:17; Zech. 2:10.

15. Brown, *Anchor Bible Gospel of John*, 33.

16. Ibid.

17. Witherington, *Jesus the Sage*, 147–208; see esp. "Jesus, the Wisdom of God," 201–208. See also Fiorenza, *Jesus: Miriam's Child, Sophia's Prophet*.

18. For similarities between the gifts promised by Wisdom in Proverbs (light, path, way, nourishment) and the seven "I am" sayings of John's Gospel, see Alyce M. McKenzie, *Preaching Biblical Wisdom in a Self Help Society* (Nashville: Abingdon Press, 2002), 204–207.

19. The idea of Jesus as Wisdom can be found, beyond John's Gospel, in a variety of references in the Synoptic Gospels: Matt.11:19, 28–30; 11:27; 12:42; Luke 10:22; 11:31, 49; 21:15.

20. "Jesus, Miriam's child and Sophia's prophet, goes ahead of us on the open-road to Galilee signifying the beginnings of the still-to-be realized *basileia* discipleship of equals" (Fiorenza, *Jesus, Miriam's Child, Sophia's Prophet*, 190).

21. Craig Koester, *Symbolism in the Fourth Gospel: Meaning, Mystery, Community* (Minneapolis: Fortress Press, 1995), 32–73. Examples in John include Nicodemus (3:1–16);

the woman at the well (4:1–42); the royal official (4:46–54); the invalid by the pool (5:1–16); the man born blind (chap. 9); and Mary, Martha, and Lazarus (chap. 11).

22. Stephen J. Patterson, *The God of Jesus: The Historical Jesus and the Search for Meaning* (Harrisburg, PA: Trinity Press International, 1998), 64. Patterson, in using the term *expendables*, is drawing on the work of sociologist of religion Gerhard E. Lenski's book, *Power and Privilege: A Theory of Social Stratification* (Chapel Hill: The University of North Carolina Press, 1984), 281–84.

23. See Matt. 18:2–5, 10, 14, 15–17; 19:13–14; Mark 9:36–37; 10:13–16; Luke 9:47–48; 18:15–17.

24. Alyce M. McKenzie, *Preaching Proverbs: Wisdom for the Pulpit* (Louisville, KY: Westminster John Knox Press, 1996), 24. This book was developed from my dissertation, "Subversive Sages: Preaching on the Proverbial Sayings of Proverbs, Qoheleth and the Synoptic Jesus."

25. This definition is attributed to Cervantes and is quoted by James Crenshaw in his *Old Testament Wisdom: An Introduction* (Atlanta: John Knox Press, 1981), 67. Miguel de Cervantes (1547–1616) was a Spanish novelist, poet, and playwright.

26. James Crenshaw refers to this portable quality when he defines the proverb as "a winged word outliving a fleeting moment" (*Old Testament Wisdom*, 67). It is likely that Crenshaw got it from biblical scholar Gunnar Hylmo (1878–1940), who uses it in describing the genre of *mashal*. Hylmo was a Swedish Old Testament scholar and theologian.

27. The term also looms large in two apocryphal Wisdom books: Ecclesiasticus (Wisdom of Jesus ben Sirach) and the Wisdom of Solomon (McKenzie, *Hear and Be Wise*, 3). Some scholars also identify several psalms as containing references to "wisdom" or wisdom themes: 1, 37:30, 49:3, 51:6, 90:12, 104:24, 105:22, 111:10 (Ibid., 188).

28. See McKenzie, *Hear and Be Wise*; see also Prov. 1:5. The word translated "skill" is *tahbulot* in Hebrew, a reference to steering flatboats on the Nile and a concept that comes to Israel from Egyptian wisdom. See also McKenzie, *Preaching Proverbs*.

29. McKenzie, *Hear and Be Wise*, 72.

30. Demotivator® posters are available at https://despair.com/collections/demotivators.

31. Other examples include "Follow me, and let the dead bury their own dead" (Matt. 8:22; Luke 9:60); "if anyone strikes you on the right cheek, turn the other also; and if anyone wants to sue you and take your coat, give your cloak as well; and if anyone forces you to go one mile, go also the second mile (Matt. 5:39–41).

32. McKenzie, *Preaching Proverbs*, 69.

33. McKenzie, *Preaching Proverbs*, 76; see also Robert Tannehill, *The Sword of His Mouth: Forceful and Imaginative Language in Synoptic Sayings* (Philadelphia: Fortress Press, 1975), 72–88.

34. C. H. Dodd, *Parables of the Kingdom*, 2nd rev. ed. (New York, Charles Scribner's Sons, 1961, originally published 1935), 5.

35. This interpretation is associated with the work of German scholar Adolf Jülicher's writing in the late 1800s. See Robert H. Stein, *An Introduction to the Parables of Jesus* (Philadelphia: Westminster Press, 1981), 52–71.

36. Amy Jill Levine, *Short Stories by Jesus: The Enigmatic Parables of a Controversial Rabbi* (New York: HarperOne, 2014), 3.

37. Alyce M. McKenzie, *The Parables for Today* (Louisville, KY: Westminster John Knox Press, 2007), 45–46.

Chapter 4: Making a Scene in the Sermon

1. Vanhoozer describes his work as a "postconservative, canonical-linguistic theology and a directive theory of doctrine that roots theology . . . firmly in Scripture" (Kevin J. Vanhoozer, *The Drama of Doctrine: A Canonical-Linguistic Approach to Christian Theology* [Louisville, KY: Westminster John Knox Press, 2005], xiii. At the same time, he seeks to preserve the contribution of the context of faith communities emphasized by George Lindbeck's cultural-linguistic understanding of doctrine in his classic *The Nature of Doctrine: Religion and Theology in a Postliberal Age* (Philadelphia: Westminster Press, 1984).

2. Vanhoozer, *The Drama of Doctrine*, xiii.

3. Ibid., 18.

4. Ibid., 13.

5. Ibid., xi.

6. Ibid., 2–3.

7. Ibid., 13–14, emphasis original.

8. Ibid., 15.

9. Ibid., 21, emphasis original.

10. Ibid., xii.

11. Ibid., 16.

12. Vanhoozer draws on the understanding of twentieth-century Roman Catholic theologian Hans Urs von Balthasar's *Theo-drama: Theological Dramatic Theory*, vols. *1–5* (San Francisco: Ignatius Press, 1988–1998). Balthasar did not think that Greek philosophical categories adequately did justice to the salvation mystery. He recast the whole drama of salvation with the help of theatrical categories, focusing on the actions of God (creation, redemption) in which the church finds itself caught up.

13. Sandra Scofield, *The Scene Book: A Primer for the Fiction Writer* (New York: Penguin Books, 2007), 12.

14. Ibid., 3.

15. Ibid., 12.

16. Ibid., 13.

17. Ibid.

18. Ibid., 177.

19. Ibid., 15.

20. Ibid.

21. Ibid., 14–18. Scofield's four elements of scene are: (1) event and emotion, (2) function, (3) structure, and (4) pulse. I've combined *pulse* with *event* and *emotion* and added a fourth element, "point of view."

22. Jordan Rosenfeld advises us that if we have to use multiple points of view within a scene, we need to use the omniscient point of view (*Make a Scene: Crafting a Powerful Story One Scene at a Time* [Cincinnati, OH: Writer's Digest Books, 2008], 227–49).

23. Fred B. Craddock, *As One without Authority* (St. Louis, MO: Chalice Press, 2001), 85.

24. Mike Graves, in *The Fully Alive Preacher: Recovering from Homiletical Burnout* (Louisville, KY: Westminster John Knox Press, 2007), seeks to reunite the vocation of preaching with the life-giving passions of the preacher's daily life. The book's title is from a quote by second-century theologian St. Irenaeus of Lyons, "The glory of God is the human being fully alive," (xiv).

25. Pulse—the wit of a young child meets the gullibility of his mother
    Purpose—to introduce the process to be followed in the rest of this chapter
    Plot—child figures out a way to put an end to his mother's pestering questions
    Point of view—the mother
26. See "The most popular talks of all time," TED, https://www.ted.com/playlists/171/the_most_popular_talks_of_all.
27. Sally Brown, "Tomorrow's Breaking News: The Horizons of North American Preaching," *Questions Preachers Ask: Essays in Honor of Thomas G. Long*, eds. Scott Black Johnston, Ted A. Smith, and Leonora Tubbs Tisdale (Louisville, KY: Westminster John Knox Press, 2016), 150.
28 Ibid., 150, emphasis original.
29. This approach calls to mind Ronald J. Allen and O. Wesley Allen's "postapologetic preaching as conversation," in which "Preachers commend something to the congregation; they do not dictate something for them." While they are "passionate about the kerygma that they proclaim . . . such passions should not give way to an arrogant sense of absolute correctness. Rather, they offer a "humble commendation of a particular perspective of Christian Faith . . . based on "the same sort of ethics needed for authentic conversation" (Ronald J. Allen and O. Wesley Allen Jr., *The Sermon without End: A Conversational Approach to Preaching* [Nashville: Abingdon Press, 2015], 103–4).
30. Thomas G. Long, "Out of the Loop: The Changing Practice of Preaching," in *What's the Shape of Narrative Preaching? Essays in Honor of Eugene L. Lowry*, eds. Mike Graves and David J. Schlafer (St. Louis, MO: Chalice Press, 2008), 128.
31. Ibid., 129.
32. Paul Scott Wilson, *Setting Words on Fire: Putting God at the Center of the Sermon* (Nashville: Abingdon Press, 2008), 26–39.
33. Paul Scott Wilson, *The Four Pages of the Sermon: A Guide to Biblical Preaching* (Nashville, TN: Abingdon Press, 1999), 90–104.
34. *TED Talks Storytelling: 23 Storytelling Techniques from the Best TED Talks*, 3rd ed. (CreateSpace Independent Publishing Platform, 2015), 45–47.
35. David J. Schlafer, *Your Way with God's Word: Discovering Your Distinctive Voice in Preaching* (Boston, MA: Cowley Press, 1995), 62–73. Schlafer describes the preacher: as poet (sermon shaped by images), as essayist (sermon shaped by arguments), and as storyteller (sermon shaped by narrative). He includes a sermon that illustrates each sermonic shape.
36. Alyce M. McKenzie, "Form Follows Function: Well-Shaped Sermons for the Twenty-first Century," *Questions Preachers Ask*, 22.
37. Marshall McLuhan, as quoted in Nicholas Carr, *The Shallows: What the Internet Is Doing to Our Brains* (New York: W. W. Norton & Company, 2010), 3; also Marshall McLuhan, *Understanding Media: The Extensions of Man* (Boston, MA: MIT Press, 1994), 18.
38. Nicholas Carr, "The Juggler's Brain," *Kappan Magazine* (December 2010/January 2011): 10, http://www.jstor.org/stable/27922479.
39. Carr, *The Shallows*, 140. Nicholas Carr is the former business editor of the *Harvard Business Review* and writes on the social, economic, and business implications of technology.
40. Ibid., 10.
41. Ibid., 142.

42. Thomas Merton, *New Seeds of Contemplation* (New York: New Direction Publishing, 2007), 104.

43. Carr, *The Shallows*, 141.

44. Ibid., 140. Carr is quoting Jordan Grafman, head of the cognitive neuroscience unit at the National Institute of Neurological Disorders and Stroke.

45. Blake Snyder, *Save the Cat: The Last Book on Screenwriting That You'll Ever Need* (Studio City, CA: Michael Wiese Productions, 2005), 1.

46. Ibid.

47. *Lisa Cron, Wired for Story: The Writer's Guide to Using Brain Science to Hook Readers from the Very First Sentence* (Berkeley: Ten Speed Press, 2012), loc. 444, Kindle, emphasis original.

48. O. Wesley Allen Jr., *The Homiletic of All Believers: A Conversational Approach to Proclamation and Preaching* (Louisville, KY: Westminster John Knox Press, 2005), 73. Allen is drawing on the insights of Arthur N. Strahler in his *Understanding Science: An Introduction to Concepts and Issues* (Buffalo, NY: Prometheus Books, 1992), 25–27. Strahler presents a reasoning circle (which he calls the induction/deduction feedback cycle) as the basis of the scientific method (see Allen, 161n7).

49. F. A. Rockwell, "Making the Scene," *Handbook of Short Story Writing*, eds. Sandra Smythe and Frank A. Dickson (Cincinnati, OH: Writer's Digest Books, 1970), 81–82. Advice from novelists and screenwriters can help us sharpen our use of scenes. F. A. Rockwell reminds fiction writers that the difference between a published story and a rejected story is that the former has better plot organization and includes scenes that give the story a colorful pictorial quality

50. Skip Press, *The Complete Idiot's Guide to Screenwriting* (Indianapolis, IN: Alpha Books, 2001), 221.

51. Karl Iglesias, *Writing for Emotional Impact: Advanced Dramatic Techniques to Attract, Engage, and Fascinate the Reader from Beginning to End* (Livermore, CA: WingSpan Press, 2005), 125.

52. Raymond Obstfeld, *Novelist's Essential Guide to Crafting Scenes* (Cincinnati, OH: Writer's Digest Books, 2000), 7–8.

53. Ibid., 2.

54. Alyce M. McKenzie, *Novel Preaching: Tips from Top Writers on Crafting Creative Sermons*, chap. 5. The chapter, "Recipes from Contemporary Preachers," sample sermons that demonstrate the sequence of each "recipe." See also Charles Denison, *The Artist's Way of Preaching* (Louisville, KY: Westminster John Knox Press, 2006), 25–34. Denison recommends the Ignatian Method of Prayer for connecting contemporary stories with biblical stories in preaching.

55. For a description of Buttrick's approach and a synopsis of one of his sermons, see McKenzie, *Novel Preaching*, 88–90.

56. For a brief, clear explanation of Buttrick's complex and highly prescriptive homiletic, see O. Wesley Allen Jr's summary of Buttrick's method in *A Renewed Homiletic* (Minneapolis: Fortress Press, 2010), 15–17.

57. Thomas H. Troeger, *Creating Fresh Images for Preaching: New Rungs for Jacob's Ladder* (Valley Forge, PA: Judson Press, 1982); *Imagining a Sermon* (Nashville: Abingdon Press, 1990); *Ten Strategies for Preaching in a Multi Media Culture* (Nashville: Abingdon Press, 1996); *So That All May Know: Preaching That Engages the Whole Congregation* (Nashville: Abingdon Press, 2008).

58. Troeger, *Ten Strategies for Preaching*, 22–29.
59. Barbara K. Lundblad, "Sermon as Movement of Images," *Patterns of Preaching: A Sermon Sampler*, ed. Ronald J. Allen (St. Louis, MO: Chalice Press, 1998), 104–109.
60. Edith Wharton, *The Writing of Fiction* (New York: Simon & Schuster, 2014), 22.
61. Leonora Tubbs Tisdale, *Prophetic Preaching: A Pastoral Approach* (Louisville, KY: Westminster John Knox Press, 2010), 80–81.
62. Ibid., 83. Blount's sermon "God on the Loose," appears in *Preaching Mark in Two Voices*, by Brian K. Blount and Gary W. Charles (Louisville, KY: Westminster John Knox Press, 2002), 28–36.
63. Carolyn Sharp, "Refuse to Be Consoled," quoted in Tubbs Tisdale, *Prophetic Preaching*, 83–84. This sermon was preached in Marquand Chapel at Yale Divinity School, September 8, 2005. Sharp is Professor of Homiletics at Yale Divinity School.
64. Bernard Grebanier, *Playwriting: How to Write for the Theater* (New York: Harper and Row,1961), 180.
65. Linda Stone, as quoted in Julie Anne Lytle, *Faith Formation 4.0* (Harrisburg, PA: Morehouse Publishing, 2013), loc. 1729–1730, Kindle. In 2014, I advised a Doctor of Ministry project by Scott Hughes, a United Methodist pastor from North Georgia. His focus was on "Creating Digital and Real Spaces for Faith Formation." The project sought to answer the question: Can Digital Technologies and Social Media Enhance Catechesis? He brought to my attention some fascinating resources on how the Web is changing the way we process life.
66. Lucius Annaeus Seneca, *Letters from a Stoic* (New York: Penguin Classics, 1969), 33.
67. Carr, *The Shallows*, 194, 199. Carr is quoting David Foster Wallace.
68. Adam Thomas, *Digital Disciple: Real Christianity in a Virtual World*. (Nashville: Abingdon Press, 2011), 65. Note: *Homo sapiens* (*Homo*=man *sapiens*=wise), which in Latin means "wise man," is the name used for modern humans, first introduced in 1758 by Carl Linnaeus.
69. Ibid., 66–67.
70. Daniel J. Siegel, *The Mindful Brain: Reflection and Attunement in the Cultivation of Well-Being* (New York: W. W. Norton, 2007), 4. Daniel J. Siegel is a professor of clinical psychiatry at the UCLA School of Medicine and executive director of the Mindsight Institute.
71. Merton, *New Seeds of Contemplation*, 104.
72. Dr. Loyer is now the lead pastor at Spry Church, a United Methodist Congregation in York, Pennsylvania.
73. Lex Loizides, "John Wesley Preaching on His Father's Grave, *Church History Review*, December 28, 2009, https://lexloiz.wordpress.com/2009/12/28/john-wesley-preaching-on-his-father%E2%80%80%99s-grave/. See also John Wesley, *The Works of the Rev. John Wesley, A.M.: Sometime Fellow of Lincoln College, Oxford* (London: Wesleyan Conference Office, 1872), 376–77.
74. Alyce M. McKenzie, *Wise Up!: Four Biblical Virtues for Navigating Life* (Eugene, OR; Wipf and Stock Publishers, 2018), 83–84.
75. Scofield, *The Scene Book*, 175–77.
76. Rosenfeld, *Make a Scene*, 227.
77. Henry H. Mitchell, *Celebration and Experience in Preaching*, rev. ed. (Nashville: Abingdon Press, 1990), 21, emphasis original.

78. Barbara Brown Taylor, "Preaching the Body," *Listening to the Word: Studies in Honor of Fred B. Craddock*, eds. Gail R. O'Day and Thomas G. Long (Nashville: Abingdon Press, 1993), 212–13.
79. Ibid., 213.
80. McKenzie, *Novel Preaching*, 28.
81. Scofield offers several literary examples of imagery in scenes on pp. 106–111 of *The Scene Book*.
82. Richard L. Eslinger, *Narrative Imagination: Preaching the Worlds That Shape Us* (Minneapolis: Fortress Press, 1995), 141–74.
83. Frederick Buechner, "A Sprig of Hope," *A Chorus of Witnesses: Model Sermons for Today's Preacher*, eds. Thomas G. Long and Cornelius Plantinga Jr. (Grand Rapids, MI: William B. Eerdmans,1994), 225.
84. Anna Carter Florence, "At the River's Edge," *A Chorus of Witness*, 171.
85. Claudette Anderson Copeland, "Tamar's Torn Robe," in Cleophus J. LaRue, ed., *This Is My Story: Testimonies and Sermons of Black Women in Ministry* (Louisville, KY: Westminster John Knox Press, 2005), 113–18.
86. Jennifer L. Lord, *Finding Language and Imagery: Words for Holy Speech* (Minneapolis: Fortress Press, 2010), 33–36.
87. Buttrick, *Homiletic*, 29.
88. William Strunk Jr., *The Elements of Style*, as quoted in Janet Burroway and Susan Weinberg, *Writing Fiction: A Guide to Narrative Craft*, 6th ed. (New York: Longman, 2003), 75.
89. John Gardner, *The Art of Fiction: Notes on Craft for Young Writers* (New York: Random House, 1984), 22–23; quoted in Burroway and Weinberg, *Writing Fiction*, 75.
90. Burroway and Weinberg, *Writing Fiction*, 75.
91. Ibid., 80.
92. Robert Alter, *The Art of Biblical Narrative* (New York: Basic Books, 1981), 114.
93. Sondra Willobee, *The Write Stuff: Crafting Sermons that Capture and Convince* (Louisville, KY: Westminster John Knox Press, 2009), 11–18.
94. Cleophus J. LaRue, "Why Bother?" This is the opening of a sermon first preached at Fifth Avenue Presbyterian Church, New York, December 7, 2008. Published in Cleophus J. LaRue, *Rethinking Celebration: From Rhetoric to Praise in African American Preaching* (Louisville, KY: Westminster John Knox Press, 2016), 75.
95. Rosenfeld, *Make a Scene*, 15.
96. Ibid., 14–15.
97. Ibid., 18.
98. Scofield, *The Scene Book*, 142–55.
99. Ibid., 144.
100. Rosenfeld, *Make a Scene*, 29.
101. Ibid., 30.
102. Ibid., 31.
103. Ibid.
104. Ibid., 35.
105. The preacher should "spurn none of these three things: that is, to teach, to delight, and to persuade" (Augustine, *On Christian Doctrine*, 1st ed., trans. D.W. Robertson Jr. [New York: Macmillan, 1989], 142).

106. Mike Graves offers an intriguing example of the power of story to teach his conviction that narrative can stir creativity (experience) and offer crucial content (exposition). He sets this exploration in the context of ongoing scenes of a professor of preaching and seven preaching students. Shaped as an account of a seminary course in narrative preaching through the use of short stories, the book skillfully interweaves experience and exposition. See Mike Graves, *The Story of Narrative Preaching: Experience and Exposition: A Narrative* (Eugene, OR: Cascade Books, 2015).

107. Joseph M. Webb, in *Preaching for the Contemporary Service* (Nashville: Abingdon Press, 2010), compares the energy and preparation of preaching to that of improvisational comedy and recommends use of a storyboard to block out and sequence the segments of the sermon.

108. Eugene Lowry, drawing on the work of Walter Ong, a pioneer in orality studies, points out that "the dominant mode of speech is time, while the dominant mode of writing is space (*The Homiletical Beat: Why All Sermons Are Narrative* [Nashville: Abingdon Press, 2012], 77).

109. I offer an exegetical process for scenic preaching in Appendix B.

110. Joseph M. Webb's *Preaching without Notes* is a helpful guide to delivering thoughtfully crafted sermons, not from a written page, but as a natural, spontaneous act of oral communication. He argues that preaching without notes is not a matter of innate talent, but the result of consistent, disciplined preparation (Nashville: Abingdon Press, 2001).

Chapter 5: Scenic Sermons

1. This is the story as told to me by Leontine Kelly in a phone conversation some years ago. It is also recounted in Bishop Kelly's daughter's book, Angella Current, *Breaking Barriers: An African American Family and the Methodist Story* (Nashville: Abingdon Press 2001), 34–35.

2. Elizabeth Ellis, "Historical Stories: Mary McLeod Bethune," in Loren Niemi and Elizabeth Ellis, *Inviting the Wolf In: Thinking about Difficult Stories* (Little Rock, AR: August House Publishers, 2001), 83–86.

3. Ibid., 86.

4. On October 1, 2017, sixty-four-year-old Stephen Paddock of Mesquite, Nevada, fired more than 1,100 rounds from his suite on the thirty-second floor of the nearby Mandalay Bay Hotel before taking his own life. His motive was unclear. The statistics given here are from https://www.thesun.co.uk/news/4593987/las-vegas-shooting-victims-names -dead-injured/.

5. The gunman in the Las Vegas massacre may have rigged his guns with devices that enable a shooter to fire bullets rapidly—called "bump stocks"—that turn semiautomatic weapons into weapons capable of mimicking automatic fire. "Twelve bump-fire stocks were found on firearms recovered from Stephen Paddock's hotel room," said Jill Snyder, the special agent in charge of the Bureau of Alcohol, Tobacco, Firearms and Explosives' San Francisco field office. Also known by the brand name Slide Fire, bump-fire stocks, or "bump stocks," modify such rifles as an AR-15 to "allow it to fire in rapid succession or automatic fire," said Sam Rabadi, a retired ATF special agent (Nichole Chavez, "What Are the 'Bump Stocks' on the Las Vegas Shooter's Guns?, CNN, October 5, 2017, https://www.cnn.com/2017/10/04/us/bump-stock-las-vegas -shooting/index.html).

6. Steve Hartman, *Leaders must do something—anything—to stop mass shootings*, CBS News, 2018, https://www.cbsnews.com/video/steve-hartman-leaders-must-do-something -anything-to-stop-mass-shootings/, accessed February 28, 2018.

7. This is an excerpt from a meditation written and preached by Reverend Don Underwood, senior pastor of Christ United Methodist Church in Plano, Texas, https://cumc .com/the-flood-2/.

8. Ibid.

9. Alyce M. McKenzie, *Preaching Proverbs: Wisdom for the Pulpit* (Louisville, KY: Westminster John Knox Press, 1996), 31.

10. Dr. Kent Ingram is the senior pastor at First United Methodist Church, Colorado Springs. He invited me to preach in connection with a workshop on preaching I had done a few days earlier at the church for pastors from the Mountain Sky Annual Conference of The United Methodist Church.

11. *The Autobiography of Benjamin Franklin* (Philadelphia: Henry Altemus, 1895), 164, emphasis original.

12. Louis R. Harlan, ed., "A Newspaper Report of an Emancipation Day Address," *The Booker T. Washington Papers: Volume 3: 1889–1895* (University of Illinois Press, 1974), 496.

13. Morna Hooker, as quoted in Bonnie B. Thurston and Judith M. Ryan, *Philippians and Philemon*, Sacra Pagina series, ed. Daniel J. Harrington (Collegeville, MN: Liturgical Press, 2005), 83. For a treatment of how Paul's original audience would have understood the cross, see Morna Dorothy Hooker, *Not Ashamed of the Gospel: New Testament Interpretations of the Death of Christ* (Grand Rapids, MI: William B. Eerdmans, 1994).

14. For exegetical insights into this passage see Bonnie B. Thurston and Judith M. Ryan, *Philippians & Philemon*, 80–91.

15. Harper Lee, *To Kill a Mockingbird* (New York: Harper & Row, 1961), 249.

16. Ibid., 248.

17. "Oral History Archives," 9/11 Memorial & Museum, https://www.911memorial.org /oral-history-archives-3.

18. Martin Luther King Jr., *Stride toward Freedom: The Montgomery Story* (Boston, MA: Beacon Press, 2010) 125.

19. Because Psalm 23 is "an American secular icon," associated since the Civil War with death and funerals, we miss the echoes that are tied to the rigors of daily living (Denise Dombkowski Hopkins, *Journey through the Psalms* [St. Louis, MO: Chalice Press, 2002], 106).

20. Jeremiah 23:1–4 and Ezekiel 34:11–16 demonstrate that where the king fails to carry out his shepherd function to provide for and protect the people, God is forced to step in as shepherd.

21. See Stephen J. Patterson, *The God of Jesus: The Historical Jesus and the Search for Meaning* (Harrisburg, PA: Trinity Press International, 1998), chap. 2.

22. See Robert Alter, *The Art of Biblical Narrative* (Philadelphia: Basic Books, 2011). David's story, says Alter, "is probably the greatest single narrative representation in antiquity of a human life evolving by slow stages through time, shaped and altered by the pressures of political life, public institutions, family, the impulses of body and spirit, the eventual sad decay of the flesh. It also provides the most unflinching insight into the cruel processes of history and into human behavior warped by the pursuit of power

(Robert Alter, *The David Story: A Translation with Commentary of 1 and 2 Samuel* [New York: W. W. Norton and Co., 1999], ix).

23. Psalm 23:3: "He leads me in right paths / for his name's sake." See Patrick Miller, *The Lord of the Psalms* (Louisville, KY: Westminster John Knox Press, 2013), 38–39.
24. Samuel Terrien, *The Psalms: Strophic Structure and Theological Commentary* (Grand Rapids, MI: William B. Eerdmans, 2003), 241.
25. John Calvin, as quoted in Brent Strawn and Roger E. Van Harn, eds., *Psalms for Preaching and Worship: A Lectionary Commentary* (Grand Rapids, MI: William B. Eerdmans Publishing, 2009), 6.
26. Ibid.
27. Dombkowski Hopkins, *Journey through the Psalms*, 107.
28. Howard Thurman, *Deep Is the Hunger: Meditations for Apostles of Sensitiveness* (Richmond, IN: Friends United Press, 1951), 160.
29. Henry Ward Beecher, *Life Thoughts: Gathered from the Extemporaneous Discourses of Henry Ward Beecher*, ed. Edna Dean Procter (London: Hamilton, Adams, & Co., 1858), 7.
30. Theodore Parker Ferris's gift for connecting with people is evident in his printed sermons. See *This Is the Day: Selected Sermons* (Dublin, NH: Yankee, 1980).
31. Thomas à Kempis, quoted in *Book of Common Worship Daily Prayer* (Louisville, KY: Westminster John Knox Press, 2018), 460.
32. Mourner's Kaddish text from https://reformjudaism.org/practice/prayers-blessings/mourners-kaddish.
33. John Wesley, "The Duty of Constant Communion," para. 1, 2, 3, 6. Text is from the 1872 edition, http://www.umcmission.org/Find-Resources/John-Wesley-Sermons/Sermon-101-The-Duty-of-Constant-Communion.
34. The Gospel lectionary text for the sixth Sunday of Easter is John 14:23–29. I decided, instead, to preach on John 14:1–7.
35. Alice Walker, "Looking for Zora," *Ms. Magazine* (1975): 74–79; 88–89.
36. Ernest T. Campbell, *Locked in a Room with Open Doors* (Waco, TX: Word Books, 1974), 20.

Bibliography

Allen, O. Wesley, Jr. *The Homiletic of All Believers: A Conversational Approach to Proclamation and Preaching*. Louisville, KY: Westminster John Knox Press, 2005.
————. *Preaching and the Human Condition: Loving God, Self, and Others*. Nashville: Abingdon Press, 2016.
————, ed. *The Renewed Homiletic*. Minneapolis, MN: Fortress Press, 2010.
Allen, Ronald J., ed. *Patterns of Preaching: A Sermon Sampler*. St. Louis, MO: Chalice Press, 1998.
Allen, Ronald J., and O. Wesley Allen Jr. *The Sermon without End: A Conversational Approach to Preaching*. Nashville: Abingdon Press, 2015.
Alter, Robert. *The Art of Biblical Narrative*. New York: Basic Books. 1981.
Alter, Robert. *The David Story: A Translation with Commentary of 1 and 2 Samuel*. New York: W.W. Norton and Co., 1999.
Andrews, William L., ed. *Sisters of the Spirit: Three Black Women's Autobiographies of the Nineteenth Century*. Bloomington: Indiana University Press, 1987.
Augustine. *On Christian Doctrine*. Translated by D. W. Robertson Jr. New York: Macmillan, 1989.
Barger Elliott, Mark. *Creative Styles of Preaching*. Louisville, KY: Westminster John Knox Press, 2000.
Blount, Brian K., and Gary W. Charles. *Preaching Mark in Two Voices*. Louisville, KY: Westminster John Knox Press, 2002.
Boadt, Lawrence. *Reading the Old Testament: An Introduction*. Nahwah, NJ: Paulist Press, 1984.
Brooks, Geraldine. *March*. New York: Penguin Books, 2005.
Brown, John. *Puritan Preaching in England: A Study of Past and Present*. New York: Charles Scribner's Sons, 1900.
Brown, Raymond E. *The Gospel According to John, 1-XII*. Vol. 29 of *The Anchor Bible*. New York: Doubleday, 1979.
Browne, Robert Eric. *The Ministry of the Word*. London: SCM Press, 1976.
Brussat, Frederic, and Mary Ann Brussat. *Spiritual Literacy: Reading the Sacred in Everyday Life*. New York: Scribner, 1998.

Burroway, Janet, and Susan Weinburg. *Writing Fiction: A Guide to Narrative Craft*. 6th ed. New York: Longman, 2003.

Buechner, Frederick. *The Gospel as Tragedy, Comedy, and Fairytale*. New York: Harper-Collins, 1977.

Buttrick, David G. *Homiletic: Moves and Structures*. Philadelphia: Fortress Press, 2008.

Camp, Claudia V. *Wisdom and the Feminine in the Book of Proverbs*. Sheffield: Almond Press, 1988.

Campbell, Ernest T. *Locked in a Room with Open Doors*. Waco, TX: Word Books, 1974.

Carr, Nicholas G. *The Shallows: What the Internet Is Doing to Our Brains*. New York: W. W. Norton & Company, 2010.

Chilcote, Paul Wesley. *John Wesley and the Women Preachers of Early Methodism*. London: Scarecrow Press, 1991.

Copeland, Claudette Anderson. "Tamar's Torn Robe." In *This Is My Story: Testimonies and Sermons of Black Women in Ministry*. Cleophus J. LaRue, ed. Louisville, KY: Westminster John Knox Press, 2005.

Craddock, Fred B. *As One without Authority*. 4th ed. St. Louis, MO: Chalice Press, 2001.

———. "Story, Narrative, and Metanarrative." In *What's the Shape of Narrative Preaching? Essays in Honor of Eugene L. Lowry*, edited by Mike Graves and David J. Schlafer. St. Louis, MO: Chalice Press, 2008.

Crenshaw, James L. *Old Testament Wisdom: An Introduction*. Atlanta, GA: John Knox Press, 1981.

Crites, Stephen. "The Narrative Quality of Experience." *Journal of the American Academy of Religion* 39, no. 3 (1971): 291–311.

Cron, Lisa. *Wired for Story: the Writer's Guide to Using Brain Science to Hook Readers from the Very First Sentence*. Berkeley: Ten Speed Press, 2012.

Current, Angella P. *Breaking Barriers: An African American Family and the Methodist Story*. Nashville: Abingdon Press, 2001.

Davis, H. Grady. *Design for Preaching*. Philadelphia: Fortress Publishers, 1958.

Denison, Charles. *The Artist's Way of Preaching*. Louisville, KY: Westminster John Knox Press, 2006.

Dickson, Frank A. and Sandra Smythe. *Handbook of Short Story Writing*. Cincinnati, OH: Writer's Digest, 1970.

Dodd, Charles Harold. *Parables of the Kingdom*. 2nd revised ed. New York: Charles Scribner's Sons, 1961; originally published 1935.

Donne, John. *Devotions upon Emergent Occasions*. Edited by Anthony Raspa. New York: Oxford University Press, 1987.

Dorff, Elliot N. *The Way into Tikkun Olam (Repairing the World)*. Woodtsock, VT: Jewish Light Publishers, 2005.

Dumbach, Annette E., and Jud Newborn. *Sophie Scholl and the White Rose*. Oxford, England: Oneworld Publications, 2006.

Dunn-Wilson, David. *A Mirror for the Church: Preaching in the First Five Centuries*. Grand Rapids, MI: William B. Eerdmans, 2005.

Edelman, Gerald M. *Second Nature: Brain Science and Human Knowledge*. New Haven, CT: Yale University Press, 2006.

Edwards, O. C., Jr. *A History of Preaching*. Nashville: Abingdon Press, 2004.

Ellsberg, Margaret R., ed. *The Gospel in Gerard Manley Hopkins, Selections from His Poems, Letters, Journals, and Spiritual Writings*. Walden, NY: Plough Publishing House, 2017.

Eslinger, Richard. *Narrative and Imagination: Preaching the Worlds That Shape Us*. Minneapolis: Fortress Press, 1995.

Ferris, Theodore Parker. *This Is the Day: Selected Sermons*. Dublin, NH: Yankee, 1980.

Fiorenza, Elisabeth Schüssler. *Jesus: Miriam's Child, Sophia's Prophet: Critical Issues in Feminist Christology*. New York: Continuum, 1995.

———. *Wisdom Ways: Introducing Feminist Biblical Interpretation*. Maryknoll, NY: Orbis Books, 2001.

Florence, Anna Carter. *Preaching as Testimony*. Louisville, KY: Westminster John Knox Press, 2007.

Franklin, Benjamin. *The Autobiography of Benjamin Franklin*. Philadelphia, Henry Altemus, 1895.

Furlong, Monica. 1975. *Puritan's Progress: A Study of John Bunyan*. London: Hodder and Stoughton, 1975.

Gardner, John. *The Art of Fiction: Notes on Craft for Young Writers*. New York: Random House, 1984,

Gilbert, Kenyatta R. *The Journey and Promise of African American Preaching*. Minneapolis: Fortress Press, 2011.

Gottschall, Jonathan. *The Storytelling Animal: How Stories Make Us Human*. New York: Houghton Mifflin Harcourt, 2012.

Grebanier, Bernard. *Playwriting: How to Write for the Theater*. New York: Harper and Row, 1961.

Graves, Mike. *The Fully Alive Preacher: Recovering from Homiletical Burnout*. Louisville, KY: Westminster John Knox Press, 2007.

———. *The Story of Narrative Preaching: Experience and Exposition: A Narrative*. Eugene, OR: Cascade Books, 2015.

Graves, Mike, and David J. Schlafer, eds. *What's the Shape of Narrative Preaching? Essays in Honor of Eugene L. Lowry*. St. Louis, MO: Chalice Press, 2008.

Greene, Dana, ed. *Evelyn Underhill: Modern Guide to the Ancient Quest for the Holy*. Albany: State University of New York Press, 1988.

Gross, Nancy Lammers. *Women's Voices and the Practice of Preaching*. Grand Rapids, MI: William B. Eerdmans, 2017.

Hall, Christopher A. "Letters from a Lonely Exile," *Christian History* 13, no 44 (1994).

Harlan, Louis R., ed. *The Booker T. Washington Papers: Volume 3: 1889–1895*. Urbana: University of Illinois Press, 1974.

Hilkert, Mary Catherine. *Naming Grace: Preaching and the Sacramental Imagination*. New York: Bloomsbury Academic Press, 1997.

Hogan, Lucy Lind. *Graceful Speech: An Invitation to Preaching*. Louisville, KY: Westminster John Knox Press, 2006.

Holbert, John C. *Telling the Whole Story: Reading and Preaching Old Testament Stories*. Eugene, OR: Cascade Books, 2013.

Hooker, Morna Dorothy. *Not Ashamed of the Gospel: New Testament Interpretations of the Death of Christ*. Grand Rapids, MI: William B. Eerdmanns, 1994.

Hopkins, Denise Dombkowski. *Journey Through the Psalms*. St. Louis, MO: Chalice Press, 2002.

Howell, Brian C. *In the Eyes of God: A Contextual Approach to Biblical Anthropomorphic Metaphors*. Eugene, OR: Pickwick Publications, 2013.

Hurlock, Kathryn. *Wales and the Crusades 1095–1291*. Cardiff: University of Wales Press, 2011.

Iglesias, Karl. *Writing for Emotional Impact: Advanced Dramatic Techniques to Attract, Engage, and Fascinate the Reader from Beginning to End.* Livermore, CA: WingSpan Press, 2005.

Johnson, Jewell. *365 Daily Devotions for Women: Inspiration from the Lives of Classic Christian Women.* Uhrichsville, OH: Barbour Publishing, 2007.

Johnston, Scott Black, Ted A. Smith, and Leonora Tubbs Tisdale, eds. *Questions Preachers Ask: Essays in Honor of Thomas G. Long.* Louisville, KY: Westminster John Knox Press, 2016.

Julian. *Julian of Norwich: Showings.* The Classics of Western Spirituality. New York: Paulist Press, 1978.

Kienzle, Beverly Mayne, and Pamela J. Walker. *Women Preachers and Prophets through Two Millennia of Christianity.* Berkeley: University of California Press, 1998.

Kim, Eunjoo Mary. *Women Preaching: Theology and Practice through the Ages.* Eugene, OR: Wipf & Stock, 2009.

King, Martin Luther, Jr. *I Have a Dream: Writings and Speeches That Changed the World.* San Francisco: HarperSanFrancisco, 1986.

———. *Stride toward Freedom: The Montgomery Story.* Boston, MA: Beacon Press, 2010.

Kinnaman, David, and Gabe Lyons. *Unchristian: What a New Generation Really Thinks about Christianity . . . and Why It Matters.* Grand Rapids, MI: Baker Books, 2012.

Koester, Craig R. *Symbolism in the Fourth Gospel: Meaning, Mystery, Community.* Minneapolis: Fortress Press, 1995.

LaRue, Cleophus James. *Rethinking Celebration: from Rhetoric to Praise in African American Preaching.* Louisville, KY: Westminster John Knox Press, 2016.

Lee, Harper. *To Kill a Mockingbird.* New York: Harper & Row, 1961.

Lee, Jarena. *Religious Experience and Journal of Mrs. Jarena Lee: Giving an Account of her Call to Preach the Gospel.* Charleston, SC: Pantianos Classics, 2017, first published in Philadelphia, 1836.

Lenski, Gerhard Emmanuel. *Power and Privilege: A Theory of Social Stratification.* Chapel Hill: University of North Carolina Press, 1984.

Lesnick, Daniel R. *Preaching in Medieval Florence: the Social World of Franciscan and Dominican Spirituality.* Athens: University of Georgia Press, 2012.

Levine, Amy-Jill. *Short Stories by Jesus: The Enigmatic Parables of a Controversial Rabbi.* New York: HarperOne, 2014.

Lindbeck, George A. *The Nature of Doctrine: Religion and Theology in a Postliberal Age.* Philadelphia, PA: Westminster Press, 1984.

Lischer, Richard. "The Limits of Story." In *Interpretation: A Journal of Bible and Theology* 38, no. 1 (1984): 26–38.

Long, Thomas G. *Preaching and the Literary Forms of the Bible.* Philadelphia: Fortress Press, 1989.

———. *The Witness of Preaching.* Louisville, KY: Westminster John Knox Press, 2016.

Long, Thomas G., and Cornelius Plantinga Jr., eds. *A Chorus of Witnesses: Model Sermons for Today's Preacher.* Grand Rapids, MI: William B. Eerdmans, 1994.

Lord, Jennifer L. *Finding Language and Imagery: Words for Holy Speech.* Minneapolis: Fortress Press, 2010.

Lose, David J. *Preaching at the Crossroads: How the World and Our Preaching Is Changing.* Minneapolis: Fortress Press, 2013.

Lowry, Eugene L. *The Homiletical Beat: Why All Sermons Are Narrative.* Nashville, TN: Abingdon Press, 2012.

———. *The Homiletical Plot: The Sermon as Narrative Art Form.* Atlanta: John Knox Press, 1980.

———. *The Sermon: Dancing the Edge of Mystery.* Nashville: Abingdon Press, 1997.

Lytle, Julie Anne. *Faith Formation 4.0.* Harrisburg, PA: Morehouse Publishing, 2013.

McFague, Sallie. *Models of God: Theology for an Ecological, Nuclear Age.* Philadelphia: Fortress Press, 2010.

McKee, Robert. *Story: Substance, Structure, Style and the Principles of Screenwriting.* New York: HarperCollins, 1997.

McKenzie, Alyce M. *Hear and Be Wise: Becoming a Preacher and Teacher of Wisdom.* Nashville: Abingdon Press, 2004.

———. *Novel Preaching: Tips from Top Writers on Crafting Creative Sermons.* Louisville, KY: Westminster John Knox Press, 2010.

———. *The Parables for Today.* Louisville, KY: Westminster John Knox Press, 2007.

———. *Preaching Biblical Wisdom in a Self-Help Society.* Nashville: Abingdon Press, 2002.

———. *Preaching Proverbs: Wisdom for the Pulpit.* Louisville, KY: Westminster John Knox Press, 1996.

Merton, Thomas. *New Seeds of Contemplation.* New York: New Direction Publishing, 2007.

Miller, Patrick D. *The Lord of the Psalms.* Louisville, KY: Westminster John Knox Press, 2013.

Mitchell, Henry H. *Black Preaching: The Recovery of a Powerful Art.* Nashville: Abingdon Press, 1990.

———. *Celebration and Experience in Preaching.* Revised ed. Nashville: Abingdon Press, 2008.

Muessig, Carolyn Anne, ed. *Preacher, Sermon and Audience in the Middle Ages: A New History of the Sermon.* Leiden, The Netherlands: Brill, 2002.

Mumford, Debra J. *Exploring Prosperity Preaching: Biblical Health, Wealth & Wisdom.* Valley Forge, PA: Judson Press, 2012.

Murphy, Francesca Aran. *God Is Not a Story: Realism Revisited.* Oxford: Oxford University Press, 2007.

Murphy, Roland E. *The Tree of Life: An Exploration of Biblical Wisdom Literature.* Grand Rapids, MI: William B. Eerdmans, 2002.

Niemi, Loren, and Elizabeth Ellis. *Inviting the Wolf In: Thinking about the Difficult Story.* Little Rock, AR: August House Publishers, 2001.

Obstfeld, Raymond. *Novelist's Essential Guide to Crafting Scenes.* Cincinnati, OH: Writer's Digest Books, 2000.

O'Day, Gail R., and Thomas G. Long. *Listening to the Word: Studies in Honor of Fred B. Craddock.* Nashville: Abingdon Press, 1993.

Old, Hughes Oliphant. *The Age of the Reformation.* The Reading and Preaching of the Scriptures in the Worship of the Christian Church, vol. 4. Grand Rapids, MI: Eerdmans, 2002.

———. *The Medieval Church.* The Reading and Preaching of the Scriptures in the Worship of the Christian Church, vol. 3. Grand Rapids, MI: William B. Eerdmans, 1999.

Osborn, Ronald E. *Folly of God: the Rise of Christian Preaching.* St. Louis, MO: Chalice Press, 1999.

Patterson, Stephen J. *The God of Jesus: The Historical Jesus and the Search for Meaning.* Harrisburg, PA: Trinity Press International, 1998.

Pasquarello, Michael, III. *Sacred Rhetoric: Preaching as a Theological and Pastoral Practice of the Church.* Eugene, OR: Wipf and Stock, 2012.

Powery, Luke A. *Dem Dry Bones: Preaching, Death, and Hope.* Minneapolis, MN: Fortress Press, 2012.

Press, Skip. *The Complete Idiot's Guide to Screenwriting.* Indianapolis, IN: Alpha Books, 2001.

Procter, Edna Dean, ed. *Life Thoughts: Gathered from the Extemporaneous Discourses of Henry Ward Beecher.* London: Hamilton, Adams, & Co., 1858.

Raboteau, Albert J. *Slave Religion: The "Invisible Institution" in the Antebellum South.* New York: Oxford University Press, 1978.

Rosenfeld, Jordan E. *Make a Scene: Crafting a Powerful Story One Scene at a Time.* Cincinnati, OH: Writer's Digest Books, 2008.

Schlafer, David J. *Your Way with God's Word: Discovering Your Distinctive Preaching Voice.* Boston, MA: Cowley Press, 1995.

Scofield, Sandra Jean. *The Scene Book: A Primer for the Fiction Writer.* New York: Penguin Books, 2007.

Seneca, Lucius Annaeus. *Letters from a Stoic: Epistulae Morales Ad Lucilium.* Translated by Robin Campbell. New York: Penguin Classics, 1969.

Siegel, Daniel J. *The Mindful Brain: Reflection and Attunement in the Cultivation of Well-Being.* New York: W.W. Norton, 2007.

Snicket, Lemony [Daniel Handler], and Brett Helquist. *The Slippery Slope.* London: Egmont, 2012.

Snyder, Blake. *Save the Cat! The Last Book on Screenwriting That You'll Ever Need.* Studio City, CA: Michael Wiese Productions, 2005.

Stanton, Elizabeth Cady, Matilda Joslyn Gage, and Ida Husted Harper, eds. *The History of Woman Suffrage.* Vol. 1. Rochester, NY: Susan B. Anthony, 1887.

Stein, Robert H. *An Introduction to the Parables of Jesus.* Philadelphia: Westminster Press, 1981.

Strahler, Arthur N. *Understanding Science: An Introduction to Concepts and Issues.* Buffalo, NY: Prometheus Books, 1992.

Strawn, Brent A., and Roger Van Harn, eds. *Psalms for Preaching and Worship: A Lectionary Commentary.* Grand Rapids, MI: William B. Eerdmans, 2009.

Strawson, Galen. "Against Narrativity." *Ratio.* 17, no. 4 (2004): 428–52.

Tannehill, Robert. *The Sword of His Mouth: Forceful and Imaginative Language in Synoptic Sayings.* Philadelphia: Fortress Press, 1975.

Taylor, Barbara Brown. *The Preaching Life.* Cambridge, MA: Cowley Publications, 1993.

Terrien, Samuel L. *The Psalms: Strophic Structure and Theological Commentary.* Grand Rapids, MI: William B. Eerdmans, 2003.

Thomas, Adam. *Digital Disciple: Real Christianity in a Virtual World.* Nashville: Abingdon Press, 2011.

Thomas, Frank A. *How to Preach a Dangerous Sermon.* Nashville: Abingdon Press, 2018.

———. *They Like to Never Quit Praisin' God: The Role of Celebration in Preaching.* Cleveland, OH: United Church Press, 1997.

Thurman, Howard. *Deep Is the Hunger: Meditations for Apostles of Sensitiveness.* Richmond, IN: Friends United Press, 1951.

Thurston, Bonnie B., and Judith M. Ryan. *Philippians and Philemon*. Sacra Pagina, ed. Daniel J. Harrington. Collegeville, MN: Liturgical Press, 2005.

Tisdale, Leonora Tubbs. *Prophetic Preaching: A Pastoral Approach*. Louisville, KY: Westminster John Knox Press, 2010.

Troeger, Thomas H. *Creating Fresh Images for Preaching: New Rungs for Jacob's Ladder*. Valley Forge, PA: Judson Press, 1982.

———. *Imagining a Sermon*. Nashville: Abingdon Press, 1990.

———. *So That All May Know: Preaching That Engages the Whole Congregation*. Nashville: Abingdon Press, 2008.

———. *Ten Strategies for Preaching in a Multimedia Culture*. Nashville: Abingdon Press, 1996.

Vanhoozer, Kevin J. *The Drama of Doctrine: A Canonical-Linguistic Approach to Christian Theology*. Louisville, KY: Westminster John Knox Press, 2005.

Von Balthasar, Hans Urs. *Theo-drama: Theological Dramatic Theory*. Vols. 1–5. San Francisco: Ignatius Press, 1988–1998.

Warnke, Frank J. *John Donne*. Twayne's English Author Series. Woodbridge, CT: Twayne Publishers, 1987.

Webb, Joseph M. *Preaching for the Contemporary Service*. Nashville: Abingdon Press, 2010.

———. *Preaching without Notes*. Nashville: Abingdon Press, 2001.

Wesley, John. *The Works of the Rev. John Wesley, A.M.: Sometime Fellow of Lincoln College, Oxford*. London: Wesleyan Conference Office, 1872.

Westermann, Claus. *Genesis 1–11: A Continental Commentary*. Translated by John J. Scullion. Minneapolis: Augsburg Publishing House, 1984.

Wharton, Edith. *The Writing of Fiction*. New York: Simon & Schuster, 2014.

Whitefield, George. *The Collected Sermons of George Whitefield (1714–1770)*. Philadelphia: The Union Press, 1904.

Wiederkehr, Macrina. *A Tree Full of Angels: Seeing the Holy in the Ordinary*. San Francisco: HarperSanFrancisco, 1990.

Wilkens, Steve, and Mark L. Sanford. *Hidden Worldviews: Eight Cultural Stories That Shape Our Lives*. Downers Grove, IL: InterVarsity Press, 2009.

Willobee, Sondra B. *The Write Stuff: Crafting Sermons That Capture and Convince*. Louisville, KY: Westminster John Knox Press, 2009.

Wilson, Paul Scott. *A Concise History of Preaching*. Nashville: Abingdon Press, 1992.

———. *The Imagination of the Heart: New Understandings in Preaching*. Nashville: Abingdon Press, 1988.

———. *Setting Words on Fire: Putting God at the Center of the Sermon*. Nashville: Abingdon Press, 2008.

———. *The Four Pages of the Sermon: A Guide to Biblical Preaching*. Nashville, TN: Abingdon Press, 1999.

Witherington, Ben III. *Jesus the Sage: The Pilgrimage of Wisdom*. Minneapolis, MN: Augsburg Fortress, 1994.

For Further Reading

Scene Is the New Story

Carr, Nicholas. *The Shallows: What the Internet Is Doing to Our Brains.* New York: W. W. Norton & Company, 2010.

Edelman, Gerald M. *Second Nature: Brain Science and Human Knowledge.* New Haven, CT: Yale University Press, 2006.

Gottshall, Jonathan. *The Storytelling Animal: How Stories Make Us Human.* New York: Houghton Mifflin Harcourt, 2012.

Siegel, Daniel J. *The Mindful Brain: Reflection and Attunement in the Cultivation of Well-Being.* New York: W. W. Norton, 2007.

Snider, Phil, ed. *The Hyphenateds: How Emergence Christianity Is Re-Traditioning Mainline Practices.* St. Louis, MO: Chalice Press, 2011.

Thomas, Adam. *Digital Disciples: Real Christianity in a Digital World.* Nashville: Abingdon Press, 2011.

The Preacher as Scene Maker

Andrews, William L., ed. *Sisters of the Spirit: Three Black Women's Autobiographies of the Nineteenth Century.* Bloomington: University of Indiana Press, 1987.

Furlong, Monica. *Puritan's Progress: A Study of John Bunyan.* London: Hodder and Stoughton, 1975.

Kienzle, Beverly Mayne, and Pamela J. Walker. *Women Preachers and Prophet through Two Millennia of Christianity.* Berkeley: University of California Press, 1998.

Kim, Eunjoo Mary. *Women Preaching: Theology and Practice through the Ages.* Eugene, OR: Wipf & Stock, 2009.

King, Martin Luther, Jr. *I Have a Dream: Writings and Speeches That Changed the World.* San Francisco: HarperSanFrancisco, 1986.

Lischer, Richard, ed. *The Company of Preachers: Wisdom on Preaching, Augustine to the Present.* Grand Rapids, MI: William B. Eerdmans, 2002.

Old, Hughes Oliphant. *The Reading and Preaching of the Scriptures in the Worship of the Christian Church.* 7 vol. Grand Rapids, MI: William B. Eerdmans, 1998–2010.

Making a Scene in the Sermon

Denison, Charles. *The Artist's Way of Preaching.* Louisville, KY: Westminster John Knox Press, 2006.

Dickson, Frank A. and Sandra Smythe. *The Writer's Digest Handbook of Short Story Writing.* Cincinnati, OH: Writer's Digest Books, 1970.

McKee, Robert. *Story: Substance, Structure, Style and the Principles of Screenwriting.* New York: HarperCollins, 1997.

Obstfeld, Raymond, *Novelist's Essential Guide to Crafting Scenes.* Cincinnati, OH: Writer's Digest Books, 2000.

Plantinga, Cornelius Jr. *Reading for Preaching: The Preacher in Conversation with Storytellers, Biographers, Poets, and Journalists.* Grand Rapids, MI: William B. Eerdmans, 2013.

Rosenfeld, Jordan E. *Make a Scene: Crafting a Powerful Story One Scene at a Time.* Cincinnati, OH: Writer's Digest Books, 2008.

Scofield, Sandra Jean. *The Scene Book: A Primer for the Fiction Writer.* New York: Penguin Books, 2007.

Sermon Collections

Allen, Ronald J., ed. *Patterns of Preaching: A Sermon Sampler.* St. Louis, MO: Chalice Press, 1998.

Alling, Roger, and David J. Schlafer, eds. *Preaching as the Art of Sacred Conversation.* Sermons That Work, 6. New York: Morehouse Publishing, 1997.

Craddock, Fred. *The Cherry Log Sermons.* Louisville, KY: Westminster John Knox Press, 2001.

Durber, Susan, and Heather Walton, eds. *Silence in Heaven: A Book of Women's Preaching.* London: SCM Press, 1994.

Kalas, J. Ellsworth. *Old Testament Stories from the Back Side: Bible Stories with a Twist.* Nashville: Abingdon Press, 1995.

Long, Thomas G., and Cornelius Plantinga Jr., eds. *A Chorus of Witnesses: Model Sermons for Today's Preacher.* Grand Rapids, MI: William B. Eerdmans, 1994.

Lundblad, Barbara K. *Marking Time: Preaching Biblical Stories in Present Tense.* Nashville: Abingdon Press, 2007.

Millhaven, Annie Lally, ed. *Sermons Seldom Heard: Women Proclaim Their Lives.* New York: Crossroad Publishing, 1991.

Mitchell, Ella Pearson, ed. *Those Preachin' Women: Sermons by Black Women Preachers.* 3 vols. Valley Forge, PA: Judson Press, 1985–1996.

Mitchell, Ella Pearson, and Jacqueline B. Glass, eds. *Those Preachin' Women.* Vol. 4. Valley Forge, PA: Judson Press, 2004.

Mitchell, Ella Pearson, and Valerie Bridgeman Davis, eds. *Those Preaching Women: A Multicultural Collection.* Valley Forge, PA: Judson Press, 2008.

Simmons, Martha, and Frank A. Thomas, eds. *Preaching with Sacred Fire: An Anthology of African American Sermons, 1750 to the Present.* New York: W. W. Norton and Company, 2010.

Taylor, Barbara Brown. *Bread of Angels.* Cambridge, MA: Cowley Publications, 1997.

———. *Gospel Medicine.* Cambridge, MA: Cowley Publications, 1995.

———. *Home by Another Way.* Cambridge, MA: Cowley Publications, 1997.

————. *Speaking of Sin: The Lost Language of Salvation.* Cambridge, MA: Cowley Publications, 2001.

Trimiew, Darryl M., ed. *Out of Mighty Waters: Sermons by African American Disciples.* St. Louis, MO: Chalice Press, 1994.

Scripture Index

Subject Index